International Monetary Power

A volume in the series

Cornell Studies in Money

edited by Eric Helleiner and Jonathan Kirshner

The Limits of Transparency: Ambiguity and the History of International Finance
by Jacqueline Best

Smoke & Mirrors, Inc.: Accounting for Capitalism
by Nicolas Véron, Matthieu Autret, and Alfred Galichon
translated by George Holoch

The Globalizers: The IMF, the World Bank, and Their Borrowers
by Ngaire Woods

International Monetary Power

edited by

DAVID M. ANDREWS

Cornell University Press   *Ithaca and London*

Cornell University Press gratefully acknowledges funding from
Scripps College, which aided in the publication of this book.

First published 2006 by Cornell University Press
Printed in the United States of America

Library of Congress Cataloging-in-Publication Data

International monetary power / edited by David M. Andrews.
    p. cm. — (Cornell studies in money)
  Includes bibliographical references and index.
  ISBN-13: 978-0-8014-4456-2 (cloth : alk. paper)
  ISBN-10: 0-8014-4456-X (cloth : alk. paper)
  1. Monetary policy.   2. International finance.   3. International
economic relations.   4. Power (Social sciences).   I. Andrews, David M.
II. Series.
  HG230.3.I577   2006
  332'.042—dc22   2006006247

Cornell University Press strives to use environmentally responsible
suppliers and materials to the fullest extent possible in the publishing
of its books. Such materials include vegetable-based, low-VOC inks
and acid-free papers that are recycled, totally chlorine-free, or partly
composed of nonwood fibers. For further information, visit our website
at www.cornellpress.cornell.edu.

Cloth printing   10 9 8 7 6 5 4 3 2 1

CONTENTS

Contributors   vi

Acknowledgments   vii

Introduction   1

Part One **Power, Statecraft, and International Monetary Relations**

1. Monetary Power and Monetary Statecraft   *7*
   David M. Andrews

Part Two **Monetary Power**

2. The Macrofoundations of Monetary Power   *31*
   Benjamin J. Cohen

3. Domestic Sources of International Monetary Leadership   *51*
   Andrew Walter

4. Below the State: Micro-Level Monetary Power   *72*
   Eric Helleiner

5. Monetary Policy Coordination and Hierarchy   *91*
   David M. Andrews

Part Three **Monetary Statecraft**

6. The Exchange-Rate Weapon and Macroeconomic Conflict   *117*
   C. Randall Henning

7. Currency and Coercion in the Twenty-First Century   *139*
   Jonathan Kirshner

8. The Limits of Monetary Power: Statecraft
   within Currency Areas   *162*
   Scott Cooper

9. Monetary Statecraft in Follower States   *184*
   Louis W. Pauly

Index   *209*

v

CONTRIBUTORS

David M. Andrews is associate professor of Politics and International Relations at Scripps College and director of the European Union Center of California.

Benjamin J. Cohen is Louis G. Lancaster Professor of International Political Economy at the University of California, Santa Barbara.

Scott Cooper is assistant professor of Political Science at Brigham Young University.

Eric Helleiner is associate professor in the Department of Political Science at the University of Waterloo.

C. Randall Henning is associate professor in the School of International Service at American University and visiting fellow at the Institute for International Economics.

Jonathan Kirshner is associate professor of Government and director of the International Political Economy Program, Einaudi Center for International Studies, Cornell University.

Louis W. Pauly is Canada Research Chair, professor of Political Science, and director of the Centre for International Studies at the University of Toronto.

Andrew Walter is senior lecturer in International Relations at the London School of Economics and Political Science.

ACKNOWLEDGMENTS

This book represents a genuinely collaborative enterprise. For some time I have puzzled over the question of international monetary power, its sources and its implications; but the topic has proved a difficult one to master. I suggested to this volume's contributors that we tackle the subject together, and they agreed. Since then, my partners have endured countless e-mail queries and comments with perfect equanimity, and I am grateful to them.

Other friends and colleagues have made valuable contributions as well. Special thanks are in order to Matthias Kaelberer, Kathleen McNamara, and Beth Simmons, each of whom helped advance this project in significant ways. Our work benefited greatly from a workshop at the European University Institute (EUI) in Florence, funded in part by the Robert Schumann Centre's Transatlantic Programme. There we received helpful guidance from Michael Artis, Jeff Chwieroth, Yi Feng, Robert Hancke, Joseph Jupille, Helen Wallace, and Clas Wihlborg. We also benefited from the unique atmosphere of the EUI, combining as it does the charms of Tuscany with the rigors of a world-class research institution, and we appreciated the hospitality of both its faculty and staff.

Roger Haydon at Cornell University Press has shepherded this project from its inception, and I am grateful for his help and guidance. A few of the chapters in this volume made their first public appearance at the annual meetings of the International Studies Association in Montreal in spring 2004, where lively discussion suggested a strong interest in its topic. Other chapters were featured in a workshop at Scripps College in Claremont, California, later that year, organized by the European Union Center of California and with the support of a grant from the Freeman Program in Asian Political Economy at the Claremont Colleges; participants included David Baldwin, Brock Blomberg, Lawrence Broz, Richard Burdekin, Mark Hallerberg, Saori Katada, David Lake, John Odell, and Thomas Willett. These are not bashful observers, and we profited from their keen insights.

Likewise a number of excellent research assistants have helped with this project, including Milinda Baker, Joslyn Barnhart, Jennifer Boyd, Laine Middaugh, Sam Schreyer, Andrea Schuster, and William Talbott. We extend our warm appreciation to Laura Burgassi, Mei Lan Goei, Filipa da Sousa, Catherine Divry, and others in San Domenico for their help in making possible the EUI workshop. Thanks are due as well to Lukas Loncko and John Harper for organizing the Claremont workshop, to Scripps College for enduring my long absence, and especially to Nancy Bekavac, Michael Lamkin, and Diane Paul for their support of this project and my many other endeavors.

Above all, I want to thank the contributors to this project. It has been a long path together, and at its end I am struck by what an honor it has been to work with such outstanding friends and scholars.

Introduction

This volume illuminates the power dimension of international monetary relations: its meaning, its sources, and its practice. Simply put, international monetary power exists when one state's behavior changes because of its monetary relationship with another state. Monetary statecraft, in turn, refers to the conscious manipulation of monetary relations in order to influence the policies of other states. Both concepts are central to understanding the changing nature of international relations in an increasingly globalized economy.

These definitions are self-consciously state-centric. Other approaches to the study of monetary power are possible, addressing different aspects of money's social and political consequences.[1] But in elucidating monetary power with an emphasis on interstate relations, the contributors to this volume have carved out an important aspect of human experience whose general contours remain underexplored. True, the concept of monetary power has been bandied about by some scholars—including Susan Strange[2] and many of the contributors to this collection[3]—

1. For example, recent work on the political economy of credit includes Andrew Leyshon and Nigel Thrift, *Money / Space: Geographies of Monetary Transformation* (New York: Routledge, 1997); Marieke de Goede, *Virtue, Fortune, and Faith: A Genealogy of Finance* (Minneapolis: University of Minnesota Press, 2005); Timothy J. Sinclair, *The New Masters of Capital: American Bond Rating Agencies and the Politics of Creditworthiness* (Ithaca: Cornell University Press, 2005). For a feminist analysis of these issues, see Linda McDowell, *Capital Culture: Gender at Work in the City* (Malden, Mass.: Blackwell Publishers, 1997).

2. Susan Strange was prolific on the subject, beginning with her "political theory of international currencies" in *Sterling and British Policy: A Political Study of an International Currency in Decline* (London: Oxford University Press, 1971), 2–40. Eric Helleiner (chap. 4 in this volume) discusses Strange's contributions and especially her notion of structural power as applied to monetary affairs.

3. Examples of related work by the contributors include David M. Andrews, "Capital Mobility and State Autonomy: Towards a Structural Theory of International Monetary Relations," *International Studies Quarterly* 38, no. 2 (1994): 193–218; Benjamin J. Cohen, *Organizing the World's Money: The Political Economy of International Monetary Relations* (New York: Basic Books, 1977); Eric Helleiner, *The Making*

1

for some time now. But the concept, and its relationship to the study of international relations more generally, has never been satisfactorily explained. This volume takes up that task.

To do so, we adopt a social power theory approach to the study of international monetary relations, treating power as a relational property.[4] Social power exists when one actor's behavior changes as a result of its relationship with another actor. International power exists when one state's behavior changes as a result of its relationship with another state. International monetary power exists when one state's behavior changes because of its monetary relationship with another state.

The resulting framework is supple enough to permit examination of claims from a number of contending perspectives yet sufficiently demanding to create a common vocabulary and basis of analysis. This is essential because the concept of international monetary power resides at the nexus of mainstream international relations theory, where questions of power figure prominently, and more specialized literatures in which the power dimension is largely ignored.[5] The subject is general neglected by the two dominant academic schools currently studying international

---

of National Money: Territorial Currencies in Historical Perspective (Ithaca: Cornell University Press, 2003); C. Randall Henning, "Systemic Conflict and Regional Monetary Integration: The Case of Europe," *International Organization* 52, no. 3 (summer 1998): 537–73; Jonathan Kirshner, *Currency and Coercion* (Princeton: Princeton University Press, 1995); Louis W. Pauly, *Who Elected the Bankers? Surveillance and Control in the World Economy* (Ithaca: Cornell University Press, 1997); Andrew Walter, *World Power and World Money: The Role Of Hegemony and International Monetary Order* (New York/London: Harvester-Wheatsheaf/St. Martin's Press, 1991).

4. Social power analysis originated in the work Harold D. Lasswell and Abraham Kaplan, especially their *Power and Society: A Framework for Political Inquiry* (New Haven: Yale University Press, 1950). Herbert A. Simon, in "Notes on the Observation and Measurement of Political Power," *Journal of Politics* 15, no. 4 (November 1953): 500–516, describes his own contributions as "a series of footnotes on the analysis of influence and power by Lasswell and Kaplan" (501). For other early work, see also Herbert Simon, *Models of Man* (New York: John Wiley, 1957); Robert A. Dahl, *Modern Political Analysis* (Englewood Cliffs: Prentice-Hall, 1963); Jack H. Nagel, *The Descriptive Analysis of Power* (New Haven: Yale University Press, 1975). In the mainstream study of international relations, Karl W. Deutsch, *The Analysis of International Relations,* 2nd ed. (Englewood Cliffs: Prentice-Hall, 1978), employs a social power approach, as do international political economy scholars Klaus Knorr, *The Power of Nations: The Political Economy of International Relations* (New York: Basic Books, 1975), and David A. Baldwin, *Economic Statecraft* (Princeton: Princeton University Press, 1985). See as well the introduction to David A. Baldwin, ed., *Neorealism and Neoliberalism: The Contemporary Debate* (New York: Columbia University Press, 1993). More recent applications to international political economy topics include George Shambaugh, *States, Firms, and Power: Successful Sanctions in United States Foreign Policy* (Albany: State University of New York Press, 1999).

5. Monetary issues figured prominently for a time in mainstream studies of international power; see, for example, Robert Gilpin, *The Political Economy of International Relations* (Princeton: Princeton University Press, 1987) as well as the case studies in Robert O. Keohane and Joseph S. Nye, *Power and Interdependence: World Politics in Transition* (Boston: Little, Brown and Company, 1977). Indeed, international monetary relations were a centerpiece of the early hegemonic stability theory literature, as discussed by Andrew Walter (chap. 3 in this volume). For some time, however, the general trend within the study of international political economy has been toward more specialized treatments of monetary issues in which power is either a secondary issue or, more typically, is not discussed at all. See, for example, the absence of the subject in William Bernhard, Lawrence J. Broz, and William Roberts Clark, eds., "The Political Economy of Monetary Institutions," special edition, *International Organization* 56, no. 4 (autumn 2002).

monetary phenomena: the optimum currency area theorists, who emphasize macro-aspects of economic interdependence,[6] and political economy theorists, who emphasize distributive concerns at the domestic level.[7] This oversight represents an important theoretical lacuna. By explicitly acknowledging the power question—the capacity of some actors to alter the behavior of others, causing them to make policy choices they would otherwise avoid—we help to close this gap.

The organization of this volume is straightforward. In part one, I provide an overview of the subject, focusing on the distinction between monetary power (a relational concept) and monetary statecraft (the deliberate manipulation of such relationships). Part two concentrates on the underlying characteristics of international monetary power. Benjamin Cohen outlines the macrofoundations of monetary power, or in other words the sources of monetary power at the macro-level. Invoking an earlier distinction he made between the transitional and continuing costs of monetary adjustment, he explains how payment of adjustment's transitional costs can sometimes be deflected to others while payment of adjustment's continuing costs can sometimes be delayed—perhaps even indefinitely. Andrew Walter discusses the domestic prerequisites of monetary leadership; he argues that currency leadership requires a relatively conservative monetary policy and institutional arrangements that facilitate highly developed financial markets. Eric Helleiner addresses the micro-level dimension of international monetary power, with attention to money's capacity to rearticulate economic interests and reconstruct political identities. David Andrews examines the hierarchical nature of international monetary relations; he contrasts monetary policy coordination efforts with trade policy nego-

6. Classic works include Robert Mundell, "A Theory of Optimum Currency Areas," *American Economic Review* 51, no. 4 (1961): 657–65; Ronald McKinnon, "Optimum Currency Areas," *American Economic Review* 53, no. 4 (1963): 717–25; Peter Kenen, "The Theory of Optimum Currency Areas: An Eclectic View," in *Monetary Problems of the International Economy,* ed. Robert Mundell and A. Swoboda, 41–60 (Chicago: University of Chicago Press, 1969). For an interesting recent revision of this approach, see Peter B. Kenen, "Currency Unions and Policy Domains," in *Governing the World's Money,* ed. David M. Andrews, C. Randall Henning, and Louis W. Pauly, 78–104 (Ithaca: Cornell University Press, 2002). For an examination of the relationship between this tradition and the works cited in the next note, see Thomas D. Willett, "Optimum Currency Area and Political Economy Approaches to Exchange Rate Regimes: Towards an Analytical Synthesis," *Current Politics and Economics of Europe* 17, no. 1 (2006): 25–52.

7. Representative works include Jeffry A. Frieden, "Invested Interests: The Politics of National Economic Policies in a World of Global Finance," *International Organization* 45, no. 4 (autumn 1991): 425–51; C. Randall Henning, *Currencies and Politics in the United States, Germany, and Japan* (Washington, D.C.: Institute for International Economics, 1994); Beth Simmons, *Who Adjusts? Domestic Sources of Foreign Policy during the Interwar Years* (Princeton: Princeton University Press, 1994); Carsten Hefeker, *Interest Groups and Monetary Integration: The Political Economy of Exchange Regime Choice* (Boulder: Westview Press, 1997); Thomas H. Oatley, *Monetary Politics: Exchange Rate Cooperation in the European Union* (Ann Arbor: University of Michigan Press, 1997); William Bernhard and David Leblang, "Democratic Institutions and Exchange-Rate Commitments," *International Organization* 53, no. 1 (1999): 71–97; William Roberts Clark and Mark Hallerberg, "Mobile Capital, Domestic Institutions, and Electorally Induced Monetary and Fiscal Policy," *American Political Science Review* 94, no. 2 (June 2000): 323–46; Lawrence J. Broz and Jeffry Frieden, "The Political Economy of International Monetary Relations," *Annual Review of Political Science* 4 (June 2001), 317–43.

tiations, explaining that, whereas the latter rely on reciprocity, the former are characterized by unilateral policy adaptations on the part of the weak.

Part three turns from monetary power to the deliberate exercise thereof, or monetary statecraft. The chapter by C. Randall Henning explores use of the "exchange-rate weapon" by the United States against its major economic partners, both historically and currently; he concludes that countermeasures adopted by Japan and the European Union have substantially diminished the utility of this instrument of monetary coercion. Jonathan Kirshner examines how heightened capital mobility and the shift to political unipolarity have influenced the practices of currency manipulation, monetary dependence, and systemic disruption; based on an original examination of a number of recent cases, he argues that, although these instances of monetary statecraft have been reshaped, they remain significant. Scott Cooper considers how both market forces and institutional rules shape the politics of formal currency areas such as the franc zone and the sterling bloc. Refining a framework originated by Kirshner, Cooper argues that monetary leaders and followers are locked in a far more complex and interdependent power relationship than is generally recognized. Louis Pauly examines the politics of exchange-rate regime choice in Austria and Canada. Although these two states occupy functionally similar positions in the global economy, they have adopted radically different strategies for limiting the influence of their giant neighbors—Germany and the United States, respectively—choices he traces to differences in the organization of their domestic political economies.

Taken together, these contributions constitute a substantial advance on previous attempts to sort out the nature and consequences of international monetary power. They are not the last word on the subject; they cannot be. But we invite other researchers to build on this edifice, as we have built on the work of others.

PART ONE

Power, Statecraft, and International Monetary Relations

CHAPTER ONE

Monetary Power
and Monetary Statecraft

David M. Andrews

On October 31, 1956, British and French military forces invaded Egypt, determined to seize the Suez Canal and humiliate Egyptian president Gamal Abdel Nasser, who had nationalized the international waterway some three months earlier. About a week after the invasion, on November 5, the pound sterling came under sustained pressure on international markets. The following day, British officials contacted their U.S. counterparts to request support; they were, instead, told that no help would be forthcoming until Britain conformed to a U.S.-sponsored UN resolution calling for an immediate ceasefire and withdrawal of its forces from Egypt. In addition to the market pressure, the British were told, the United States would block the United Kingdom's access even to its own reserves in the International Monetary Fund (IMF). On the other hand, if London withdrew its forces the United States would not only cooperate with the United Kingdom at the IMF but would provide additional resources in the form of an immediate export-import credit.

"This was blackmail," recalled Richard A. Butler, a senior adviser to Prime Minister Anthony Eden and former chancellor of the Exchequer. "But we were in no position to argue."[1] Harold Macmillan, his successor as chancellor, agreed and then delivered the bad news to the war cabinet. The run on the pound, he explained, had been "viciously orchestrated" by the United States and would end only if a ceasefire were ordered by midnight that evening.[2] In fact, Britain capitulated ahead of schedule, announcing a cease-fire at 5 p.m. on November 6—despite the entreaties

For helpful comments on earlier versions of this chapter I am grateful to the contributors to this project as well as to the participants in the Florence workshop, the Claremont workshop, and a seminar at Brigham Young University.

1. Richard A. Butler, *The Art of the Possible: The Memoirs of Lord Butler* (Boston: Gambit, 1972), 195.
2. Alistair Horne, *Harold MacMillan*, volume 1: 1894–1956 (New York: Viking, 1989), 440.

of its French ally. "Thus the United States," as Jonathan Kirshner observes, "was able to stop a military invasion in its tracks."[3]

This episode gives rise to certain questions. What circumstances allowed U.S. authorities to achieve this stunning shift in British foreign policy? What lessons can be drawn from this incident, as well as from other instances of monetary statecraft? More generally, what are the sources of international monetary power? How can it be exploited, and what are its limits?

In this chapter, I provide an introduction to the subject and survey our collective findings. The first two sections discuss international monetary power as a relational concept and the different forms it can assume. The remainder of the chapter distinguishes monetary power from monetary statecraft, examines monetary statecraft more closely, and discusses limits to the exercise of monetary power.

Power and International Monetary Relations

As explained in the introduction to this volume, we understand international monetary power as a relational property; it is manifest when one state's behavior changes because of its monetary relationship with another state. In defining monetary power in this fashion, we are adopting a particular view of causality. To say that state A has power over state B is to make the claim that A's relationship with B is causing B to behave in a certain way with respect to policy C. Of course, A may not be the sole cause of B's behavior; social reality is complex and explanations are therefore typically multivariate in nature. But the claim does imply a counterfactual corollary: B's relationship with A is causing B to behave differently than would otherwise be the case. Unless this corollary obtains, the claim that A has power over B is meaningless.[4]

Accordingly, claims regarding power require a certain precision if they are to be evaluated. Specifically, claims about an actor's power must be described in terms of scope (that is, power with respect to which policies or behaviors?) and domain (power over which other actors?).[5] In assessing questions of scope and domain, it is useful to consider just how monetary power—understood as a relational property— manifests itself.

Monetary relations can alter policy behavior both directly and indirectly. Indirect means of influence involve issue linkage—connecting outcomes on subject x (regarding monetary affairs) to outcomes on subject y (on some unrelated topic), or

---

3. Jonathan Kirshner, *Currency and Coercion: The Political Economy of International Monetary Power* (Princeton: Princeton University Press, 1995), 64–70, quotation on 70.

4. Although the emphasis here is on the observable, *behavior* can instead be understood very broadly, as including "beliefs, attitudes, opinions, expectations, emotions, and/or predispositions to act"; see David A. Baldwin *Economic Statecraft* (Princeton: Princeton University Press, 1985), 20n.42.

5. These terms date back to Harold D. Lasswell and Abraham Kaplan, *Power and Society: A Framework for Political Inquiry* (New Haven: Yale University Press, 1950). Even contingent claims require qualification in terms of scope and domain; see the discussion in David A. Baldwin, ed., *Neorealism and Neoliberalism: The Contemporary Debate* (New York: Columbia University Press, 1993), 16–17.

vice versa. Plainly governments can and sometimes do seek to gain leverage by linking monetary behavior to other matters, as the Suez example demonstrates; indeed the availability and utility of such linkages is the major reason why high politics cannot be separated from low politics.[6]

Linking monetary relations to states' foreign policy objectives was a major focus of Jonathan Kirshner's 1995 study *Currency and Coercion;* in the present volume, Kirshner (chap. 7) evaluates the continuing relevance of such efforts in light of changes to global political and economic relations. But linkage strategies involving monetary relations cannot be properly understood without first understanding power relations within the scope of monetary policy itself; otherwise, we cannot understand when and why such efforts succeed. We are therefore concerned, first and foremost, with the power implications intrinsic to international monetary relations. For example, national authorities will at least occasionally have different preferences regarding currency use, currencies' mutual values, payments financing, and liquidity provision.[7] How will the resulting collision of preferences be resolved?

To illustrate this problem, consider another example of monetary statecraft, once again involving the major economic powers of the day—in this case, the United States, West Germany, and Japan in the mid-1970s. Upon assuming office, economic officials in the Jimmy Carter administration were not satisfied with the pace of global economic recovery from the recession caused by the first oil crisis. However, the Carter team preferred not to stimulate the U.S. economy in isolation, which would have aggravated the current account deficit. Instead, they advocated stimulus within countries with current account surpluses—Germany and Japan in particular—on the theory that these "locomotives" should drive global recovery. When the governments in Bonn and Tokyo resisted this notion, U.S. officials let it be known that they would be content to allow and even to encourage the dollar to depreciate against their currencies. In the face of the subsequent appreciation of the yen, the Japanese government committed, in a bilateral agreement in early 1978, to a program of fiscal stimulus; the German government agreed to similar measures at the Bonn summit of 1978. Although the latter development was part of a larger, more balanced package (in which the United States agreed to decontrol oil prices and France and Italy agreed to conclude the Tokyo round of trade negotiations), the Germans almost certainly would not have consented to stimulate their economy in the absence of deliberate U.S. pressure on the dollar-deutschmark exchange rate.[8]

In short, the monetary policy preferences of the United States prevailed—al-

6. A distinction coined by Stanley Hoffmann, "Obstinate or Obsolete? The Fate of the Nation-State in Western Europe Today," *Daedalus* 95, no. 3 (1966): 862–916.

7. Note that in developing this list we confine ourselves to finance's monetary dimension; for treatments of broader issues of international credit, see the references in the introduction to this volume.

8. I. M. Destler and Hisao Mitsuyu, "Locomotives on Different Tracks: Macroeconomic Diplomacy, 1977–1979," in *Coping with U.S.-Japanese Economic Conflicts*, ed. I. M. Destler and Hideo Sato (Lexington: Lexington Books, 1982), 243–70; Robert D. Putnam and C. Randall Henning, "The Bonn Summit of 1978: A Case Study in Coordination," in *Can Nations Agree? Issues in International Economic Cooperation*, ed. Richard N. Cooper, Robert D. Putnam, C. Randall Henning, and Gerald Holtham (Washington, D.C.: Brookings Institution, 1989), 12–140.

though admittedly not without some offsetting concessions from Washington. But those concessions, although real, were not the heart of the matter. Why was the United States able to pressure its largest economic partners into altering their domestic policies? More generally, how is the pursuit of different national monetary preferences resolved in an interdependent setting? What are the characteristics of power in such interactions? Satisfactory answers to these questions are necessary to improve our understanding both of monetary relations between states and of international relations more generally.

Forms of International Monetary Power

Pathways for the exercise of monetary power are to be found both at the state or macro-level and through nonstate actors at the micro-level. These two dimensions of monetary power are, of course, connected: micro-level behavior can result in pressure for changes in macro-level policy, and vice-versa. Still, the two can be distinguished for analytical purposes, and by distinguishing between them we can better understand the power implications of each.

At the macro-level, the problem of adjustment to balance-of-payments disequilibrium is central to discussions of monetary power. Payments imbalances (or prospective imbalances) can result in pressures on states to abandon preferred policies; witness the events leading to the Bonn summit, as already discussed. This problem is ubiquitous among politically independent states, whether they organize their monetary systems nationally or collectively.[9] But the problem of adjustment is particularly pronounced in modern democracies because the expectations of electorates regarding national economic policy performance have risen dramatically. In such societies, resistance to changing domestic policy because of external pressures has become increasingly pronounced in the last hundred-odd years. As a result, the distribution of adjustment costs among states is intensely contested.

Of course, there are technical aspects of this distribution that are uncontroversial. Payments deficits result from the national absorption of resources in excess of current income; it therefore follows that a return to balance requires the deficit state to reduce its absorption of resources relative to income.[10] From the standpoint of traditional economic theory, therefore, real adjustment—as opposed to financing a continuation of the imbalance—always results in a reduction in a deficit state's absorption relative to its income. Less of the deficit state's national income is spent and more saved.

As we will see, however, neither standard economic theory nor modern political economy makes strong positive claims about precisely how the interstate adjustment process actually occurs—in other words, about the path for return to payments

9. Even the participants in a monetary union experience the problem of payments imbalances as part of their dealings with the outside world.

10. A qualifier is in order; sometimes payments deficits result from states borrowing from abroad to finance productive development at home, in which case the imbalance is temporary and self-correcting. For a more complete discussion, see Benjamin J. Cohen (chap. 2 in this volume).

equilibrium. This omission is of more than merely academic interest: at stake is the capacity of national authorities to make basic decisions about their national economies—about taxing and spending; about the level of interest rates; and about inflation, employment, and growth—independently of external influences.[11] To put it bluntly, will payments balance be restored by inflating surplus economies or by disinflating deficit economies? Questions like this are intensely political, and power relations play a central role in their resolution.

Adjustment is therefore a central feature of monetary relations bearing on power; but it is not the only such issue. At the micro-level, the organization of a monetary system, whether national or collective, can shape private-sector behavior and even individual consciousness in ways that, in turn, influence policy choices. Likewise, international monetary relations—relations between monetary systems—can help rearticulate economic interests and redefine social identity. Our examination of monetary power therefore examines not only the logic of monetary adjustment; we consider as well the implications of interstate monetary relations for individual and collective behavior, preferences, and even self-understanding. To ignore these features of the monetary landscape would be to grossly underestimate the reach of international monetary power.

A more complete discussion of these issues follows; but suffice it to say that, at the macro-level, the key issue is who *pays* the costs of adjustment. Adjustment costs are not uniform; some are continuing, others transitional. Monetary power at the macro-level consists of the capacity either to delay payment of adjustment's continuing costs or to deflect its transitional costs on to others. Different mechanisms are associated with these two capacities, each with distinctive sources.

At the micro-level, by contrast, the chief issue is who *benefits* from the organization of international monetary affairs. For example, specific producer and consumer interests may have different preferences (with varying levels of intensity) for exchange-rate levels or for particular exchange-rate regimes.[12] But static analysis of these and related matters is often insufficient to assess power relations. Why? Because monetary relations sometimes encourage substate actors to rearticulate their interests or even to reconstruct their self-conceptions. Such changes can then have serious repercussions for the economic, social, and even political allegiances of individuals and groups. As at the macro-level, different mechanisms—rooted in different sources—exist for accomplishing these varied micro-level tasks.

Attention to these different pathways for influence is critical given our understanding of international monetary power—that is, a relational property that exists whenever one state's behavior changes because of its monetary relationship with another state. Analysis must therefore be multidimensional, as monetary power can as-

11. A less conspicuous distributional concern at the interstate level involves the benefits derived from seigniorage—that is, the revenues to public authorities deriving from the difference between the nominal value of currencies and the costs of their production. See the discussion in Benjamin J. Cohen, *The Geography of Money* (Ithaca: Cornell University Press, 1998), 39–42, 123–25.

12. This is a central concern of political economy theorists focusing on domestic distributional concerns (see references in the introduction to this volume). For a summary, see Lawrence J. Broz and Jeffry Frieden, "The Political Economy of International Monetary Relations," *Annual Review of Political Science* 4 (June 2001), 317–43.

Table 1.1 Forms of international monetary power

	Level of analysis			
	Macro-level		Micro-level	
Power to . . .	deflect the transitional costs of adjustment	delay the continuing costs of adjustment	rearticulate actor interests	reconstruct actor identities
Primary mechanisms	Passivity with respect to adjustment pressures, thus encouraging other states to bear the brunt of price and income changes required for mutual adjustment	Drawing down reserves or borrowing from abroad, thus postponing real adjustment	Adoption of an extraterritorial currency for at least some purposes, resulting in:	
			Reduction of mutual transaction costs; trade diversion; and formation of new private sector coalitions	Collective experience of monetary phenomena; symbolic role of money in identity formation
Principal sources	Fundamental economic characteristics (esp. relative economic size and openness)	Overall liquidity position (foreign reserves plus access to international credit)	Functional attractiveness of extra-territorial currencies; side payments from interested parties to key decision makers	
	Credibility of policy framework; quality of financial market institutions			

sume different forms depending on the nature of the relationship in question. Four distinct forms (or types) of international monetary power are summarized in table 1.1; the following sections survey each in more detail.

The Macro-Dimension: Who Pays?

Despite the centrality of monetary adjustment to international economic theory, the standard literature provides very little guidance about the precise route that adjustment will take.[13] Neither economics nor political science makes clear claims about exactly who adjusts to whom.[14] Indeed, lacking a strong positive model about

13. Optimum currency area theory is a partial (but only partial) exception, and even its highly qualified claims are primarily exhortatory: it offers a framework for determining how governments *should* organize their monetary affairs, not how they *do* organize them. See the references in the introduction to this volume.

14. Despite its title, *Who Adjusts? Domestic Sources of Foreign Economic Policy during the Interwar Years* (Princeton: Princeton University Press, 1994) by Beth Simmons does not take up this question. Its discussion is limited to differences in states' willingness to comply with a given set of adjustment rules rather than addressing how those rules were arrived at or whom they benefited.

how adjustment takes place, even prescriptive arguments about the adjustment process are generally weak.[15]

Among the very few works to address this issue seriously is a 1966 article by one of the contributors to this project, Benjamin Cohen.[16] In this unjustly neglected work, Cohen explicitly distinguishes between continuing and transitional adjustment costs. The *continuing* cost of adjustment is the cost that prevails after all change associated with the return to payments equilibrium has occurred. This cost must be paid by the (formerly) deficit state—because by definition deficit states absorb resources in excess of their income, and a return to balance means that this state of affairs has ceased. The *transitional* cost of adjustment, by contrast, refers to the cost of the change itself—that is, the cost associated with restoring payments balance. Economic theory provides no guidance whatsoever as to how this cost will be paid; its distribution is, as Cohen argues (chap. 2 in this volume), "up for grabs."

This distinction is critical. Although the costs associated with the transition to payments equilibrium are by definition temporary, the relevant time horizon for national leaders is often limited to that transitional period. Leaders care about the costs of transition and generally prefer to have others pay them—to externalize adjustment costs. They cannot, however, all be successful in this endeavor; hence, international monetary relations have an inherently competitive dimension. The results of that competition are likely to be decided on the basis of power.

In returning to this subject, Cohen explicitly addresses the power implications of his earlier analysis. Corresponding to the different forms of adjustment costs, he argues, are two very different forms of monetary power: the Power to Delay payment of the continuing costs of adjustment, and the Power to Deflect adjustment's transitional costs.

Because it serves the interests of deficit countries to postpone the payment of the continuing costs of adjustment for as long as possible, the Power to Delay has enormous significance. The most critical determinants of this capacity, Cohen argues, are financial variables—above all, a country's international liquidity position, which encompasses both foreign reserves and access to external credit. The more liquidity a country has at its disposal, the longer it can postpone adjustment of its balance of payments. The Power to Deflect, on the other hand, concerns the capacity of states to pass on the transitional costs of adjustment to their economic partners. Instead of deriving from financial variables, this capacity originates in more fundamental economic variables that distinguish one national economy from another. Two fea-

---

15. There is a large literature on macroeconomic policy coordination that discusses how adjustments should be made; see references in Thomas D. Willett, "Developments in the Political Economy of Policy Coordination," *Open Economies Review* 10, no. 2 (May 1999): 221–53. But, as Richard N. Cooper puts it, "Ideally, responsibility for adjustment between deficit and surplus countries would be divided according to some world welfare criteria, but we have no such criteria." "Comments on Adjustment Responsibilities," in *The International Monetary System: Problems and Proposals,* ed. Lawrence H. Officer and Thomas D. Willett, 135–38 (Englewood Hills: Prentice-Hall, 1969), quotation on 136.

16. Benjamin J. Cohen, "Adjustment Costs and the Distribution of New Reserves," *Princeton Studies in International Finance,* no. 18 (1966).

tures in particular stand out: the relative openness and degree of adaptability of each individual economy.

Thus understood, the Power to Delay the continuing costs of adjustment can be enhanced by improving the state's international liquidity position; the Power to Deflect the transitional costs of adjustment can likewise be magnified by altering the state's underlying economic characteristics.[17] But these are not trivial undertakings: none of the associated variables is subject to easy manipulation. Although states may jostle for position within what Cohen calls "the currency pyramid," it is difficult to replace a monetary leader.[18]

In fact, even modest differences in initial economic and financial conditions are likely to result in highly asymmetrical relations among monetary players; the resulting hierarchy is characterized by what I call (chap. 5 in this volume) "passive leadership" at the top and policy subordination by follower states. The subject of monetary leadership is therefore an important one. Andrew Walter (chap. 3 in this volume) distinguishes between two aspects of international monetary leadership—currency leadership and liquidity leadership. Walter argues that currency leadership, which occurs when a national currency plays a dominant role as an anchor, vehicle, and investment currency for international transactions between public or private actors in the world economy, is logically prior to liquidity leadership, which occurs when one or more countries provide short- and longer-term liquidity to the world economy in a stabilizing, countercyclical fashion. Walter identifies the domestic monetary and financial arrangements necessary for developing and sustaining such leadership. In particular, he argues, currency leaders need institutional arrangements that make the conservative commitments of monetary policy makers credible and that facilitate the emergence of well-developed financial markets.

Within the resulting international monetary hierarchy, improvement relative to others is generally possible only at the margins or over the long haul. That said, important changes can result from negotiating new political arrangements within states (or among them) that reduce national vulnerability to external influences. This was certainly the case with the introduction of Economic and Monetary Union (EMU) in Europe. C. Randall Henning (chap. 6 in this volume) examines instances of significant, long-term changes in monetary and other economic arrangements in both Europe and Japan, and the circumstances that prompted them. Having been exposed repeatedly to U.S. monetary statecraft (as in the run-up to the Bonn summit), both European and Japanese authorities embarked on projects to deploy countermeasures; EMU was one of these.

Thus, although it is difficult to engineer changes in the power position of states in the international monetary arena are difficult to engineer, it is not impossible. Henning's chapter assesses the effectiveness of ongoing efforts to this end by the leading economic partners of the United States.

17. Or by altering the political domain of a currency, as, for example, through the formation of a currency union.
18. Cohen, *Geography of Money,* 113–18.

The Micro-Dimension: Who Benefits?

Standard economic studies of international monetary relations have tended to focus almost exclusively on the macro-level questions previously raised. The political economy literature, on the other hand, has recently begun to explore micro-level questions, especially those related to the aggregation and mediation of economic interests (primarily at the national level) with respect to exchange-rate policy.[19] This literature has important implications for the study of international monetary power, although most of those implications remain unexplored.

Some initial observations have been offered, however, and much of the most sophisticated analysis along these lines has been done by Jonathan Kirshner. Drawing on the work of Albert Hirschman, Kirshner directs attention to "the transformation of interests that results from participation in a currency system," a process he calls "entrapment."[20] Membership in a currency area can divert trade and strengthen private-sector coalitions with close economic ties to the dominant state; it can also lead member governments to acquire an interest in the stability and value of the dominant state's currency.[21] These forms of dependence can reinforce the power of the dominant state in indirect ways that, although difficult to measure, may nevertheless be highly significant.[22] Put differently, money has the Power to Rearticulate the economic interests of important societal actors.[23]

Kirshner's analysis suggests that currency areas amount to a political exchange of sorts, in which monetary leaders provide certain benefits to followers either directly (for example, by pooling their foreign-exchange reserves with smaller members) or indirectly (in the form of side payments). For their part, followers cede control over certain of their internal policies; they also incur opportunity costs with respect to the resources extracted by the leader. Focusing on the domestic distribution of the costs and benefits of currency-area membership provides insights into when such an exchange is likely to prove stable. Scott Cooper (chap. 8 in this volume) examines the dynamics of these relationships, with attention to how currency areas create opportunities for both leaders and followers to engage in monetary statecraft.

But the micro-dimension of international monetary power is not limited to the rearticulation of economic interests; it also entails the Power to Reconstruct, at least at the margins, societal actors' very sense of identity. For example, Eric Helleiner has argued that the use of a common money may foster a sense of community be-

19. See the references in the introduction to this volume.

20. Kirshner, *Currency and Coercion*, 117–19, quotation on 118; Albert O. Hirschman, *National Power and the Structure of Foreign Trade* (Berkeley: University of California Press, 1969).

21. Currency areas may entail the use of a common currency, as is the case with the CFA (Communauté financière d'Afrique) franc zone in West Africa, or the tying together of national currencies through an exchange-rate mechanism, as prevailed in the European Monetary System prior to the shift to EMU.

22. Kirshner, *Currency and Coercion*, 167, 268. Indeed, Kirshner argues (169, 249, 267) that the goal of currency entrapment has been the most important reason why dominant states have created currency areas, as Britain, France, and Germany did during the 1930s.

23. For a parallel argument about the effects of international trade, see Scott C. James and David A. Lake, "The Second Face of Hegemony: Britain's Repeal of the Corn Laws and the American Walker Tariff of 1846," *International Organization* 43, no. 1 (1989): 1–29, especially 3–9.

cause money acts, like language, as a basic medium of social communication.[24] As with language, a common currency can foster a sense of common identity, especially as individuals experience monetary phenomena together. Helleiner (chap. 4 in this volume) expands on these points and discusses how the reduction of transaction costs within a currency bloc, the development of a common interest in the value and stability of the core currency, the collective experience of monetary phenomena, and the symbolic role of money can work together to alter both interests and identity. In a fashion analogous to endogenous optimum currency area theory, he argues that a currency union at once requires a degree of social trust and mutual identification among its users and that it can help generate that trust.[25]

Monetary Power versus Monetary Statecraft

To summarize, international monetary power can assume any of a number of different forms: the Power to Deflect the transitional costs of monetary adjustment, the Power to Delay payment of adjustment's continuing costs, the Power to Rearticulate actors' economic interests, and the Power to Reconstruct actors' social identities. Regardless of the form it assumes, however, monetary power must be distinguished from monetary statecraft. Although monetary power exists whenever a state's behavior changes because of its monetary relationship with another state, monetary statecraft has a more restricted meaning: the conscious manipulation of monetary relations in order to affect the policies of other states.

Put differently, monetary power does not correspond to control; it corresponds, instead, to influence. This distinction, which hinges on the notion of intent, is essential to power analysis. To illustrate, if a parent behaves badly, this behavior may cause the parent's child to behave badly as well. This may not be the parent's intent; the parent may be saddened at this outcome, or may remain oblivious to it. Nevertheless, the child's poor behavior may reflect the parent's power or influence, understood as a relational property.

Thus, it is one thing to claim that power exists; this refers to a kind of relationship. But efforts to exploit this relationship—that is, to manipulate it in order to pursue specific objectives—are quite another matter.[26] Such undertakings—or in-

24. Eric Helleiner, "National Currencies and National Identities," *American Behavioral Scientist* 41, no. 10 (1998): 1409–36; Eric Helleiner, *The Making of National Money: Territorial Currencies in Historical Perspective* (Ithaca: Cornell University Press, 2003), 100–120.

25. On endogenous optimum currency-area theory, see Jeffrey A. Frankel and Andrew K. Rose, "The Endogeneity of Optimum Currency Area Criteria," *The Economic Journal* 108, no. 449 (1998): 1009–25. On money and social trust, see Cohen, *Geography of Money*, 10–13; Matthias Kaelberer, "The Euro and European Identity: Symbols, Power and the Politics of European Monetary Union," *Review of International Studies* 30, no. 2 (April 2004): 161–78; Andrew Walter (chap. 3 in this volume).

26. Alternatively, some discussions of power assert that intent is essential to the concept. For example, Bertrand Russell, in *Power: A New Social Analysis* (London: Unwin Books, 1962), holds that "power may be defined as the production of intended effects" (25). Robert Dahl's "intuitive idea of power,"

fluence attempts—are purposeful acts; they are means toward an end, intended to bring about desired changes in the behavior of others. These influence attempts are sometimes called statecraft.

Statecraft consists of the art of conducting state affairs; gradually the use of the term has come to refer almost exclusively to a state's foreign relations. Building on an analytical foundation originally developed by Harold D. Lasswell, David Baldwin devised a fourfold division of policy instruments available to officials wishing to exercise influence abroad, composed of propaganda, diplomacy, economic statecraft, and military statecraft. Baldwin describes economic statecraft as "influence attempts relying primarily on resources which have a reasonable semblance of a market price in terms of money."[27] Monetary statecraft, we submit, is a subset of this category; it refers to influence attempts that rely primarily on the manipulation of monetary relations between states.

How would we know if monetary power is being intentionally harnessed—that is, if a change in an actor's behavior is the result of statecraft? Returning to the example introduced earlier—A's power over B with respect to issue C—merely asserting that B's new behavior conforms to A's preferences is not sufficient to establish deliberate manipulation. It may well be that A had no intention of altering B's behavior—that is, A made no explicit influence attempt. If so, it may still be the case that A has power over B (understood as a causal description of their relationship).[28] But absent an undertaking, the mere alignment of a less powerful actor's behavior with a more powerful actor's preferences is insufficient to establish conscious design on the part of that more powerful agent.

In short, power can exist even absent purposeful efforts to exploit it. Several of the contributors to this volume, especially David Andrews and Eric Helleiner, draw attention to the indirect and even nonintentional exercise of power.[29] But in order for these discussions to have concrete meaning, they rely on the distinction between power as a relational property—the power to act and to avoid being acted upon—and the deliberate exploitation of such a relationship.

---

namely that "A has power over B to the extent that he can get B to do something that B would not otherwise do"—although less clear on this point—also appears to incorporate intent as a matter of definition. "The Concept of Power," *Behavioral Science* 2 (1957): 201–15; quotation on 202–3. Such views are significantly different from Herbert Simon's claim, in *Models of Man* (New York: Wiley, 1957), that "for the assertion, 'A has power over B,' we can substitute the assertion, 'A's behavior causes B's behavior'" (5). Following Simon, we distinguish between power as a relational property, which is an assertion of a causal relationship without reference to intent, and the instrumental use of power.

27. Baldwin, *Economic Statecraft*, 13–14; Harold Lasswell, *Politics: Who Gets What, When, How* (New York: Meridian Books, 1958), 204–5 (in a postscript to a volume originally published in 1936).

28. If B's behavior with respect to issue C is different than it would be absent B's relationship with A. Unless this obtains, the statement that A has power over B with respect to issue C is devoid of meaning.

29. As do James and Lake, "The Second Face of Hegemony," in their discussion of coercive hegemony: "The invisible hand of market power, moreover, need not be exercised consciously by the hegemon" (8).

Elements of Monetary Statecraft

What aspects of interstate monetary relations are subject to deliberate manipulation? In addressing this question, we identify two broad categories: currency relations and financial relations (with the latter limited to its monetary aspects).[30] Within the broad category of currency relations, we distinguish between policies regarding currency values and those regarding currency use. Within the broad category of financial relations, we distinguish between policies regarding payments financing and those regarding liquidity provision.

These distinctions have to do with the means associated with monetary statecraft; but the manipulation of monetary relationships can also be usefully classified, even though with reservations, with respect to its immediate ends. Those ends, or objectives, may be primarily internal or external in their orientation.[31] For example, authorities may desire to lower interest rates without incurring substantial collateral costs (e.g., capital outflows); here the objective is primarily internal, even though the pursuit of that objective may involve the use of controls on external capital movements. On the other hand, national authorities might want to encourage their economic partners to stimulate their economies or perhaps to warn some state against devaluing the exchange rate of its currency. It might be argued that the ultimate purpose behind even these last actions is internal—that is, the real aim of stimulating economic activity elsewhere is to expand national export markets, and the purpose of defending stable exchange rates is to protect existing markets.[32] But certainly the immediate objectives of such actions are external.

Table 1.2 summarizes the resulting typology. Four policy areas—the manipulation of currency values, currency use, payments financing, and liquidity provision—are conjoined with the internal/external dichotomy regarding their immediate orientation. The resulting range of eight general policy objectives, and some of the associated policy strategies, is discussed in greater detail later; first, however, I briefly survey the major points of this schema.

With respect to currency values, national authorities might have the internal objective of insulating domestic monetary policy, an ambition that could be pursued by deploying a system of capital controls (although other strategies are available as well); alternatively, authorities might have the external objective of manipulating currencies' exchange rates, possibly in order to promote exports but also in order to exact concessions on other issues. With respect to currency use, authorities might wish to restrict external employment of the national currency, in order to preserve

30. Without this constraint, financial relations would be far too broad a category to be usefully construed as a subset of monetary affairs. On the political economy of credit more generally, see the references in the introduction to this volume.

31. As the discussion in the remainder of this paragraph suggests, describing the ultimate orientation of policy as either internal or external is more challenging; hence our focus on immediate objectives.

32. In turn, it might be argued that a still deeper motivation is to secure the reelection of the government, and so on.

Table 1.2 Objectives and instruments of monetary statecraft

		Policy area			
		Currency relations		Financial relations	
		Currency value	Currency use	Payments financing	Liquidity provision
Immediate orientation of policy	Primary internal	Domestic policy insulation (e.g., via capital controls)	Restricting external employment of the currency	Developing and maintaining access to external sources of payments financing with minimal policy constraints	Ensuring that domestic access to official liquidity is not a policy constraint
		Example: Malaysia following the Asian currency crisis	Example: German policy under the EMS	Example: IMF net reserve positions	Example: Creation of SDRs
	Primary external	External currency manipulation (e.g., talking the dollar down)	Promoting external employment of the currency	Providing limited and conditional access to payments financing	Exploiting others' reliance on official liquidity
		Example: U.S. policy prior to Bonn summit	Example: U.S. policy after World War II	Example: Financial aspects of the Suez crisis	Example: U.S. opposition to the formation of an Asian Monetary Fund

EMS, European Monetary Systems
SDRs, Special Drawing Rights

domestic autonomy; on the other hand, there are substantial incentives to enhance the external employment of the national currency, not least the profits deriving from seigniorage.[33] With respect to financial relations, likely debtors may seek to ensure access to payments financing and to develop sources of official liquidity, in order to buffer themselves against the whims of creditors. Those same potential creditors, on the other hand, have the opposite set of incentives: to exploit others' reliance on payments financing and to provide liquidity in limited amounts and subject to some form of conditionality.

Table 1.2 includes illustrations of strategies associated with these objectives; these examples are intended to be broadly suggestive, not exclusive or exhaustive. Some of these cases have already been discussed; others are noted in the pages that follow.

33. See note 11.

Currency Relations: Domestic Policy Insulation and Exchange-Rate Manipulation

One possible objective of monetary statecraft is to insulate domestic monetary policy from external pressures, or in other words to preserve monetary autonomy, to the fullest extent possible. A state could do this by becoming a regional or global monetary leader and encouraging follower states to adapt to its policy preferences; but, as a matter of definition, not all states can be monetary leaders. For the vast majority of states, the prospects for policy insulation depend instead on the availability of intermediate options for productive engagement with the global economy—options between the logical extremes of complete integration, on the one hand, and autarky, on the other.

A prominent policy tool available to authorities seeking such a balanced outcome is the use of capital controls.[34] Capital controls may induce a great deal of evasion, but that does not mean that they are never effective; in recent years, the Chilean experience, among others, has demonstrated that the use of selective controls can produce certain positive results.[35] And though capital controls remain a blunt instrument for insulating domestic policies from external influences, they may form part of a more comprehensive strategy that includes securing cheap and reliable access to payments financing and international liquidity (as discussed later).

Malaysia's imposition of a capital control regime following the Asian currency crisis, and the response of U.S. authorities to that development, is discussed by Kirshner (chap. 7 in this volume). But capital controls are not the only means whereby national authorities can enhance domestic policy autonomy. Alternatively, authorities may pursue a strategy of exchange-rate floating, an approach that reduces reliance on both capital controls and external financing; Louis Pauly (chap. 9 in this volume) reviews the Canadian experience on this front.

As Pauly notes, the choice of strategy—the search for a reasonably stable solution to the problems of the "messy middle" between the "corner solutions" of exchange-rate fixing and floating[36]—will depend critically on the characteristics of the state's domestic political economy. For example, Austria's corporatist political economy made possible a strategy entirely at odds with the Canadian approach. By comparing postwar monetary policy in these two small economies, Pauly is able to survey

---

34. This was well understood by the designers of the Bretton Woods institutions, as Eric Helleiner demonstrates in *States and the Re-emergence of Global Finance: From Bretton Woods to the 1990s* (Ithaca: Cornell University Press, 1994). But the IMF's Articles of Agreement failed to realize in full the shared goals of Maynard Keynes and Harry Dexter White with respect to capital controls; see David M. Andrews, "The Bretton Woods Agreement as an Invitation to Struggle," in *The Economy as a Polity: The Political Constitution of Contemporary Capitalism*, ed. Christian Joerges, Bo Stråth, and Peter Wagner, 77–97 (London: University College London Press, 2005).

35. The Chilean experience suggests that controls can help change the composition of capital flows in helpful ways; they were less successful in limiting exchange-rate appreciation. For a more general discussion, see Benjamin Cohen, *The Future of Money* (Princeton: Princeton University Press, 2004), 104–21.

36. David M. Andrews, C. Randall Henning, and Louis W. Pauly, eds., *Governing the World's Money* (Ithaca: Cornell University Press, 2002), 4–5.

the means at the disposal of monetary followers seeking to buffer the influence of monetary leaders. Depending on their internal characteristics, he argues, states in broadly similar international situations may choose dramatically different strategies for limiting the influence of powerful partners.

Another element of monetary statecraft is the manipulation of currencies' external values, or exchange rates. This is a broad category of policy activities with any of several possible objectives.[37] Those objectives may be benign, as in efforts to stabilize a currency's external value (whether unilaterally or as part of a pegged exchange-rate regime); or they may be sinister, as in efforts to undermine a particular national economy or to disrupt a given international regime.[38] Often the objective is of an intermediate nature—coercive without being destructive—as was the case with U.S. policy prior to the Bonn summit and, in fact, more generally in the cases surveyed by Henning (chap. 6 in this volume).

Regardless of the goal, the most direct mechanism for exchange-rate manipulation is foreign-exchange market intervention using national reserves (or, in explicitly predatory actions, counterfeiting the currency of a country targeted for disruption). Less direct mechanisms include arranging credit to pursue additional market interventions, persuading other public authorities (e.g., foreign central banks) to intervene in the exchange market in support of shared objectives, or persuading private actors to engage in speculative activities in support of policy goals (e.g., "talking the dollar down").[39] Conversely, authorities might endeavor to persuade public or private actors *not* to engage in any of these actions.

Kirshner (chap. 7) and Henning (chap. 6 in this volume) address external currency manipulation as an objective of monetary statecraft in the face of changing circumstances. Kirshner argues that the political attractiveness of currency manipulation depends in part on environmental characteristics, including the degree of capital mobility (influencing the means by which this objective can be achieved) and the overall distribution of power within the international system (influencing the policy objectives of states). On balance, however, he finds that opportunities for politically motivated currency manipulation continue to abound. Henning draws somewhat different conclusions, arguing that the employment of the exchange-rate weapon creates its own resistance and, more specifically, that authorities in Japan and Europe have now substantially insulated themselves from this form of coercion emanating from the United States.

---

37. Kirshner, *Currency and Coercion*, defines currency manipulation as "actions taken to affect the stability or value of target currencies" (8). National authorities do not typically want their currency to be relatively costly or cheap as an end in itself; nevertheless, they sometimes desire to manipulate their currencies' values in order to achieve other objectives, such as promoting exports or maintaining a supply of affordable imports. See Broz and Frieden, "Political Economy of International Monetary Relations," especially 319, 331–35.

38. Or, as in the case of "strategic disruption," to extract side payments because of credible threats to engage in such disruption. For a discussion, see Kirshner, *Currency and Coercion*, 171–73.

39. Once again, *in extremis* authorities might encourage other parties to counterfeit a targeted currency; Jonathan Kirshner (chap. 7 in this volume) provides examples and a discussion.

Currency Relations: Influencing Currency Use

Another channel of monetary statecraft involves the promotion (or discouragement) of a currency's external use. Rather than seeking to influence a currency's external value, the aim here is to influence its external employment—the variety of purposes to which it is put and the variety of locales in which it functions.[40] Increased external use enhances the issuing state's capacity to extract wealth from abroad (through seigniorage); it may also allow the issuing state to enjoy some of the benefits associated with currency entrapment, as previously described. Thus, there are powerful arguments in favor of expansion of external use.[41]

But the widespread employment of a given national currency outside the borders of the issuing authority is not necessarily an unalloyed benefit; it can impose certain costs as well. Certainly the problems experienced by postwar Britain in managing the sterling balances held by other members of the Commonwealth suggest the enormous potential costs of allowing a national money to serve as a reserve currency.[42] This lesson was not lost on West German policy makers when the external use of the deutschmark threatened to expand during the 1970s and 1980s as a result of the currency's pivotal role in the European Monetary System (EMS), and German authorities took active measures to discourage this outcome. Japanese officials were likewise wary about an international role for the yen.[43]

Understanding these different policy preferences requires grappling more carefully with the power implications of external use. For example, although enhanced foreign use can result in increased seigniorage, it also entails at least a potential future cost: should the foreign holders decide (en masse) to dump these holdings in favor of another currency and should these foreign holdings be significant, the effects on the currency's value could be considerable. Calculations vary as to the likelihood of this outcome and its expected effects should it occur, as Cooper explains in his discussion of the politics of currency areas (chap. 8 in this volume). National authorities have therefore varied substantially in their approach to this matter, with some—like the British during World War II—actively promoting their currencies' employment abroad. Certainly U.S. authorities were not averse to expanding the dollar's role as an international currency after 1945.[44] Other states—notably Germany, Japan, and Switzerland during the 1970s and 1980s—have taken steps to limit foreign use of the national currency.[45]

40. On the dynamics and scale of currency internationalization (the use of a currency for cross-border transactions) and currency substitution (the use of a currency to perform some or all of the traditional functions of money within a foreign state), see Cohen, *Geography of Money*, 92–118.

41. On the other hand, some of the benefits of entrapment can be achieved without requiring enhanced external use of a nation's currency (e.g., by promoting stable exchange rates with selected partners); see, in this regard, note 21.

42. For discussions of these difficulties, see Benjamin J. Cohen, *The Future of Sterling as an International Currency* (London: Macmillan, 1971); Susan Strange, *Sterling and British Policy: A Political Study of An International Currency in Decline* (London: Oxford University Press, 1971).

43. C. Randall Henning, *Currencies and Politics in the United States, Germany, and Japan* (Washington, D.C.: Institute for International Economics, 1994), 316–20.

44. Ibid., 320–21.

45. Even strict neutrality with respect to external use constitutes a policy decision; this is the case

The techniques associated with currency promotion, at least in the present day, are typically indirect; they tend to involve persuasion of one form or another.[46] As Walter notes (chap. 3 in this volume), the most powerful form of persuasion is to have an attractive currency, supported by an appropriate policy mix and a credible set of domestic institutions; but these conditions are hardly susceptible to easy manipulation. Instead, official decisions to "dollarize" (a term sometimes employed to describe substitution of the domestic currency, even when the substitute is not the greenback) often involve side payments. These may be relatively transparent, as with arrangements for access to lender-of-last-resort facilities within a currency area, or more opaque, as with the military arrangements that sometimes accompany currency use decisions.[47] The point is that policy decisions to adopt another state's currency for certain purposes, or even as legal tender, are apt to involve multiple considerations.[48]

Financial Relations: Control of Payments Financing and Liquidity Provision

Although international financial relations are a broad subject extending well beyond the ambit of this study, there are aspects of financial relations that impinge directly on monetary policy and international monetary relations—especially payments financing and the provision of official liquidity. In fact, the distinction between these two areas is a fine one, having to do primarily with the ways in which payments deficits can be financed (and, hence, real adjustment can be avoided). The essential distinction here is between liability financing and asset financing. Liability financing means running up external liabilities by borrowing; asset financing is about drawing down existing savings or reserves. Either method can be used to finance deficits, each with its own advantages and disadvantages.

By payments financing, then, we mean liability financing—that is, access to external credit; examples include currency-swap arrangements between central banks and borrowing from the IMF. By liquidity provision, we mean asset financing—that is, accumulating reserve assets or their equivalents; examples include unconditional lines of credit—which amount to the creation of new assets—and the distribution of Special Drawing Rights (SDRs), a reserve asset created in the 1960s by the member states of the IMF in an attempt to reduce reliance on the dollar.[49]

---

with the European Central Bank (ECB), whose policy with respect to the euro (at least in its official articulation) is neither to promote nor to discourage its foreign employment through specific measures.

46. This was not always the case; during the colonial era, efforts to enforce the external use of particular currencies were sometimes both direct and forceful.

47. Of course, even more blatant side payments, such as bribes to individual decision makers, are not out of the question, especially in currency areas involving states with weak administrative and legal safeguards.

48. As a general matter, efforts to influence private decisions about currency use offer reduced opportunities for side payments, given the diffuse nature of the targeted audience. Such opportunities nevertheless exist when crucial decisions are centralized in the hands of major market actors.

49. For a comprehensive exposition of the origins of the SDR, see John S. Odell, *U.S. International Monetary Policy: Markets, Power, and Ideas as Sources of Change* (Princeton: Princeton University Press,

What are the objectives of monetary authorities with respect to these instruments? In general, authorities from deficit states, or from states where authorities regard future deficits as likely, would like to ensure that internal policies will not be constrained by the absence of liquidity (regardless of its source—that is, regardless of whether it takes the form of payments financing or official liquidity provision). In this respect, their objectives are similar to those previously discussed with respect to domestic policy insulation; the difference is the means that are employed to secure this objective. Instead of (or in addition to) seeking to insulate their economies from external influence through the use of capital controls and related instruments, authorities may hope to develop arrangements that will secure a supply of liquidity that is both reliable and inexpensive. Examples of such arrangements include member states' net reserve positions at the IMF, from which they can borrow without conditions.

Authorities from surplus states, on the other hand, are understandably interested in controlling the access of outsiders to their resources or even to the resources of others. This interest derives in the first instance from their fiduciary responsibilities: they want to make sure that policies are in place to ensure repayment. In addition, there is a natural temptation to exploit others' reliance on these resources in order to accomplish ancillary objectives; examples include IMF loan programs, which are typically associated with conditionality. As Kirshner (chap. 7 in this volume) discusses, IMF negotiations over aid to South Korea in the wake of the Asian financial crisis covered a range of topics well beyond the fund's normal remit, topics that had long been on the wish list of the U.S. Treasury.

The conflicting objectives of debtors and creditors have been one of the defining features of international monetary politics. Certainly the Suez case demonstrates the substantial leverage that a creditor state (the United States) was able to impose on a debtor (the United Kingdom).[50] And just as concerns about the provision of international liquidity led to the introduction of SDRs during the 1960s, similar worries—and especially the widespread view among Asian governments that the United States abused its influence in the IMF during the currency crises of the 1990s— have led to more recent pressures for the formation of an Asian Monetary Fund, a subject discussed by both Henning and Kirshner.

The Limits to Monetary Statecraft

The preceding sections have outlined our understanding of power generally, of monetary power in particular, and of the elements of monetary statecraft. We have

---

1982), 79–164. Some hoped that the European Currency Unit (ECU) would likewise serve as a source of official liquidity within the EMS; instead, this pseudo-currency acted merely as an accounting instrument.

50. There is some dispute as to whether the United States helped precipitate sterling's problems in this episode. There is no doubt, however, that Washington took advantage of the resulting situation, as described at the beginning of this chapter.

distinguished between power itself and efforts to harness it—that is, efforts by a powerful actor to sway others' behavior in particular ways. That distinction becomes especially important as we discuss the limits to monetary statecraft.

Monetary statecraft entails the employment of policy tools for instrumental purposes; but this is easier said than done. In fact, among the central findings of our study are the substantial impediments to the efficient exercise of monetary power as a deliberate instrument of economic statecraft. Above all, the same quality of publicness that led Joanne Gowa to distinguish the domestic politics of money from its policy counterparts—for example, trade or industrial policies—has parallel implications for the study of monetary statecraft.[51] As a result, the tools of monetary statecraft—especially those tools having to do with currency relations—are often too blunt to be effective when they would most be desired and too diffuse to be directed at particular targets without incurring substantial collateral damage.[52]

To illustrate this problem, consider a final case, one that some commentators regard as the exercise of monetary power par excellence: the 1971 closure of the "gold window," the facility at the U.S. Treasury through which foreign central banks could convert their dollar holdings into gold. Many scholars argue that this development demonstrated the capacity of the United States to rewrite the rules of the Bretton Woods system unilaterally—changes that were later reluctantly ratified by Washington's allies in the Smithsonian Agreement. As Susan Strange later put it, "to decide one August morning that dollars can no longer be converted into gold was a progression from exorbitant privilege to super-exorbitant privilege; the US government was exercising the unconstrained right to print money that others could not (save at unacceptable cost) refuse to accept."[53]

This case does indeed demonstrate U.S. economic power; but a closer look at the facts reveals distinct limits to the ability of the United States to manipulate monetary relations. The August 15, 1971, announcement that the gold window would be closed—subsequently referred to in Japan as "the Nixon shock"—was preceded by a meeting at Camp David of top U.S. economic officials. Although there were prominent clashes at this meeting between Federal Reserve chairman Arthur Burns and Secretary of Treasury John Connally, perhaps the most interesting role was played by Treasury Undersecretary for Monetary Affairs Paul Volcker. Volcker had been a consistent advocate of the Bretton Woods system, and of fixed exchange rates, since

51. Joanne S. Gowa, "Public Goods and Political Institutions: Trade and Monetary Policy Processes in the United States," *International Organization* 42, no. 1 (winter 1988): 15–32.

52. Although focusing on the domestic implications of this observation, Broz and Frieden, "Political Economy of International Monetary Relations," note that "exchange rate policy is less excludable than trade policy" (328). For a more general discussion of the characteristics of public goods (including their nonexcludability), see Duncan Snidal, "Public Goods, Property Rights, and Political Organizations," *International Studies Quarterly* 23, no. 4 (December 1979): 532–66; for the degree to which different policy areas have these characteristics, see Duncan Snidal, "The Limits of Hegemonic Stability Theory," *International Organization* 39, no. 4 (autumn 1985): 579–614.

53. Susan Strange, "The Persistent Myth of Lost Hegemony," *International Organization* 41, no.: 4 (1987): 551–74, quotation on 569. For classic political science analyses of the closing of the gold window, see Joanne S. Gowa, *Closing the Gold Window: Domestic Politics and the End of Bretton Woods* (Ithaca: Cornell University Press, 1983); Odell, *U.S. International Monetary Policy*, 165–291.

his days at the New York Federal Reserve. But at the Camp David meeting, he wavered. "I hate to do this, to close the window. All my life I have defended exchange rates, but I think it is needed. . . . But don't let's close the window and sit—let's get other governments to negotiate new rates."[54]

Volcker's statement reveals the central dilemma for the U.S. team. Reviewing this period many years later, Volcker wrote that America's partners, and Japanese officials in particular, "misunderstood our intentions" when the gold window closed.

> The Japanese assumed we simply wanted to avoid gold sales. They would have been perfectly happy to buy and hold dollars; what they did not want was a change in the exchange rate. But that, of course, was exactly what we had decided was essential. What we did not really want, and really had been forced upon us, was a change in the official price of gold that a succession of administrations had pledged was inviolate.[55]

Why did Volcker believe a change in the gold price was undesirable but ultimately acceptable, whereas a negotiated change in exchange rates was highly desirable but impossible? Because "I did not believe, and John Connally certainly did not believe, that we could go to the Japanese and the Europeans and say, in effect, 'Look, contrary to all we've said for seven years, we want a big realignment of exchange rates. Let's arrange it this weekend before the markets open on Monday.'"[56] Pressed on this issue at the Camp David meeting, Volcker was forced to concede that negotiating a realignment would be an impossible task. "They [the Japanese and Europeans] certainly would have refused." Indeed, "they would also immediately have been placed in an intolerable position."[57]

Volcker therefore reluctantly endorsed the course of unilateral action. Closing the gold window was not the outcome U.S. officials wanted, but it was the one they controlled, and they could use it to help bring about the changes that they really desired: "a big shift in exchange rates, trade liberalization by [U.S. economic partners], and more help on our overseas defense costs as well."[58]

But if closing the gold window was not the policy objective, neither was it an adequate tool to bring about the policy changes the United States desired. Volcker later confessed his naïveté on this matter: "I thought we could wrap up an exchange rate realignment and start talking about reform [of the international monetary system] in a month or two; say, by the IMF meeting in late September." On the other hand,

54. William Safire, *Before the Fall: An Inside View of the Pre-Watergate White House* (Garden City, N.Y.: Doubleday, 1975), 513–15.

55. Paul A. Volcker and Toyoo Gyohten, *Changing Fortunes: The World's Money and the Threat to American Leadership* (New York: Times Books, 1992), 80–81.

56. Ibid., 78. Such a timetable would have been necessary because extended talks on the subject would become public knowledge and precipitate yet another run on the dollar.

57. Volcker added, "How could they continue to hold and buy dollars in the market and not convert them into gold? How could we possibly avoid leaks of information and enormous speculation? And how would we cope with that situation—other than to suspend gold payments right away, with the appearance of defeat and the loss of initiative." Volcker and Gyohten, *Changing Fortunes*, 78.

58. Ibid., 81.

"Connally assumed from the start that it would take months to put the other countries in a mood to accept sufficiently large exchange rate changes."[59]

In fact, Connally (together with Nixon) had foreseen the end game to these negotiations in a way that Volcker did not. Much to Volcker's consternation, "a lot of time was spent at Camp David in dealing with what to me was a side issue"—a series of import surcharges imposed at the time of the gold window's closure, and legal justifications for these tariffs (which violated international trade agreements to which the United States was a party). Volcker initially attributed this discussion entirely to a campaign promise the president had made to textile manufacturers, a "pledge that the president apparently felt more strongly about than gold."[60] But the import surcharge turned out to be crucial in the negotiations leading to the eventual ratification of the U.S. reform agenda because, in the ensuing negotiations, lifting this tax was the only concession that the United States team (as led by Connally) was prepared to make. The gold window was not reopened, the dollar was devalued against gold, and a substantial realignment against the Japanese and European currencies was agreed on, all in exchange for relief on the import surcharges—much as Nixon and Connally had envisioned.[61]

Again, interpreters of this episode have made much of the ability of the United States to rewrite the rules of the international monetary system at the drop of a hat. In fact, that redrafting took months to negotiate and ultimately depended on trade concessions—lifting the Nixon surcharge—for its success. Put differently, the dollar's central role in the world monetary system was not a sufficient basis to renegotiate even the terms of that role, much less the comprehensive package of concessions sought by Washington. Only in conjunction with targeted trade sanctions was the Nixon team able to bring about the Smithsonian Agreement; the monetary options were too blunt, and too indiscriminate, to be effective negotiating tools.

This is not always the case; often monetary relations can be manipulated as an effective instrument of statecraft. But because the capacity of governments to discriminate in such efforts—to target particular actors while shielding others—is limited (especially with respect to currency relations), monetary threats are sometimes less attractive—and less credible—than certain other forms of economic coercion.[62] Certainly the moments when the deliberate application of monetary pressure can be

59. Ibid., 80.
60. Ibid., 79.
61. The United States largely realized its goals with respect to exchange-rate realignment, whereas trade liberalization concessions by its partners were minimal and military offset negotiations remained more or less continual. But, much to the administration's consternation, there was no formal devaluation of the U.S. dollar against the currency of its largest trading partner—Canada—because authorities in Ottawa refused to end their exchange-rate float. For a discussion, see Louis Pauly (chap. 9 in this volume).
62. For example, a large body of recent scholarly work has addressed the implications of a strategic understanding of power for the assessment of international economic sanctions. These studies call into question the prior consensus, widely held by mainstream international relations scholars, that sanctions are ineffective as policy tools. See, for example, Alistair Smith, "The Success and Use of Economic Sanctions," *International Interactions* 21, no. 3 (1996): 229–45; T. Clifton Morgan and Anne C. Meiers, "When

decisive—as in the Suez case—are rare. Hence, although the power element in international monetary relations is ubiquitous, opportunities to engage successfully in monetary statecraft are not.

As states and citizens struggle to organize their societies to meet the challenges of the twenty-first century, they will need to take international monetary power into account. Likewise, and despite its limitations, monetary statecraft will at least periodically shape behavior in its intended targets. In this volume, we have outlined a framework for understanding both monetary power and monetary statecraft, and the relationship between them. Future research should examine the limits to monetary statecraft more closely—a subject this volume only begins to explore—because the exercise of monetary power is bound to remain a salient feature of international relations.

Threats Succeed: A Formal Model of the Threat and Use of Economic Sanctions," paper presented at the 95th annual meeting of the American Political Science Association, Atlanta, Georgia, September 1999; Daniel W. Drezner, *The Sanctions Paradox: Economic Statecraft and International Relations* (New York: Cambridge University Press, 1999); Dean Lacy and Emerson M. S. Niou, "A Theory of Economic Sanctions" (unpublished manuscript), Duke University, Durham, North Carolina, 2000; Daniel W. Drezner, "The Hidden Hand of Economic Coercion," *International Organization* 57 (summer 2003): 643–59.

PART TWO

Monetary Power

CHAPTER TWO

The Macrofoundations
of Monetary Power

Benjamin J. Cohen

What are the foundations of monetary power? David Andrews (chap. 1 in this volume) distinguishes between two pathways for the exercise of monetary power: the macro-level, linked to the problem of balance-of-payments disequilibrium; and the micro-level, working through the capacity of money to alter actor interests and identities. The purpose of this chapter is to promote a clearer understanding of the sources of power at the macro-level pathway—what we may call the macrofoundations of monetary power. Building in good part on earlier contributions of my own,[1] I argue that the central issue at the macro-level is the distribution of the burden of adjustment to external imbalance. The macro-level dimension of monetary power consists, first and foremost, of a capacity to *avoid* payments adjustment costs, either by delaying adjustment or by deflecting the burden of adjustment on to others. Ceteris paribus, the greater is a state's capacity to avoid adjustment costs, relative to that of other states, the greater is its power at the macro-level.

The devil, of course, is in the details. What do we mean by adjustments costs? What are the sources of the capacity to avoid adjustment costs—the macrofoundations of monetary power? And what are the limits of that capacity? The first of these questions is addressed in first three sections of this chapter, and the subsequent questions are addressed in sections four and five. Section six concludes.

The Burden of Adjustment

Analysis at the macro-level, I submit, must begin by focusing on the distribution of the burden of adjustment to external imbalance. The underlying source of power at

---

1. Including, especially, Benjamin J. Cohen, "Adjustment Costs and the Distribution of New Reserves," *Princeton Studies in International Finance*, no. 18 (1966).

this level is a state's relative capacity to avoid adjustment costs, either by delaying the adjustment process or by deflecting the burden of adjustment to others.

Autonomy and Influence

At the most general level, power in international relations is defined as the ability to control, or at least influence, the outcome of events. In operational terms, this naturally equates with a capacity to control the behavior of actors—"letting others have your way," as diplomacy has jokingly been defined. A state, in this sense, is powerful to the extent that it can effectively pressure or coerce outsiders, in short, to the extent that it can exercise leverage or enforce compliance. As Andrews points out (chap. 1 in this volume), a common synonym for this meaning of power is, simply, *influence*.[2]

But influence is not the only relevant meaning of power. There is also a vital second meaning, corresponding to the dictionary definition of power as a capacity for action. A state is also powerful to the extent that it is able to exercise policy independence—to act freely, insulated from outside pressure in policy formulation and implementation. In this sense, power does not mean influencing others; rather, it means not allowing others to influence *you*—others letting you have *your* way. A useful synonym for this meaning of power is *autonomy*.

The distinction between the two meanings is critical. Influence and autonomy may be understood as two distinct dimensions of power, which we may label, respectively, the external dimension and internal dimension. Both are based in social relationships and can be observed in behavioral terms. Both are also unavoidably interrelated. They are not, however, of equal importance. Logically, power begins with autonomy, the internal dimension. Influence, the external dimension, is best thought of as functionally derivative—inconceivable in practical terms without first attaining and sustaining a relatively high degree of policy independence at home. As the saying goes in American football, the best offense starts with a good defense. It is possible to think of autonomy without influence; it is impossible to think of influence without at least some degree of autonomy.

This does not mean that autonomy must be enjoyed in *all* aspects of international affairs or in *all* geographic relationships in order to be able to exercise influence in *any* aspect or relationship. Neither domain nor scope needs to be universal for power to be effective. States can successfully apply leverage in selected issue areas or relationships even while themselves being subject to pressure or coercion in others. But

---

2. The careful reader will note that, in a previous essay, I proposed the term *authority* rather than *influence* for this meaning of power. See Benjamin J. Cohen, "Money and Power in World Politics," in *Strange Power: Shaping the Parameters of International Relations and International Political Economy*, ed. Thomas C. Lawton, James N. Rosenau, and Amy C. Verdun, 91–113 (Aldershot: Ashgate, 2000). I am now persuaded, however, that, because of the inferences of legitimacy associated with the notion of authority, the term *influence* is preferable. For more on the ties between monetary authority and legitimacy, which are an important part of the micro-level pathway of power, see especially Andrew Walter (chap. 3) and Louis Pauly (chap. 9 in this volume).

it does mean that in a *given* issue area or geographic relationship, power begins at home. First and foremost, policy makers must be free (or at least relatively free) to pursue national objectives in the specific issue area or relationship without outside constraint, to avoid compromises or sacrifices to accommodate the interests of others. Only then will a state be in a position, in addition, to enforce compliance elsewhere. Autonomy, the internal dimension, may not be *sufficient* to ensure a degree of foreign influence. But it is manifestly *necessary*—the essential precondition of influence.

The Core of Monetary Power

Autonomy, of course, is prized by governments in every aspect of international relations. Its salience, however, is most evident in economic relations, which by definition create a condition of interdependence with other states that is both active and ongoing. Economic relations involve transactional linkages, creating a web of mutual dependencies. Mutual dependencies, however—as Robert Keohane and Joseph Nye long ago reminded us in their classic *Power and Interdependence,* first published in 1977[3]—are rarely symmetrical. Opportunities are created, therefore, for an exercise of influence by those who are less dependent—in short, by those with relatively greater autonomy. The lower the degree of a state's dependence on a relationship, relative to others, the greater will be its ability to manage existing connections to its own advantage.

And in no area of economic relations is the salience of autonomy more evident than in the realm of monetary affairs, where states are inescapably linked through the balance of payments. The risk of unsustainable payments disequilibrium represents a constant threat to policy independence. Excessive imbalances automatically generate mutual pressures to adjust, to help move the balance of payments back toward equilibrium. But adjustment can be inconvenient or even costly in both economic and political terms. No government likes being forced to compromise key policy goals for the sake of restoring external balance. All, if given a choice, would prefer to see others make the necessary sacrifices. At the macro-level of monetary affairs, therefore, monetary power consists of the capacity to avoid the burden of adjustment required by payments imbalance.

The core importance of autonomy in this regard has not always been fully appreciated in the scholarly literature. Indeed, most students of monetary power (including most of the contributors to this volume) prefer to stress the external dimension—the capacity to control the behavior of others in one way or another—rather than the internal dimension. But we cannot ignore the functionally derivative nature of the external dimension. In practice, power in a given issue area such as monetary relations logically begins with autonomy—the preservation of key policy goals at home. That is the necessary condition. Only if a state is actually able to avoid

---

3. Robert O. Keohane and Joseph S. Nye, *Power and Interdependence: World Politics in Transition,* 3rd ed. (New York: Longman, 2001).

the burden of adjustment domestically will it be in a position, in turn, to exert influence elsewhere. Hence, if we are interested in getting to the very core of power at the macro-level, we must go first to the internal dimension, as I propose here. Above all, what matters for the exercise of power abroad is practical freedom of action at home.[4]

The Two Modes of Influence

But we cannot ignore the external dimension entirely. Because monetary relations are inherently reciprocal, a potential for influence, in a real sense, is created automatically whenever practical policy independence is achieved. By definition, a capacity to avoid adjustment costs implies that if payments equilibrium is to be restored, others must adjust instead—at least part of the burden will be diverted elsewhere. Hence, a measure of influence is necessarily generated as an inescapable corollary of the process. That too matters for analytical purposes.

But it is also important to keep the matter in perspective. The influence that derives automatically from a capacity to avoid adjustment costs represents at best a contingent aspect of power because it can be said to exist at all only because of the core dimension of autonomy. Moreover, the impacts involved are diffuse and undirected. That is very different from what is conventionally meant by the external dimension of power, which most often is understood to imply some degree of direct focus or deliberate intent—what Andrews (chap. 1 in this volume) calls a "purposeful act." From a political economy point of view, the difference is critical.

Essentially, the difference goes to the contrast between what Scott James and David Lake label the first and second faces of hegemony (or power): the first face of direct government-to-government influence, which is exercised through positive or negative sanctions; and the second face of market leverage, which favorably alters incentive structures.[5] Correspondingly, we may think in terms of two modes in the exercise of influence: passive and active. The influence generated as a corollary of the adjustment process is exercised passively, even unpremeditatedly, and is best understood simply as the alter ego of autonomy. Alternatively, influence may be exercised actively, targeted at specific countries and applied with self-conscious purpose—in

---

4. Implicit in this formulation, of course, is an assumption that, in responding to external imbalance, the country is already at internal balance—that is, that domestic policy goals are already being achieved in spite of (or perhaps because of) the external imbalance. Hence, any compromise of (deviation from) current policy would in fact be considered a sacrifice. Implicit also is an assumption that domestic policy goals are defined by a political process rather than by pure economic calculation. No presumption is made that freedom of action at home will be used in a manner that meets the test of economic rationality.

5. Scott James and David Lake, "The Second Face of Hegemony: Britain's Repeal of the Corn Laws and the American Walker Tariff of 1846," *International Organization* 43, no. 1(1989): 1–30. In all, James and Lake identify three faces of hegemony, drawing, as they readily admit, on an earlier literature going back to Peter Bachrach and Morton Baratz, "The Two Faces of Power," *American Political Science Review* 56, no. 4 (December, 1962): 947–52. The third face added by James and Lake, which stresses the hegemon's use of ideas and ideology to influence opinion, is more a part of the micro-level pathway of power and is not directly considered here.

the language of Andrews (chap. 1 in this volume), a deliberate "influence attempt." Both modes of influence begin with autonomy as a basic and necessary condition, and in both cases other states may feel compelled to adjust. But, whereas in the passive mode the pressures exerted on others are market-driven, operating through hegemony's second face, in the active mode the pressures are exerted directly by government, hegemony's first face.

In a sense, passive influence in the adjustment process is relatively uncontroversial, broadly accepted as an unavoidable, if regrettable, consequence of inequality—a veritable fact of life. Active influence attempts, by contrast, are apt to become far more politicized because they are both elective and purposeful. The active mode seeks to compel others to bear the burden of adjustment, taking us well beyond the notion of influence as simply an incidental by-product of autonomy. The active mode, in effect, aims to translate passive influence into practical control through the instrumental use of power. That is a very big difference, indeed.

The Two Hands of Monetary Power

The bottom line is clear. Whereas payments disequilibria are necessarily shared—one nation's deficit is someone else's surplus—the costs of adjustment need not be shared at all. Governments thus have every incentive, ceteris paribus, to maximize their capacity to avoid adjustment costs—their autonomy—relative to others. The greater the relative capacity to avoid adjustment costs, the greater is a state's monetary power.

My focus here on adjustment costs is hardly novel, of course. Other scholars have also placed the distribution of the burden of adjustment at the heart of their comments on monetary power, including David Andrews,[6] Randall Henning,[7] Jonathan Kirshner,[8] Michael Webb,[9] and of course the late Susan Strange.[10] But most treatments until now have been regrettably ambiguous about what is meant by adjustment costs, leaving the analysis incomplete. We still lack a full understanding of what, precisely, the notion of burden is supposed to mean in the context of payments adjustment. Hence, we still lack a full understanding of the macrofoundations of monetary power as well.

To help promote a fuller understanding, I propose to resurrect a distinction that I first outlined in a much earlier attempt to explore the concept of adjustment

6. David M. Andrews, "Capital Mobility and State Autonomy: Toward a Structural Theory of International Monetary Relations," *International Studies Quarterly* 38, no. 2 (1994): 193–218.

7. C. Randall Henning, "Systemic Conflict and Regional Monetary Integration: The Case of Europe," *International Organization* 52, no. 3 (1998): 537–73.

8. Jonathan Kirshner, *Currency and Coercion: The Political Economy of International Monetary Power* (Princeton: Princeton University Press, 1995).

9. Michael C. Webb, "Capital Mobility and the Possibilities for International Policy Coordination," *Policy Sciences* 27, no. 4 (1994): 395–423.

10. See, especially, Susan Strange, *States and Market,* 2nd ed. (London: Pinter Publishers, 1994). For an evaluation of Strange's thoughts on monetary power, see Cohen, "Money and Power in World Politics"; Eric Helleiner (chap. 4 in this volume).

costs.[11] Specifically, I distinguish between two distinctly different kinds of adjustment cost—one continuing, the other transitional. Corresponding to each of the two kinds of adjustment cost is a very different kind of monetary power, which we may call the two "hands" of power.[12] At the macro-level, monetary power is fundamentally dual in nature. On the one hand, states have the Power to Delay; on the other hand, they have the Power to Deflect. A two-fisted government prefers both.

The continuing cost of adjustment, we shall see, may be defined as the cost of the new payments equilibrium prevailing after all change has occurred. The Power to Delay is the capacity to avoid the continuing cost of adjustment by *postponing* the process of adjustment.

The transitional cost of adjustment, by contrast, may be defined as the cost of the change itself. When the process of adjustment cannot be put off, the Power to Deflect represents the capacity to avoid the transitional cost of adjustment by *diverting* as much as possible of that cost to others.

The Continuing Cost of Adjustment

To understand the Power to Delay, we must begin with the concept of adjustment. By definition, adjustment imposes on deficit countries a real economic loss that will persist indefinitely once the process is complete. This is the continuing cost of adjustment. Nothing suits the interest of deficit countries more than a capacity to postpone adjustment for as long as possible.

Payments Adjustment

The standard measure of *balance* in the balance of payments is the current account, which comprises all transactions relating to a country's current national income and expenditures—imports and exports of goods (merchandise trade) and services ("invisibles") plus unilateral transfers. Adjustment, correspondingly, is the process by which imbalances in the current account—surpluses or deficits—are reduced or eliminated. Import and/or export volumes adjust to restore payments equilibrium. Countries with deficits experience a decline of imports of goods and services relative to exports; countries with surpluses experience the reverse.

Not all imbalances need to be eliminated, of course. Standard economic theory teaches that many current-account imbalances are simply the result of what may be regarded as a kind of rational intertemporal trade—deficit countries borrowing resources from the rest of the world for productive investment at home and surplus countries investing savings abroad today to support greater domestic consumption tomorrow. Such imbalances, in principle, are sustainable indefinitely and require no

---

11. Cohen, *Adjustment Costs.*

12. My choice of the term *hands* here, while perhaps a bit whimsical, is intended to be consistent with the anatomical bent of the faces-of-power literature.

adjustment at all. In practice, however, many imbalances go well beyond what can be readily sustained for all kinds of reasons—for example, because borrowed funds are not invested productively or because of financial-market limitations. In such instances, which are all too frequent in the real world, adjustments of trade volumes are indeed required.

Adjustments of trade volumes, however, are impossible, without a corresponding reallocation of productive resources;[13] and in a market setting, resource reallocations will not occur without the stimulus of a change of prices or income. The required price and income changes may be promoted directly by means of so-called expenditure-changing policies that aim to alter the overall level of spending, such as monetary and fiscal policy; or they may be promoted more indirectly via a change of the exchange rate—which in the traditional economics literature is referred to as an expenditure-switching policy, promoting adjustment via an altered ratio of prices between tradable and nontradable production.[14] Formally, adjustment may be defined as "a marginal reallocation of productive resources and exchanges of goods and services under the influence of changes in relative prices, incomes, and exchange rates."[15] This is the classical concept of "real" adjustment, the basic tool of open-economy macroeconomics.

Real adjustment is necessarily a mutual process, reflecting the reciprocal nature of monetary relations. Just as one economy cannot be in deficit without others being in surplus, so resources cannot be reallocated in one without equivalent and offsetting reallocations elsewhere. Should a deficit country move resources into export production that were previously employed in producing for the home market, surplus countries will also find themselves obliged to shift resources about as they begin to receive additional imports. Likewise, should a deficit country increase output in import-competing industries, surplus countries will find themselves exporting less and thus with additional resources for use in nontraded production. In either case, the reallocation of resources is complementary; the process of adjustment is shared.

Redistributing the Pie

However, although the process of adjustment is necessarily shared, the same need not be true of the burden of adjustment. In fact, once equilibrium is restored, the deficit country will unavoidably suffer a real economic loss, which will persist indefinitely. This is the continuing cost of adjustment, which is always borne wholly by deficit countries.

13. *Reallocation of resources* should be understood to mean not only switches from one type of employment to another but also switches to or from unemployment.

14. The efficacy of exchange-rate changes will depend, of course, on the extent of pass-through—that is, the degree to which domestic tradable-goods prices actually move in response to changes of nominal currency values. In practice, pass-through may be limited or delayed considerably. Trade restrictions or capital controls may also be regarded as expenditure-switching policies but are not directly considered here.

15. Cohen, *Adjustment Costs*, 3.

To comprehend why, assume a simple two-country model of payments imbalance. For the deficit country, adjustment requires a reduction of imports relative to exports, which is possible only if its real national absorption of goods and services, the sum total of spending by all domestic residents, is reduced relative to that of the surplus country. At the new payments equilibrium, therefore, the deficit country must be worse off than the surplus country, in the sense that it will now receive a smaller proportion of the combined output of the two economies. That is what I mean by the continuing cost of adjustment. I label it a *continuing cost* because it is open-ended—the ongoing sacrifice imposed by the new equilibrium that prevails after all change has occurred.

In absolute terms, the magnitude of the continuing cost may vary considerably, depending on the particulars of the approach to adjustment. The required change in the current account can be accomplished via a very different combination of changes in real national income and absorption in deficit countries—for example, a reduction of absorption relative to a more or less stable national income; an absolute loss of national income as well as absorption (via unemployment or an unfavorable movement of the terms of trade); an increase of national income, all of which, however, is absorbed abroad; or even an absolute increase of absorption as well as national income. Whatever the approach taken, however, the bottom line remains the same. At the new equilibrium, deficit countries will receive a smaller share of combined world output—a thinner slice of the pie. That is a sacrifice no matter how you cut it.

Deficit countries, therefore, have every incentive to put off the process of adjustment for as long as possible. Delay pays. As long as there is no change in the status quo, there will be no redistribution of the pie—hence no new burden. The scale of a state's Power to Delay is indicated by its capacity, in relative terms, to effectively postpone the payments adjustment process.

The Transitional Cost of Adjustment

But that is only one hand of monetary power. The continuing cost of adjustment involves an ongoing sacrifice imposed by the new equilibrium prevailing after all change has occurred, that is, after the adjustment process is concluded. But the process itself also imposes a sacrifice—the cost that must be incurred to make the necessary change. Each adjustment implies transition, a once-for-all phenomenon; and each transition has its own cost, separate and quite distinct from the presumed burden of the new equilibrium obtaining after the transition is complete. That is what I call the transitional cost of adjustment—in effect, the price of getting from here to there. Governments have every incentive to avoid this cost, too. No country wants to make more sacrifices than absolutely necessary.

The Adjustment Process

To illustrate the nature of the transitional cost of adjustment, consider a worker who, having lost a job and being unable to find a comparable one, finally accepts a lower-paying position. This process of adjustment imposes two costs on the worker. The more obvious one is the real sacrifice implied by the new position, namely, the difference between the new wage and the previous wage. This is an open-ended phenomenon, a loss of income that will go on as long as the worker remains in the new position—the continuing cost of adjustment. But, in addition, the worker must have suffered some loss of income during the period of enforced idleness. There may have been some real cost incurred in searching for a new job, investing in new skills, or moving to a new location. This is a once-for-all phenomenon, a singular loss of income associated with the process of change itself. That is what I mean by the transitional cost of adjustment.

The question is, who pays? In the illustration, the burden falls on the worker. But this need not always be so. The government, for instance, might provide unemployment compensation, job training, or other forms of adjustment assistance, thus shifting at least some of the cost to the taxpayer. Alternatively, part of the burden might be borne by the worker's former employer in the form of a generous severance package or even by private charitable organizations dedicated to aiding the involuntarily unemployed. In fact, the distribution of the transitional cost of adjustment is, a priori, indeterminate. Unlike the continuing cost of adjustment, which is never shared, the transitional cost is, in effect, up for grabs.

Recall that the process of balance-of-payments adjustment necessarily involves a realignment of relative prices, incomes, or exchange rates sufficient to generate the required reallocation of resources at the margin. The greater the changes of prices, incomes, or exchange rates required, the greater is the transitional cost of adjustment. In principle, payments equilibrium can be restored either by real depreciation—policies of monetary deflation or nominal currency devaluation / depreciation—in deficit countries or by real appreciation—monetary inflation or nominal currency revaluation / appreciation—in surplus countries. Implications for the distribution of the burden of adjustment differ greatly depending on which route is taken. Both economic and political elements of cost are involved.

Fixed versus Floating Exchange Rates

The circumstances under which this transition takes place matter, of course. Consider first a world in which nominal exchange-rate changes are ostensibly ruled out—in today's terminology, a world of "hard" pegs. In that case, distributional implications are reasonably straightforward. With formal devaluations or revaluations ruled out, payments equilibrium can only be restored through expenditure-changing policies. That is, adjustment will be accomplished through either a market-driven fall of prices and incomes in deficit countries, reinforced by restrictive monetary and fiscal policies, or a market-driven rise of prices and incomes in surplus countries, reinforced by more expansionary monetary and fiscal policies. In the former case, it is plainly the deficit countries that bear the burden of adjustment. Economically, deflationary conditions will almost certainly result in higher unemployment, slower growth, and perhaps even recession before a new equilibrium can be established. Politically, austerity is bound to erode a government's popularity with voters. Conversely, in the latter case, it is the surplus countries that pay the price. Accelerated inflation reduces purchasing power and can distort investment incentives. It also tends to be politically unpopular.

Alternatively, consider a world of exchange-rate flexibility, where nominal exchange-rate changes are possible—in today's terminology, a world of "soft" pegs or some manner of floating. In this case, distributional implications are more complex because governments are no longer limited to expenditure-changing policies alone. Policy makers now can "pick their poison," as a recent International Monetary Fund (IMF) study puts it.[16] External adjustment can be allowed to impact prices and incomes in the domestic economy either directly with the nominal exchange rate fixed, indirectly via the expenditure-switching effect of exchange-rate movements, or via some combination of the two. In such a world, two separate aspects of the process are influential in determining the costs involved—one involving any movements of exchange rates that do occur, the other involving the degree of domestic price and income changes that ultimately are required, whether nominal exchange rates move or not.

Suppose some exchange-rate movements do occur as part of the adjustment process. Who bears the onus of responsibility? A realignment of rates may be the result of deliberate policy decisions (formal devaluation / revaluation) or may be essentially market driven (nominal depreciation / appreciation). Either way, governments may be held accountable for triggering or tolerating changes in a currency's nominal value.

Does this matter? In a hypothetical two-country world, where currency values are the inverse of one another, it should make no difference who is seen as responsible for the change. Exchange-rate movements would be symmetrical, a decline of one country's money necessarily equivalent to a rise of the other's. But in the real world of more than 150 currencies, by contrast, the distinction can matter a great deal. The evolution of a given money's value in relation to any other single currency, its bilateral exchange rate, may be substantially different from the evolution of its value against the population of currencies in general—called the effective exchange rate. A change in one money's effective exchange rate, even if sizable, may have little impact on individual bilateral rates if spread broadly enough. Conversely, even a small change in an effective exchange rate may have a very large impact elsewhere if it is concentrated on just one or two bilateral rates. In short, exchange-rate movements may be anything but symmetrical. As a practical matter, therefore, some governments may be exposed to much more criticism than others, even if they are not the first mover.

Essentially, this is a political issue. Exchange-rate changes are difficult to ignore. An exchange rate is like the eye of a needle through which prices of all domestic goods and services are linked and compared with the prices of foreign output. Because this

16. Shigeru Iwata and Evan Tanner, "Pick Your Poison: The Exchange Rate Regime and Capital Account Volatility in Emerging Markets," International Monetary Fund, Working Paper 03/92 (Washington, D.C., 2003).

role makes the exchange rate a critical variable in determining the pattern of resource allocation as well as the level and distribution of income, governments have every reason to avoid the onus of responsibility insofar as possible. Nominal exchange-rate changes can generate a considerable backlash among voters, especially (but not exclusively) in small economies, for symbolic as well as material reasons. Devaluation or depreciation is typically interpreted as a defeat for a government's policies, damaging its reputation and credibility. Conversely, revaluation or appreciation may be resented for its potentially painful impacts on balance sheets and the earning capacity of key sectors of the economy. As a practical matter, few governments wish to be blamed for a sizable change in the value of the national currency.

The second aspect of the transition process in a world of floating rates concerns the degree of impact on the domestic economy. Once adjustment is under way, who experiences the greatest price or income changes? Governments may also be held accountable for any domestic austerity or inflation that results from the process of restoring external equilibrium.

This matters because we know that domestic impacts, too—not just exchange-rate movements—may be anything but symmetrical. In practice, prices and incomes may change much more in some countries than in others, depending on circumstances. Adjustment in one country could generate relatively little macroeconomic change at home but considerable price and income pressures abroad, effectively diverting much of the pain of adjustment elsewhere; or, conversely, most of the impact could be bottled up domestically, whether exchange rates move or not. As with exchange-rate movements, few governments wish to be blamed for a sizable impact on the domestic economy.

Summary

Overall, then, the distribution of the transitional cost of adjustment depends on both aspects of the process: first, who bears the onus of responsibility for any exchange-rate changes that occur; and second—whether exchange rates change or not—who is forced to experience the biggest direct changes of domestic prices and income. In monetary affairs, these are the price of getting from here to there, which are also sacrifices no matter how you cut it. No wonder governments want to avoid the transitional cost of adjustment, too, deflecting as much as possible to others! The scale of a state's Power to Deflect is indicated by its capacity, in relative terms, to effectively divert the transitional cost of adjustment to others.

The Power to Delay

What, then, are the sources of monetary power at the macro-level? What are its limits? States obviously differ greatly in their relative capacity to avoid the burden of adjustment. It is equally obvious that there are limits to the autonomy of even the most powerful states. How can all this be explained?

Given the dual nature of the macro-level pathway, it should not be surprising that separate factors might be at work in each of the two hands. Most critical for the Power to Delay, I suggest, are financial variables—above all, a country's international liquidity position, which encompasses both foreign reserves and access to external credit. The more liquidity there is at a country's disposal, relative to other states, the longer it can postpone adjustment of its balance of payments. Most critical for the Power to Deflect, by contrast, are more fundamental structural variables, also defined in relational terms, that determine how much real sacrifice will be required once the process of adjustment begins. It should also not be surprising that there might be distinctly different limits to each of the two hands of monetary power.

International Liquidity

A country's international liquidity comprises all available sources of internationally acceptable liquid assets. Before the postwar revival of global capital markets, the term was generally assumed to be synonymous with the sum of a country's international reserve assets. But once financial globalization began to take hold, the meaning of the term was expanded to include access to external credit as well, extended to the government or to the private sector. Today, international liquidity is generally defined to encompass the full array of international means of payment owned by or available to a country's public authorities and residents.

The ultimate purpose of international liquidity is financing: to cover deficits in the balance of payments, via either a net reduction of external claims (owned reserves) or a net increase of external liabilities (borrowing). The availability of financing to an economy, relative to others, can have a significant impact on the timing of adjustment and, hence, on the distribution of adjustment costs among deficit countries. More liquidity means more capacity to stave off any unwelcome reallocation of resources. Every deficit country has an obvious incentive to postpone the continuing cost of adjustment for as long as possible. The longer one deficit country can manage to put off adjustment, the greater will be the pressure on other deficit countries to bear the burden instead.

Of course, surplus countries too may have an incentive to delay the adjustment process—for example, if they believe that once the process begins, it is they who will be compelled to bear the bulk of the transitional cost of adjustment. Moreover, should that be their preference, surplus countries also have a greater ability to delay adjustment because it is almost always easier to absorb surpluses than to finance deficits. The motivation of surplus countries, however, is unlikely to be as intense as that of deficit countries, which have *both* costs to worry about. Moreover, even surplus states must anticipate the possibility that, sooner or later, they will suffer deficits, too. Hence, all states have a rational interest in acquiring and maintaining a healthy international liquidity position, on which the Power to Delay depends.

What, then, are the limits of this hand of monetary power? This requires a closer look at each of the two main components of international liquidity: owned reserves and borrowing capacity. The conditions affecting each are similar but not identical.

Owned Reserves

Superficially, it might seem that a government would want to hoard as many reserves as possible; insulation from payments pressures would be maximized by the largest possible stockpile of usable liquid assets. But that neglects the cost involved in acquiring reserves, which must be balanced against the benefit of greater autonomy. Reserves can be accumulated either as a result of current-account surpluses or by borrowing. Both strategies mean a reduction of real national absorption, either directly as a result of reduced imports relative to exports or indirectly as a result of increased interest payments. Neither, therefore, is likely to be pursued without limit because the cost of acquiring reserves could turn out to be greater than the loss of absorption that might be required by adjustment. Economic theory has long argued that rational policy makers can be expected to seek an *optimal* level of reserves rather than a *maximum*.

Optimality, however—like beauty—lies in the eye of the beholder. Different policy makers can make very different calculations, depending on their subjective evaluations of the costs and benefits involved. And these evaluations, in turn, will very much depend on politics, international as well as domestic. A government that feels beholden to constituencies that would be especially hurt by a reduction of payments deficits, such as large-scale importers, would be likely to discount the cost of hoarding additional reserves. By contrast, a government that feels it can count on foreign allies to bail it out in the event of a payments emergency would be less inclined to invest in new reserves. A priori, therefore, no generalization is possible about where the limits are likely to be found in this context. All we know for sure is that the appetite for owned reserves will be considerably short of infinite. Hence, the Power to Delay by this means will be short of infinite, too.

Borrowing Capacity

In most respects, much the same also can be said about external borrowing. Here, too, it might appear that a government would want to make as much use as possible of borrowing capacity to finance deficits. The more liquidity that can be raised externally, either by the government itself or by the private sector, the longer adjustment can be postponed. But that too neglects the costs involved. These costs include not just the direct debt-service payments that would be required by foreign loans; even more critically, they include possible policy compromises that could become necessary if the country finds itself overextended to foreign creditors.

External credit can be raised from a variety of sources, of course. But whatever the source, the liquidity provided can turn out to be too much of a good thing should the level of borrowing appear to rise beyond the economy's capacity to service the debt. For poorer and less developed countries, the main source of external credit is the public sector—governments of the more advanced industrial economies or multilateral agencies like the IMF. Overextension to public-sector creditors usually means that the borrower ends up negotiating a stabilization program, either bilaterally with creditor governments, multilaterally through the mechanisms of the so-called Paris Club, or with the IMF, with all the attendant conditionality. For middle-income emerging markets or more advanced economies, the main source of external credit is the global capital market. Overextension to private creditors usually means, eventually, a loss of perceived creditworthiness, which can lead to a sudden halt in new lending just when it might be most needed. Worse, excessive borrowing risks provoking panicky withdrawals and crisis, as capital importers around the world have sadly learned, from Mexico in 1994–95 to east Asia in 1997–98 to Argentina early in the new millennium. Reputation in financial markets, as we know, is a fragile flower, difficult to cultivate but easy to uproot. Painful policy adjustments may be required to restore a country's access to private investment.

Whatever the source of credit, therefore, autonomy may eventually have to be sacrificed for the sake of restoring external balance—a direct loss of power. Hence, with borrowing too, just as with owned reserves, rational policy makers can be expected to seek an optimum rather than a maximum. And here too, calculations of optimality will very much depend on politics.

But there is also a big difference. The calculations demanded here are inherently more complex than they are with owned reserves because they necessarily involve tricky questions of probability and risk. With reserves, evaluations of prospective costs are relatively straightforward. Little risk is associated with hoarding reserves, and the real losses from deficit reduction or interest payments can be estimated with a reasonable degree of certainty. With external credit, by contrast, nothing is certain because borrowing capacity is by definition subjective in nature, often fluctuating widely, and even wildly, in response to the fickleness of creditor governments or changing sentiment in the marketplace. Because of this uncertainty, generalizations about limits are even more difficult than they are with the reserve component of liquidity.

In effect, limits are not set by borrowers at all. Rather, they are set by creditors, both public and private. It is they who gain the power that overextended debtors lose. The challenge for borrowers is hard enough when dealing with creditor governments, whose decisions may be ruled as much by politics as economics. Calculations are even more difficult when it comes to market actors, who are constantly judging what they perceive as the quality of policy performance in individual economies. Financial markets are like a perpetual opinion poll. If a country is currently able to avoid a deficit reduction owing to ready access to credit, it is because the markets have given it their Good Housekeeping Seal of Approval. Conversely, if a country finds itself no longer able to put off an adjustment owing to a cessation of lending, it is the markets that are enforcing a limit on its Power to Delay. The more states relay on borrowing capacity rather than owned reserves for their international liquidity, the greater is the role of creditors, public and private, in determining who ultimately will be forced to undergo real adjustment.

Two implications follow. First, it seems clear that the distribution of the continuing cost of adjustment among deficit countries will be heavily influenced, if not largely determined, by creditor perceptions of debt-service capacity, which tend to favor the relatively wealthy. Ceteris paribus, the Power to Delay should be greatest in the advanced industrial economies—the nations that enjoy the highest standing as international borrowers. The Power to Delay will be least in poorer and less developed economies that have limited access, at best, to foreign finance. Second, it also seems clear that the distribution of the continuing cost among deficit countries is apt to be highly volatile, given the persistent threat of rapid swings of sentiment about the "soundness" of policy in one economy or another. The perpetual opinion poll often changes its mind—and when it does, the ability to postpone adjustment through borrowing is changed as well. Taken together, these two observations suggest that, although wealthier economies may be the most favored in this context, there is no fixed pattern involved. What creditors giveth by way of a Power to Delay, they may also taketh away.

The Special Case of the United States

Finally, this brings us to the special case of the United States, with its unparalleled capacity to postpone adjustment. Since 1981, the U.S. current account has been in deficit in all but one year (the recession year of 1991)—a record unlike that of any other country. The United States clearly enjoys more Power to Delay than anyone else. How can this be explained?

The answer lies in the unique status of the dollar as the world's preeminent international currency—indeed, the world's only truly *global* currency. The United States enjoys the most Power to Delay because the greenback is "king of the world," as one journalist has put it, "the world's bedrock currency."[17] Global popularity translates directly into a sustained demand for the dollar or dollar-denominated claims, which in turn enables the United States to finance deficits, in effect, with its own money. A need for international liquidity in the conventional sense is obviated when national liquidity is all that is required.

But there is also a downside to this privilege. Dollar accumulation around the world is no more than a form of external borrowing by the United States. In acquiring dollars or dollar-denominated claims, foreigners automatically extend credit to the U.S. economy; in the case of greenback notes, the credit is even interest-free. As with all external borrowing, therefore, there is a potential limit, set by the willingness of foreigners to go on lending. The ability of the United States to postpone adjustment ultimately rests on that same perpetual opinion poll, that is, on the judgments of agents elsewhere, including not only private-market actors using the dollar for investment purposes but also foreign central banks using the dollar for their reserves. Should the perpetual opinion poll lose its faith in the dollar—ceasing to lend or, worse, seeking to liquidate past investments—the United States could find itself under great pressure to reverse its current deficit. Today, many believe, the danger is even greater now that a potentially attractive alternative to the greenback

17. Rick Hampson, "Whatever They Think of America, People and Nations the World Over Prefer the Greenback," *USA Today,* December 26, 2001, p. A01.

is available in the form of Europe's new joint currency, the euro.[18] The U.S. Power to Delay is by no means limitless.

The Power to Deflect

The Power to Deflect, by contrast, derives not from financial variables but, rather, from more fundamental structural variables that distinguish one national economy from another. Two features in particular stand out: the degree of openness and the degree of adaptability of each individual economy.

Some observers might wish to add a third feature: whether an economy happens to be in surplus or deficit. But that would be a mistake. Initial payments positions obviously are relevant to the distribution of the continuing cost of adjustment and therefore to the Power to Delay. But when it comes to the transitional cost of adjustment, as indicated, distribution is effectively up for grabs.

At issue, to repeat, are two questions. First, who bears the onus of responsibility for any exchange-rate changes that may occur? Second, whether exchange rates change or not, who is forced to experience the greatest direct changes of domestic prices and income? These are the two critical aspects of the adjustment process that bear on the distribution of the transitional cost. Each may fall on either surplus or deficit countries.

Sensitivity and Vulnerability

In an attempt to explore some of these issues in 1966,[19] I suggested the notion of adjustment vulnerability, defined as the proportion of the transitional cost of adjustment borne by each economy. In essence, adjustment vulnerability might be understood as an inverse measure of what I here call the Power to Deflect. But I would not use the term adjustment vulnerability today because it unfortunately obscures a now more familiar distinction, first introduced by Keohane and Nye in *Power and Interdependence* (1977), which helps us to understand why the two structural features of openness and adaptability, defined in relational terms, are of greatest salience in determining the Power to Deflect.

In exploring the nature of interdependence, Keohane and Nye broke ground in distinguishing between the two critical dimensions of sensitivity and vulnerability. Sensitivity interdependence, as Keohane and Nye put it, involves the susceptibility of an economy to impacts from the outside—the degree to which conditions in one country are liable to be affected, positively or negatively, by events occurring elsewhere. Vulnerability, by contrast, involves the reversibility of impacts from the outside—the degree to which (or, in other words, the cost at which) a country is capable

---

18. Not everyone agrees with this assessment of the euro's potential attractiveness. For a more skeptical view, see Benjamin J. Cohen, "Global Currency Rivalry: Can the Euro Ever Challenge the Dollar?" *Journal of Common Market Studies* 41, no. 4 (2003): 575–95.

19. Cohen, *Adjustment Costs.*

of overriding or accommodating to the effects of events occurring elsewhere. The distinction is relevant here because it highlights the fact that every adjustment process can be decomposed into two separate elements: stimulus and response. The stimulus is the initial impact of disequilibrium on an economy; response refers to the ease with which the initial impact can be reversed. The sensitivity-vulnerability dichotomy neatly captures these two elements for analytical purposes.[20]

Openness and Adaptability

The Power to Deflect is a function of both elements of the adjustment process, stimulus *and* response. Openness matters to the Power to Deflect because it is the key determinant of an economy's sensitivity, relative to others, to payments disequilibrium (stimulus). Adaptability matters because it is the key determinant of an economy's relative vulnerability to disequilibrium (response).

Of these two structural variables, openness is clearly the easier to identify empirically. A standard measure of openness is the ratio of foreign trade to gross domestic product (GDP). The logic of its salience here is equally clear. The more open an economy, the greater is the range of sectors whose earning capacity and balance sheets will be directly impacted by adjustment once the process begins. This is true whether exchange rates remain pegged or are allowed to move. Either way, openness makes it difficult for an economy to avert at least some significant impact on prices and income at home.

In addition, if exchange rates move, governments in open economies are likely to come in for more criticism than would policy makers in more closed economies. Openness, ceteris paribus, also broadens the range of domestic constituencies that will take an active interest in the value of the country's currency. In a relatively closed economy, even fairly substantial exchange-rate movements may leave the largest part of the population unaffected and therefore indifferent, effectively insulating the government from criticism. In a more open economy, by contrast, where more interest groups will be directly affected, even small movements may lead to widespread opprobrium for policy makers, even if the government had nothing to do with starting the process in the first place. A high degree of openness makes it difficult to suppress widespread domestic repercussions when exchange rates change. It therefore makes it difficult for the authorities to deflect blame for any inflation or austerity that may result.

Adaptability is more difficult to identify empirically—it is an admittedly amorphous concept that, in fact, encompasses a myriad of qualities at the microeconomic

20. Much credit for recognizing the usefulness of the sensitivity-vulnerability dichotomy in this context goes to David Andrews, who has highlighted the notions of monetary sensitivity and vulnerability in a series of papers going back to "Bargaining Power and Policy Interdependence: Monetary Diplomacy in the Postwar International System," a paper presented at the 1997 annual meeting of the American Political Science Association. The point has also figured prominently in extended private correspondence between the two of us over many years. I am happy to acknowledge my intellectual debt to him on this point.

level, such as factor mobility, informational availabilities, and managerial resilience. Still, the logic of its salience, too, is clear. For any given degree of openness, the adaptability of an economy determines how readily diverse sectors can reverse a disequilibrium without large or prolonged price or income changes. At issue is allocative flexibility. The more easily productive resources can switch from one activity to another, overriding or accommodating to outside pressures, the less likely it is that domestic repercussions will involve serious pain; hence, the less likely it is, as well, that the process of adjustment will generate widespread resentment or protest. Conversely, the greater the rigidities characteristic of an economy's labor or product markets, the more serious will be resulting market dislocations and therefore the potential for political fallout. Adaptability, like beauty, may be one of those properties that is difficult to define, yet we know it when we see it and we know that it is important.

Implications

Again, two implications follow. First, it seems clear that the distribution of the transitional cost of adjustment is likely to favor larger and more diversified economies. Large size, as measured by GDP, generally means a relatively lower degree of openness. Greater diversification in production means that the economy offers more opportunities for alternative employment when adaptations are required. Smaller and less developed economies, conversely, are likely to be the least favored in the adjustment process. Some three decades ago, in the midst of the massive dislocations generated by the first oil shock, I wrote about what appeared to be a "cascading" of the burden of adjustment among oil-importing countries, with the poorest and least developed economies being forced to bear the greatest burden of all.[21] "Power economics," I called it then. Today, with the wisdom of hindsight, I would call it a manifestation of the Power to Deflect.

The second implication is that, unlike the continuing cost of adjustment, the distribution of the transitional cost of adjustment can be expected to be comparatively stable over time rather than volatile. Structural variables such as openness or adaptability tend to change relatively slowly, to the extent that they change at all. The Power to Deflect, accordingly, is likely to change slowly, if at all, as well.

From Passive to Active Mode

Finally, we return to the measure of influence that is inherent in the Power to Deflect. Although the essence of the Power to Deflect is a capacity to avoid the transitional cost of adjustment (autonomy), the practical effect, as we have noted, is to divert the burden elsewhere, compelling others to bear it instead—a form of influence. In and of itself, the influence that is generated in this manner, which I have de-

---

21. Benjamin J. Cohen, "Mixing Oil and Money," in *Oil, the Arab-Israel Dispute, and the Industrial World: Horizons of Crisis*, ed. J. C. Hurewitz, 195–211 (Boulder: Westview Press, 1976).

scribed as the alter ego of autonomy, is passive and diffuse, essentially a product of market forces. But a more active mode is also possible, as many authors emphasize.[22] The active mode, stressing the direct use of positive or negative sanctions in government-to-government relations, seeks to translate passive influence into practical control through the instrumental use of power. What is the connection between the two modes?

The connection, clearly, lies in the politics of interstate relations and, especially, in what Andrews (chap. 1 in this volume) calls monetary statecraft. The active mode—"influence attempts that rely primarily on the manipulation of monetary affairs," to quote Andrews—is optional. It is also purposeful, seeking to enforce compliance by way of pressure or coercion. In other words, it is policy-contingent. This means that it is not enough simply for a state to enjoy the structural characteristics essential to the Power to Deflect. Relative openness and adaptability are necessary conditions but hardly sufficient. One can think of a number of larger and more diversified economies that seem capable of diverting the transitional cost of adjustment to others, including, especially, the advanced industrial countries. But not many of these are known to engage in direct arm-twisting to get their way on monetary issues. Beyond a capacity for influence, a government must also have the motivation to put its Power to Deflect to active use—an understood framework of policy goals. Motivation will reflect a host of considerations peculiar to an individual country, involving foreign-policy strategy and domestic institutions as well as underlying constituency politics and political culture. As several of the contributions to this volume make clear, there is no certainty at all that the capabilities created by the Power to Deflect will be actively exploited.

Conclusion

To summarize, we may say that the macrofoundations of monetary power are best understand as being dual in nature. At the macro-level, monetary power is deployable with two hands: the Power to Delay, aimed at avoiding the continuing cost of adjustment; and the Power to Deflect, aimed at avoiding the transitional cost of adjustment. The Power to Delay is largely a function of a country's international liquidity position relative to others, comprising both owned reserves and borrowing capacity. The Power to Deflect has its source in more fundamental structural variables: the relative degree of openness and adaptability of the national economy. The Power to Delay is limited only by the government's appetite for reserves and by the willingness of foreign agents to lend. The Power to Deflect is limited by the economy's underlying attributes and endowments.

Accordingly, it should be no surprise that states vary greatly in their monetary power, implying a systematic element of hierarchy in monetary relations. In fact,

22. Including most of the contributors to this volume; for a prominent exception, see Eric Helleiner (chap. 4 in this volume).

monetary relations have always tended to be distinctly hierarchical, taking the shape of what I have elsewhere described as a Currency Pyramid—narrow at the peak, where one or a few countries dominate, and increasingly broad below.[23] Ultimately, for all states, the issue is adjustment costs. Relative standing in the Currency Pyramid depends on the relative capacity to avoid the burden of payments adjustment, making others pay instead.

Recently, David Lake challenged international relations theorists to pay more heed to the element of hierarchy in international relations.[24] In the light of current scholarship, he argues, state sovereignty can no longer realistically be regarded as an absolute principle—quite the contrary, in fact. In his words: "Hierarchy is, and always has been, part of international relations. . . . Our theories of international relations would be improved by explicitly incorporating variations in hierarchy."[25] The analysis here does just that for theories of monetary relations, incorporating variations in hierarchy by exploring the underlying sources of monetary power. The practical importance of the analysis lies in its identification of the key factors that determine the relative power of individual states, all of which are amenable to public policy to a greater or lesser extent.

The positioning of states in the Currency Pyramid directly reflects their access to both hands of monetary power. At the peak of the Pyramid is the United States, long acknowledged as the most powerful state in monetary affairs. The analysis in this essay suggests that the dominant position of the United States, which many describe as a hegemony, should be attributed to the country's unique combination of relevant capabilities—the special privilege that it enjoys in financing deficits, due to the global role of the dollar, as well as the notable adaptability of its domestic economy, which also happens to be relatively closed as compared with most other nations. Conversely, the lowly status of many poor developing nations would appear to relate directly to their lack of international liquidity as well as, typically, to the relatively high openness and low allocative flexibility of their economies. In between, rankings may be said to depend on how the key liquidity and structural factors stack up in each individual country. If governments wish to elevate their standing in the Currency Pyramid, it is these factors that must be addressed.

23. Benjamin J. Cohen, *The Geography of Money* (Ithaca: Cornell University Press, 1998); *The Future of Money* (Princeton: Princeton University Press, 2004).

24. David A. Lake, "The New Sovereignty in International Relations," *International Studies Review* 5, no. 3 (2003): 303–23.

25. Ibid., 304.

CHAPTER THREE

Domestic Sources of International Monetary Leadership

Andrew Walter

Currency leaders enjoy various forms of influence and power. The "exorbitant privilege" of currency leaders, above all the ability to finance external deficits by issuing IOUs and thereby to delay adjustment, has in particular received great attention in the literature. But what produces currency leaders? What, in other words, are the sources of this central aspect of international monetary power? In the preceding chapter, Benjamin Cohen outlines the macrofoundations of international monetary power—that is, the general characteristics of states that allow them to delay payment of the continuing costs of adjustment or to deflect the transitional costs thereof. Cohen locates the principal sources of the Power to Deflect in states' fundamental economic characteristics, in particular in their relative economic size and openness. He goes on to identify the primary sources of the Power to Delay in states' overall liquidity position (the sum of their foreign reserves and access to international credit).

In this chapter, I build on this contribution while drawing attention to other elements of the literature on monetary policy. I do so in order to argue that there are two additional prerequisites of international monetary leadership, having to do with domestic policies and institutional arrangements. First, currency leadership requires a relatively conservative monetary policy from the leader that is credibly embedded in its domestic political and economic institutions. This credible policy framework helps to produce willing followership on the part of the key audience, private market agents, as well as other national monetary authorities. Second, currency leadership also depends on a related set of institutional arrangements that facilitate the emergence of highly developed financial markets. I dis-

I thank Eric Helleiner, Randy Henning, Jerry Cohen, Jonathan Kirshner, Scott Cooper, Bob Hancké, and various other participants at the Florence conference for their very helpful comments on an earlier draft. Special thanks are due to David Andrews for his detailed comments. None are responsible for any remaining errors.

cuss other prerequisites for monetary leadership also, but the main focus is upon these two.

Currency leadership is a form of monopoly power, and the leader may try to exploit this power to achieve particular ends. In the short run, an established leader may use this monopoly power to exert substantial influence over other states' policies, even if this attempt is seen as illegitimate by followers. For example, the United States was able to exploit its currency leadership position in the 1960s and 1970s, delaying the continuing costs of adjustment and deflecting the adjustment's transitional costs on to others. In the long run, however, the persistent exploitation of monopoly power may undermine the foundations of currency leadership itself. For example, excessively expansionary U.S. monetary policy in the late 1970s threatened to undermine the willingness of private market agents to continue to hold dollar assets, requiring a shift back to a more conservative and credible U.S. monetary policy after 1979. The British case in the early twentieth century also demonstrates that fundamental shifts in the leader's domestic institutional framework can result in a rapid erosion of the status of the lead currency, particularly when potential rival currencies exist. Hence, monetary leadership can only be sustained through the ongoing persuasion of market agents. A corollary of the argument is that international currency promotion is extraordinarily difficult and is an option available only to very few states.

The rest of this chapter is organized around three main questions. First, what is the nature of international monetary leadership? This section is mainly concerned with definitions and in situating the argument in relation to the existing literature on leadership and hegemony. Second, what is the nature of monetary followership for both other states and private sector actors? Third, what are the limits to monetary leadership, and, as regards the theme of this volume, to the power that monetary leaders enjoy? A final section concludes.

What Is Monetary Leadership?

Monetary power has long been associated with the role of dominant or hegemonic countries in the international political economy.[1] This idea has a longer heritage than so-called hegemonic stability theory, but it achieved its fullest expression in this theory from the mid-1970s. Charles Kindleberger himself, on which much of this literature draws, employs the term leadership rather than hegemony.[2] He argues that international monetary leaders, such as pre-1914 Britain and the post-1945 United

1. See, for example, Robert Gilpin, *US Power and the Multinational Corporation* (New York: Basic Books, 1975); *The Political Economy of International Relations* (Princeton: Princeton University Press, 1987). For a critical review of this literature and its empirical claims, see Barry J. Eichengreen, "Hegemonic Stability Theories of the International Monetary System," in *Can Nations Agree? Issues in International Economic Cooperation*, ed. Richard N. Cooper, 255–98 (Washington D.C.: Brookings Institution, 1989); Andrew Walter, *World Power and World Money* (New York/London: Harvester Wheatsheaf, 1993).

2. Charles P. Kindleberger, *The World in Depression, 1929–1939* (London: Allen and Unwin, 1973); "International Public Goods without International Government," *American Economic Review* 71, no. 6 (1986): 1–13.

States, provided a collective good in the form of a common currency and a countercyclical monetary stabilization policy at the international level. As David Lake observes, collective goods or leadership theory is more applicable to international money than to trade, where, he argues, hegemonic coercion is more relevant.[3] Here, I follow Lake and Kindleberger in employing the term international monetary leadership rather than hegemony. Nevertheless, I argue that the foundations of such leadership can also create the preconditions for the exercise of coercive, exploitative hegemonic power.[4]

Most now accept that hegemonic stability theory erred in overlooking domestic factors, not least in the hegemon itself. However, leadership theory also typically ignores domestic factors, making it poorly equipped to explain the nature and sources of monetary leadership.[5] First, such models exclude private-sector actors, a key constituency among monetary followers that has received surprisingly little attention in the hegemony/leadership literature.[6] Second, such models omit the domestic political and institutional factors that are basic preconditions of monetary leadership.[7]

I explore both of these issues in the following section and argue that these aspects relate to an important element of *legitimacy* enjoyed by the leader that helps explain why followership can be largely voluntary in nature. Persuasion is more typical of monetary leadership than is explicit (hegemonic) coercion. Market agents, in particular, are difficult to coerce and must generally be persuaded of the advantages of using and holding the lead currency. However, the dividing line between persuasion and coercion, particularly of other states, is often difficult to draw in practice.

Despite some similarities, my argument differs in emphasis from that of John Ruggie[8] and John Ikenberry and Charles Kupchan,[9] who argue that authoritative leadership of the Weberian variety derives from normative convergence between the leader and its followers. Although some degree of intellectual and normative convergence was evident in the British and U.S. cases of international monetary leadership, I argue here that an element of divergence is essential to successful monetary leadership. A successful monetary leader needs, among other things, to be *more* conservative in its monetary policies and financial institutions than most other countries.

3. David A. Lake, "Leadership, Hegemony, and the International Economy: Naked Emperor or Tattered Monarch with Potential?" *International Studies Quarterly* 37, no. 4 (1993): 459–89, especially 460. On international leadership and trade, see Stephen D. Krasner, "State Power and the Structure of International Trade," *World Politics* 28 (1976): 317–47. On public goods approaches, see Duncan Snidal, "The Limits of Hegemonic Stability Theory," *International Organization* 39, no. 4 (1985): 579–614.

4. In developing a theory of international monetary leadership, I also fill a gap in my own earlier work *World Power and World Money*, 249–57), which argues that hegemonic stability theory cannot explain the historical cycle of international monetary stability and instability.

5. See, for example, Snidal, "Limits of Hegemonic Stability Theory."

6. Joanne S. Gowa, "Hegemons, IOs and Markets: The Case of the Substitution Account," *International Organization* 38, no. 4 (1984): 661–83, and Benjamin J. Cohen, *The Geography of Money* (Ithaca: Cornell University Press, 1998), are exceptions.

7. For a similar argument, see J. Lawrence Broz, "Origins of the Federal Reserve System: International Incentives and the Domestic Free Rider Problem," *International Organization* 53 (1999): 39–70.

8. John G. Ruggie, "International Regimes, Transactions and Change: Embedded Liberalism in the Postwar Economic Order," *International Organization* 36, no. 2 (1982): 379–415.

9. John G. Ikenberry and Charles A. Kupchan, "Socialization and Hegemonic Power," *International Organization* 44, no. 3 (1990): 283–315.

It is also necessary to distinguish between two aspects of international monetary leadership: currency leadership and liquidity leadership.[10] Currency leadership occurs when a national currency plays a dominant role as an anchor, vehicle, and investment currency for international transactions among actors, both public sector and private sector, in the world economy.[11] Liquidity leadership occurs when one or more countries provide short- and longer-term liquidity to the world economy in a stabilizing, countercyclical fashion. The consensus now differs from Kindleberger's original contention that there could be only "one stabilizer" in the area of liquidity provision.[12] Liquidity leadership tends to be provided collectively rather than singly, in contrast to currency leadership.[13] Given the primary focus of this volume on monetary rather than financial issues, and that currency leadership is logically prior to liquidity leadership, I focus here on currency leadership.[14]

Why Follow the Leader?

The literature has tried to explain currency followership in two main ways, which roughly correspond to rationalist and constructivist approaches. The first and most common approach focuses on the material incentives for followers that the leader directly or indirectly provides. The second focuses on the way in which followers, through a process of normative socialization, come to accept the leader's economic policy preferences as being in their own interest. I focus here on followership by other major states because once they decide to follow the leader, the remaining smaller countries have little choice.[15]

10. Charles P. Kindleberger sees both of these as important aspects of international monetary leadership, but places most emphasis on the second; see his *The World in Depression, 1929–1939* (London: Allen and Unwin, 1973); "International Public Goods without International Government." See also, Lake, "Leadership, Hegemony, and the International Economy," 462–63.

11. For an extensive treatment, see Benjamin J. Cohen, *The Future of Money* (Princeton: Princeton University Press, 2004).

12. Kindleberger, *World in Depression,* 305. There was no good theoretical foundation for this argument; see, for example, Russell Hardin, *Collective Action* (Baltimore: Johns Hopkins University Press, 1982); Snidal, "Limits of Hegemonic Stability Theory."

13. J. Lawrence Broz, "The Domestic Politics of International Monetary Order: The Gold Standard," in *Contested Social Orders and International Politics,* ed. D. Skidmore (Nashville: Vanderbilt University Press, 1997), 53–91; Eichengreen, "Hegemonic Stability Theories."

14. When follower countries hold a center country's liabilities as foreign exchange reserves, producing international currency leadership, they are also likely to favor liquidity provision in this currency. There can be reverse linkages between the two. As I argue later in this chapter, collective liquidity provision in the British case before 1914 and the U.S. case in the 1960s helped to maintain a single-currency leadership.

15. Cohen, *Future of Money,* distinguishes between tighter and looser forms of state followership, from "dollarization" to simple pegging to an anchor currency. Here, for simplicity, I focus on the latter because it is the most common form of followership by other major states. For a discussion of dollarization, see Eric Helleiner (chap. 4 in this volume).

Material Incentives

Standard leadership theory has not explored why states follow the leader. Indeed, this is a trivial question in a public goods framework because follower countries have no material incentive not to consume the public good. The nature of the exchange-rate system, the mode, degree of institutionalization and conditionality attached to international liquidity provision, and so on are all second-order questions for public goods theory.[16] However, these kinds of details matter considerably for follower-ship in practice. Britain and the United States both provided currency leadership in their respective eras of preeminence, but the much greater role for key currencies in the post-1945 period produced a more highly skewed distribution of adjustment costs than under the pre-1914 gold standard.[17] Similarly, any government that has accepted conditions on borrowing from a major creditor country or through the International Monetary Fund (IMF) and World Bank can tell us that the details matter greatly.

Allied to public goods theory is the idea that the use of a single money, like the spread of English as a global language or eBay as an Internet auction platform, has positive network externalities: the more actors that use it, the greater the benefit to all users.[18] This has some important implications. First, it usefully emphasizes the benefits of a single international currency to *private*-sector agents, not other states. Indeed, it is typically private market agents, rather than public authorities in other states, that confer key currency status on a particular currency. Second, because money has some of the qualities of a natural monopoly, it suggests that monetary leadership may persist even when the original conditions producing it have changed. As with all monopolies, there exists an ever-present temptation for the monopolist to exploit its position. This potential for abuse helps to explain why most followers tend to diversify their currency portfolios somewhat rather than relying completely on a single international currency.[19]

Still left unanswered, however, is why a particular currency and country come to lead in the first place. There are two main kinds of material incentives to followers: those that derive from the fundamental economic characteristics of states relative to one another and those that derive from the perceived relative monetary advantages of domestic policies and institutions in the leading country itself.

In terms of international incentives, the size of a particular country, its importance in international trade, and its initial ability to run current-account surpluses provide incentives for other countries and private-sector agents to use its currency

16. Lake, "Leadership, Hegemony, and the International Economy," 484.

17. A gold-exchange standard, in contrast to a gold standard, allows key currency countries to delay adjustment and to deflect costs on to other countries.

18. Charles P. Kindleberger, "The Politics of International Money and World Language," *Princeton Essays in International Finance* 61 (1967); Paul De Grauwe, *International Money: Post-War Trends and Theories,* 2nd ed. (Oxford: Oxford University Press, 1996), 2.

19. See Cohen, *Geography of Money;* Peter Lindert, "Key Currencies and Gold, 1900–1913," *Princeton Essays in International Finance* 24 (August 1969).

in third-party transactions and to hold assets denominated in its currency.[20] A substantial export dependence on the leader's market may provide a powerful material incentive to follow the leader generally on economic policy matters. However, trade patterns are not the only factor in currency leadership. In the later stages of the British and U.S. leadership eras, other countries came to challenge their dominant international trading positions, but the challenge to their currency leadership role was in both cases much less severe. Hence, some countries are much more important in international trade than in international money, notably Germany before 1914 and Japan since the 1970s.

A similar incentive for currency followership is produced by the asymmetries of financial development in the world economy. The existence of relatively deep, stable, efficient, and open financial markets in one country will encourage both public- and private-sector agents to have confidence in transacting in and holding assets denominated in its currency. Of course, the role of London and New York in the respective currency leadership of Britain and the United States has long been recognized, and currency leadership contributed to their financial development. However, we still need to explain why these countries achieved relative financial development prior to their currency leadership.

Before turning to this, there is a third, noneconomic incentive for monetary followership. International security relationships may create supplementary incentives for followership by states (although not for private-sector agents, or at least not directly). Although security factors tend to receive attention mainly in the literature on hegemony and international trade,[21] U.S. currency leadership in the 1950s and 1960s cannot be understood without them. West Germany's commitment to the U.S. dollar was substantially reinforced by its dependence on the U.S. security umbrella. The Blessing letter of March 1967, in which the Bundesbank's president pledged not to convert Germany's dollar reserves into gold (as the disloyal French had been doing with their own dollar holdings), must be understood in this context. The Atlantic alliance subsequently became less of a constraining factor, as détente was consolidated and as German fears of the inflationary consequences of a pure dollar standard (from 1968) came to the fore.

Still, although security incentives for followership may help when economic incentives are weak or diminishing, they are unlikely to play a central role for long. Although it is difficult to imagine how a country could attain international monetary leadership without playing an important role in international trade, security incentives for followership may not be necessary. The British-led international gold standard before 1914 owed little to security alliances. Indeed, ad hoc central bank cooperation during this era seemed relatively insulated from the more fluid great-power alliances of the time. French and Russian financial assistance to the Bank of

20. Broz, "Origins of the Federal Reserve System," 48; Cohen, *Future of Money*, 11; Cohen (chap. 2 in this volume).

21. Joanne S. Gowa, *Allies, Adversaries and International Trade* (Princeton: Princeton University Press, 1994); Krasner, "State Power"; Lake, "Leadership, Hegemony, and the International Economy," 470–72.

England in the Barings crisis of 1890, despite their unresolved imperial rivalries with Britain, is indicative.[22] Like trade incentives, security incentives provide insufficient explanations of monetary leadership and followership.

In the absence of supportive domestic monetary policies and institutions, the economic factors already discussed are not sufficient to produce willing followers of potential monetary leaders. As Cohen notes, a viable lead currency must have a "proven track record of relatively low inflation and inflation variability."[23] But what assures market agents that such a track record will be reproduced in the future? There is now a good deal of literature, much of it stemming from the seminal article by Douglas North and Barry Weingast,[24] that focuses on the domestic institutional foundations of financial development. In this view, the founding of institutions of limited government in late-seventeenth-century Britain, by substantially reducing the likelihood of default against private-sector creditors, was a key step in the development of deep money and capital markets in London.[25] The implication of this argument is that in the modern world, international monetary leaders are likely to arise only under conditions of limited, constitutional government. A complementary theory is that financial development is a product of a society's legal institutions.[26] These authors find from cross-country evidence that English common law, with its bias in favor of creditor rights, is most conducive to financial-sector development and that the French civil law system is least conducive.[27] Although this legal origin theory has been subject to criticism, the point that financial development is favored by strong protection of creditor rights is less controversial.

For monetary followers—the willing users of another country's currency—it is not only the potential for outright default that matters but also the potential for partial default via inflation. The use of fiat money creates a potential for inflation, and a commitment to a low-inflation monetary policy is unlikely to be credible in the absence of institutional factors that constrain its use.[28] This could include the delegation of monetary policy to an independent central bank or the support of a dominant political constituency for conservative monetary policies.[29] Either way, private-sec-

22. Charles P. Kindleberger, *A Financial History of Western Europe* (London: Allen & Unwin, 1984), 282, claims that the Bank of England's refusal to accept the Prussian National Bank's offer of financial assistance in 1873 was driven by strategic or political sensitivities. This remains an underexplored aspect of international monetary cooperation and conflict.

23. Cohen, *Future of Money*, 10.

24. Douglass North and Barry Weingast, "Constitutions and Commitment: The Evolution of Institutions Governing Public Choice in Seventeenth-Century England," *Journal of Economic History* 49, no. 4 (1989): 803–32.

25. For a further development and modification of this argument, see David Stasavage, *Public Debt and the Birth of the Democratic State: France and Great Britain, 1688–1789* (Cambridge, UK: Cambridge University Press, 2003).

26. Rafael La Porta, Florencio Lopez-de-Silanes, and Andrei Shleifer, "Law and Finance," *Journal of Political Economy* 106, no. 6 (1998): 1113–55.

27. The German and Scandinavian legal systems occupy an intermediate position.

28. Finn Kydland and Edward S. Prescott, "Rules Rather than Discretion: The Inconsistency of Optimal Plans," *Journal of Political Economy* 85, no. 3 (1977): 473–92.

29. On the former, see Kenneth Rogoff, "The Optimal Degree of Commitment to an Intermediate Monetary Target," *Quarterly Journal of Economics* 100, no. 4 (1985): 1169–89; on the latter, see Adam

tor agents must be assured that institutional mechanisms that assure policy consistency are in place. Britain's limited government and limited franchise helped to entrench the position of those in society who favored a relatively conservative or "hard" monetary policy, reinforced by the adoption of the gold standard in 1713. This conservative financial clique also dominated the Bank of England, a crucial institutional development that preceded the emergence of deep financial markets in Britain. As a result, the credibility of Britain's commitment to a conservative monetary policy, except during emergencies such as the Napoleonic Wars, was largely unquestioned until World War I.[30]

By extension, this argument might apply to the case of U.S. financial development, given the way in which its institutional framework famously decentralizes political power.[31] However, without a central bank until 1914, the decentralized political institutions of the United States and its much larger economy could not alone foster financial development.[32] Despite a very shaky start by the Federal Reserve, the design of the U.S. central banking constitution also served, if not always consistently, to put into place a monetary framework that offset political pressures for inflation.[33] It also helped to stabilize a previously volatile domestic financial sector and, in particular, to provide New York bankers with the short-term discount market they needed to assure liquidity for international holders of dollars, as the Bank of England had long done for London's financiers.[34] Of course, the disruptive effects of World War I also played an important role in accelerating the rise of New York relative to London.

In the early twentieth century, the domestic political and institutional framework that had facilitated Britain's adherence to the gold standard began to change.[35] This eventually proved disastrous for Britain's position, given the emergence of a serious challenge to its monetary leadership by the United States. In a series of related de-

---

Posen, "Central Bank Independence and Disinflationary Credibility: A Missing Link?" *Oxford Economic Papers* 50, no. 3 (1998): 335–60.

30. Barry J. Eichengreen, *Golden Fetters: The Gold Standard and the Great Depression, 1919–1939* (New York: Oxford University Press, 1992), chap. 2; Giulio M. Gallarotti, *The Anatomy of an International Monetary Regime: The Classical Gold Standard, 1880–1914* (New York: Oxford University Press, 1995).

31. See Kenneth A. Schultz and Barry R. Weingast, "The Democratic Advantage: Institutional Foundations of Financial Power in International Competition," *International Organization* 57, no. 1 (2003): 3–42.

32. Broz, "Origins of the Federal Reserve System"; Daniel Verdier, "Capital Mobility and the Origins of Stock Markets," *International Organization* 55, no. 2 (2001): 327–56. The U.S. public debt market was still very small in 1914, casting doubt on the applicability of the North and Weingast thesis.

33. Jon Faust, "Whom Can We Trust to Run the Fed? Theoretical Support for the Founders' Views," *Journal of Monetary Economics* 37, no. 2 (1996): 267–83.

34. Broz, "Origins of the Federal Reserve System."

35. Some earlier works on sterling's decline tend to emphasize economic factors or international political factors. For the former, see, for example, Benjamin J. Cohen, *The Future of Sterling as an International Currency* (London: Macmillan, 1971); for the latter, see, for example, Susan Strange, *Sterling and British Policy: A Political Study of an International Currency in Decline* (London: Oxford University Press, 1971).

velopments, the extension of the franchise after World War I, the rise of the trade union movement and the Labour Party, and the rise of Keynesian economic ideas eventually threatened Britain's political commitment to the gold standard.[36] Furthermore, the loss of outright veto power by the House of Lords in 1911 centralized political power in the hands of the British prime minister and Cabinet. In combination with a wider franchise and the rise of the unionized left, the potential for inflation was now much greater and sterling's credibility as an international currency was undermined.[37] Capital controls, imposed in the name of national macroeconomic stabilization during and after World War II, reflected this new reality and were another blow to sterling's international role. Allied with Keynesian economic policy ideas and a now wholly subordinate Bank of England, successive British cabinet governments after 1945 pursued macroeconomic policies that by the 1960s had almost completely undermined Britain's pretensions to currency leadership. Nevertheless, although Britain no longer satisfied the first domestic prerequisite of monetary leadership (that is, as a provider of relatively conservative monetary policy), the second (as a provider of conservative financial institutions) remained largely intact. London subsequently flourished as an open center for international finance, but only by specializing in offshore finance conducted in other currencies, above all the US dollar. Despite the City of London's position as a global financial center, Britain was no longer a global currency leader; a small if lingering international role for sterling was confined to the remnants of the British empire and some overly loyal former dominions.

The erosion of the credibility of the U.S. commitment to a stable currency after 1945 was much less marked than in the British case. The monetary link to gold, albeit in altered form, remained important for U.S. policy, in marked contrast to Britain. By the end of the war, the United States owned about three-quarters of the world's monetary gold, and the Franklin D. Roosevelt administration wanted to preserve the "economic power" this represented.[38] The U.S. domestic institutional structure was also a crucial aspect of the comparative resilience of its monetary leadership. In the New Deal years and in the immediate postwar years, the U.S. Federal Reserve had been politically subordinated to the government.[39] From the time of the U.S. Treasury–Federal Reserve Accord of March 1951, the latter was able, with the support of the Treasury, to regain independent control over interest rates.[40] The result was low levels of inflation relative to those in most other major economies (see fig. 3.1). The Federal Reserve's conservative stance was generally supported by suc-

36. Eichengreen, *Golden Fetters;* Beth A. Simmons, *Who Adjusts? Domestic Sources of Foreign Economic Policy during the Interwar Years* (Princeton: Princeton University Press, 1994); Robert Skidelsky, *John Maynard Keynes: Vol. 2. The Economist as Saviour, 1920–1937* (London: Macmillan, 1992).

37. Alec Cairncross and Barry Eichengreen, *Sterling in Decline: The Devaluations of 1931, 1949 and 1967,* 2nd ed. (Houndmills, UK: Palgrave, 2003), xv, xx.

38. Robert Skidelsky, *John Maynard Keynes: Vol. 3. Fighting for Britain, 1937–1946* (London: Macmillan, 2000), 317.

39. Milton Friedman and Anna J. Schwartz, *A Monetary History of the United States, 1867–1960* (Princeton: Princeton University Press, 1963), 532–33.

40. Ibid., 610–26.

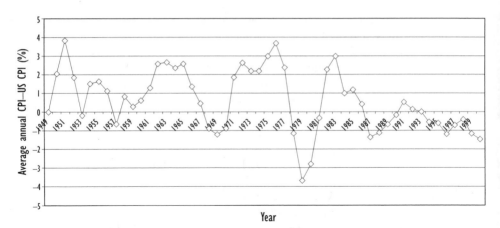

Figure 3.1 Average inflation differential of ten major economies (Canada, Japan, Belgium, France, Germany, Italy, the Netherlands, Sweden, Switzerland, and the United Kingdom) average inflation differential over the United States, 1949–2000. CPI, consumer price inflation. (*Source:* International Monetary Fund, *International Financial Statistics,* CD-ROM, consumer price inflation.)

cessive administrations. Congress was relatively inactive during this period in monetary and exchange-rate policy because of the low incentives for collective action in these policy areas; this, too, favored monetary conservatism.[41] In the Dwight D. Eisenhower years, the fixed gold price was seen by the administration as one of the foundations of good economic housekeeping. In the 1960s, beginning with John F. Kennedy, the commitment to the fixed $35-per-ounce gold price became a matter of high politics.

However, from the mid-1960s, with productivity growth falling, political pressure on the Federal Reserve to deliver on jobs and growth increased. With the steady erosion of the external gold constraint on U.S. policy, successive administrations from 1962 onward were accused of exploiting their ability, due to the international reserve role of the dollar, to export inflation abroad and to shift the costs of adjustment to others.[42] The Federal Reserve Board remained committed to the fixed gold price and to a low inflation policy, but by the early 1970s it had well and truly lost this battle.[43] U.S. willingness to exploit its powerful position increasingly alienated loyal allies of a more conservative monetary bent, with the Germans floating the deutschmark against the dollar in March 1973. By 1978, the steadily falling dollar suggested that financial markets had also lost confidence in U.S. macroeconomic policy. Only Paul Volcker's dramatic reassertion of the U.S. Fed's autonomy and a policy of mon-

41. As Joanne S. Gowa argues, in "Public Goods and Political Institutions: Trade and Monetary Policy Processes in the United States," *International Organization* 42, no. 1 (1988): 15–32, this contrasts with greater political activism in finance.

42. See De Grauwe, *International Money*, 32–39.

43. Charles A. Coombs, *The Arena of International Finance* (New York: John Wiley, 1976).

etary conservatism from 1979 succeeded in restoring the underpinnings of the dollar's international position.[44]

To summarize the argument of this section, monetary followership by private- and public-sector agents occurs in part because of the monetary policy credibility and the high financial development that flow from the leader's domestic institutional arrangements. Of course, domestic institutions for monetary and financial conservatism are unlikely to produce international monetary leadership without sufficient economic size and an important international trading position; Switzerland since 1945 is a case in point. Furthermore, as the Volcker shift demonstrates, individuals as well as institutions matter.[45] However, even though domestic political, legal, and economic institutions are not determinant, they nevertheless give greater purchase on why, during the past two centuries, Britain and then the United States were the countries both able and willing to provide international monetary leadership and why others were bound to follow. Indeed, if we accept that financial development helped to promote the general preeminence of the large Anglo-Saxon countries in both the economic and security realms, domestic institutions should be seen as all the more crucial.[46]

Normative Convergence through Socialization

Material incentives for followership, both international and domestic in origin, can only get us so far in explaining the details of international monetary organization and followership. Such theories lack an account of the economic and political ideas that give substantive content to the preferences of actors and to the institutional particularities of the day.

Ruggie, together with Ikenberry and Kupchan, is most often associated with the theory that leadership is based on normative convergence between elites in the major countries.[47] Following Polanyi,[48] Ruggie argues that British leadership in the nineteenth century was founded on the then dominant norms of laissez-faire and monetary discipline. This consensus broke down in the interwar period, but the ex-

44. Paul Volcker and Toyoo Gyoten, *Changing Fortunes: The World's Money and the Threat to American Leadership* (New York: Times Books, 1992), chap. 6.

45. In this case, ideology probably did not play an important part. It is clear from Volcker's memoirs that he was not an ideological monetarist but, rather, a pragmatic central banker determined to put an end to the inflationary psychology that had become entrenched in the United States in the 1970s; ibid., 163–77.

46. Schultz and Weingast, "Democratic Advantage."

47. Ruggie, "International Regimes, Transactions and Change"; Ikenberry and Kupchan, "Socialization and Hegemonic Power." By contrast, Gramscians tend to talk less about "norms" than of "hegemonic ideologies" and emphasize the coercive aspects of ideational power. See Stephen Gill, "Globalization, Market Civilization, and Disciplinary Neoliberalism," *Millennium* 24, no. 3 (1985): 399–423; Robert W. Cox, *Production, Power, and World Order: Social Forces in the Making of History* (New York: Columbia University Press, 1987).

48. Karl Polanyi, *The Great Transformation: The Political and Economic Origins of Our Time* (Boston: Beacon Press, 1944).

periences of depression and war eventually resulted in a "shift in what we might call the balance between 'authority' and 'market' [that] fundamentally transformed state-society relations, by redefining the legitimate social purposes in pursuit of which state power was expected to be employed in the domestic economy."[49] For Ruggie, this "embedded liberal" compromise fundamentally distinguished U.S. leadership from the British version that preceded it.

Nevertheless, it remains the case that British and U.S. monetary leadership in their respective periods rested on *relative* monetary conservatism. Britain, or more specifically the Bank of England, the City, and the Treasury, adhered more strictly to monetary orthodoxy before 1914 than did the governments of Germany and France, whose much wider electoral franchises made them more sensitive to the real economic consequences of strict monetary orthodoxy.[50] The reason for this asymmetry is obvious: if a prospective monetary leader were not relatively conservative in orientation, it is unlikely private-sector agents would be willing to follow in the initial stages. Money is, after all, a social convention whose value in exchange and as a store of value depends on it being in comparatively short supply relative to other goods, services, and assets, including other monies.

Given the less conservative monetary reputation of the United States after 1945, this argument may seem surprising. But after the war, the relative inflation performance of the United States was exceptional for a few decades, particularly in the 1950s. It was comparable with that of West Germany and Switzerland until the late 1960s and much better than Britain's (see fig. 3.2). Nor should the degree to which the United States in the 1960s achieved this good performance by exporting some of its monetary inflation abroad be exaggerated. After all, the Swiss and West Germans, whose currencies tended to bear the brunt of dollar weakness, enjoyed good inflation performance through the mid-1960s despite rapid growth and considerable resistance to currency revaluation.[51]

Certainly, there was a general deterioration in inflation performance in the mid-1960s, but it is not until the late 1960s that U.S. inflation began to look "out of control" by comparison with the low-inflation Germans and Swiss (if not by British standards). By the early 1970s, the U.S. reputation for relative monetary conservatism had well and truly been squandered, and the Swiss and Germans broke away from their inflationary dollar pegs. Surprisingly for many at the time, however, there was no general private-sector (or public-sector) abandonment of the dollar. In the late 1970s, with the U.S. currency depreciating quickly and with the U.S. government offering foreign currency–denominated bond issues and pondering (only to reject) the possibility of a Substitution Account, the dollar's international position appeared to many to be under serious threat.[52] This perception was surely correct

49. John G. Ruggie, "International Regimes, Transactions and Change," 386.

50. Broz, "Domestic Politics of International Monetary Order."

51. The burden of inflation in the Bretton Woods system fell largely on the commodity money, gold, the dollar (and deutschmark) price of which came under growing pressure in the late 1960s and soared in the 1970s.

52. Gowa, "Hegemons, IOs, and Markets," 664.

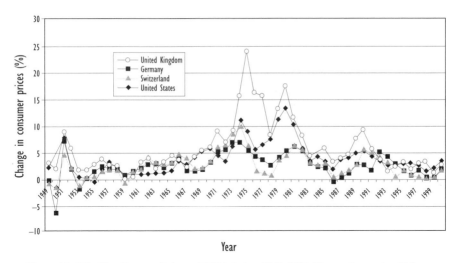

Figure 3.2 U.S., West German, Swiss, and UK inflation, 1949–2000. (*Source:* International Monetary Fund, *International Financial Statistics,* CD-ROM, consumer price inflation.)

because a shift to foreign currency borrowing by the United States would have undermined a key aspect of its monetary power: its ability to borrow, well beyond the capacity of any other country, enormous amounts of money cheaply from foreigners in U.S. dollars, the repayment of which can take place (if necessary) in currency that the government can print.

However, the dramatic tightening of monetary policy undertaken by a new Federal Reserve chairman, Paul Volcker, in retrospect proved sufficient to restore both the conservative monetary reputation of the Fed in the eyes of international financial markets and the international role of the dollar. By 1983, U.S. inflation was back down to near-Germanic levels and has more or less stayed there since, despite periodic bouts of fiscal profligacy. The role of the dollar in private international financial markets has since undergone a minor secular decline, but it remains by some margin the leading international currency; I have more to say on this subject in my concluding remarks. The dollar continues to be the preeminent international currency, I might add, in spite of considerable swings in its external value over time vis-à-vis other major currencies.

Not only do private-sector agents tend to expect relative (although not excessive) conservatism from monetary leaders; the monetary authorities of the follower states do as well. British governments fulfilled such expectations before 1914 and tried, at great cost to the domestic economy and ultimately in vain, to do so again over the years 1925–31. Those countries that followed the United States after 1945 also expected conservatism from the center country. This was obscured during the period of the postwar "dollar shortage," but from around 1951 other governments came to rely heavily on relative U.S. monetary conservatism. Indeed, in the debates over the problems of the gold-exchange standard in the 1960s, it often seemed as if the Europeans expected the United States to sacrifice its own domestic growth and employment goals in order to shore up both the system and their own economic strategies.[53] This may seem hypocritical because most European countries were at the time engaged in full-employment and high-growth policies that also had inflationary consequences. Ruggie is right that the end of gold-dollar convertibility was consistent with the maintenance of embedded liberalism,[54] but followership in the Bretton Woods system was also based on a U.S. commitment—and a related follower expectation—precisely *not* to exploit the full possibilities of U.S. monetary autonomy.

This bargain broke down in the early 1970s as the Richard Nixon administration exploited the possibilities of monetary autonomy, but the asymmetry of expectations on which it was based persisted well after the demise of the gold-exchange standard system. It was evident in European support for a Special Drawing Rights (SDR) standard in the international monetary reform negotiations during 1972–74.[55] When European countries again tried to convince the United States to move toward an SDR standard via the Substitution Account proposal in the late 1970s, the emphasis was still on the need for the United States to adopt relatively conservative monetary policies for the general good. The views of a German economist writing at the time would have been widely shared by central bankers and finance ministers in other major countries: "Monetary stability . . . can only be achieved by an economic policy which engenders trust and convinces the market that the world's major currency is once again capable of exercising its function as a store of value."[56]

The international political economy literature has commonly seen Lyndon Johnson's Great Society program and pro-growth policies as the key reasons for the eventual breakdown of the system, even though they reflected a normative convergence on the part of the United States toward European policy objectives.[57] Ronald McKinnon, a U.S. economist and a proponent of a formal dollar standard in the 1960s, argues that "America's principal international monetary obligation was not the *pro forma* link to gold but rather to maintain stable dollar prices of internationally tradable goods as well as an open capital market."[58] This encapsulates well the conservative "obligation" of the currency leader from the point of view of the followers, public and private sector alike. What was so shocking to U.S. allies was that, after Eisenhower, the U.S. government increasingly seemed ready to abandon good economic housekeeping for objectives that the followers shared. By the time of Nixon,

53. President de Gaulle would have retorted that the United States needed only to scale back its imperialist ambitions abroad. However, most European governments strongly favored a continuing U.S. troop presence on their own continent; this included France, albeit with reservations. Japan did as well.

54. Ruggie, "International Regimes, Transactions and Change," 408.

55. John Williamson, *The Failure of World Monetary Reform, 1971–74* (New York: New York University Press, 1977).

56. Dieter Gehrmann, "Substitution Account: No Solution for International Monetary System," *Intereconomics* 3 (May–June 1980): 114; cited in Gowa, "Hegemons, IOs and Markets," 665n.16.

57. See, for example, David P. Calleo, *The Imperious Economy* (Cambridge, Mass.: Howard University Press, 1982), 35.

58. Ronald I. McKinnon, *Money in International Exchange: The Convertible Currency System* (New York: Oxford University Press, 1979), 261.

the United States went to war on such double standards. As John Connally, Nixon's abrasive Treasury secretary, memorably said in 1971, "the dollar may be our currency but it's your problem."[59]

It might be argued that this interpretation is inconsistent with the West German position, especially that of the conservative Bundesbank. However, political resistance in West Germany to currency revaluation was strong, both in the Bundesbank and in the influential banking and industrial sectors. A majority on the Bundesbank council resisted pressure from the West German government in 1971 to move to a floating rate system, instead favoring exchange-rate fixity with the dollar and capital controls as a means of remaining within the Bretton Woods system.[60] Even in the Bundesbank, then, the incentives to continue to follow the U.S. leader remained strong until the last great dollar crisis of the Bretton Woods system in March 1973.[61] By then, the United States had forfeited its claims to monetary conservatism in German eyes and had joined the ranks of the merely average Organization for Economic Cooperation and Development (OECD) country.

West Germany's role in subsequent moves toward European monetary integration also supports the argument made here. Through the "snake" and later the European Monetary System (EMS), West Germany made a successful bid for European monetary leadership that lasted for about two decades (although the precise number of followers fluctuated considerably during this time). Although other Europeans often complained about the Bundesbank's "obsession" with low inflation, the Bundesbank and the deutschmark increasingly consolidated their undisputed leadership positions within the European system. In the French franc crisis of 1982–83, President François Mitterrand finally opted to follow the German leader by reversing his earlier expansionary policies and pursuing a policy of convergence through the "franc fort" policy. In the absence of a deep elite commitment to the broader European integration process, this difficult choice may not have been made.

The main threat to the EMS came in the wake of German reunification, when a ballooning fiscal deficit threatened to undermine the Bundesbank's monetary conservatism. In 1993, in a moment of hubris or desperation, the French government made the mistake of suggesting that the French franc should succeed to currency leadership within Europe (the *grande gaffe*). The argument assumed that the French were now *more* monetarily conservative than the Germans. Private-market agents, the ultimate arbiters, did not agree, looking to Bundesbank leadership that the latter was willing to provide.[62]

59. Cited in Harold James, *International Monetary Cooperation since Bretton Woods* (Washington, D.C.: International Monetary Fund, 1996), 210.

60. Ibid., 214–16; David Marsh, *The Bundesbank: The Bank That Rules Europe* (London: Mandarin, 1992), 180–93.

61. Among these incentives, in addition to those already mentioned, may have been the deep acceptance by European elites of U.S. values that flowed from the postwar U.S.-dominated occupation and reconstruction of West Germany. See Ikenberry and Kupchan, "Socialization and Hegemonic Power," 304.

62. See Barry J. Eichengreen, *Globalizing Capital (Princeton: Princeton University Press, 1996)*, 174. In the same manner as Paul Volcker during 1979–80, the Bundesbank successfully put down this challenge at considerable cost to the German and European economies.

This episode also suggests, as does the U.S. case of fiscal profligacy since the 1960s, that fiscal balance is less important to monetary leadership vis-à-vis market agents than is the absence of monetary accommodation. Indeed, currency leadership can make it easier for the leader to finance domestic dis-saving by borrowing from abroad. Fiscal deficits also deepen the bond market in the center country and hence promote followership. However, very large fiscal deficits in the center country, by raising real interest rates in the entire system, erode the legitimacy of the monetary leader vis-à-vis other countries. Thus, the first prerequisite of international monetary leadership might be extended to the pursuit of conservative macroeconomic policy in general, but, within the macroeconomic policy mix, monetary conservatism remains the most important element. It is also clear that monetary conservatism is a relative rather than an absolute concept—its meaning depends considerably on the intellectual climate and policy practices of the time.

Monetary Leadership, Power, and Their Limitations

As the cases of the United States since the 1960s and Germany in the early 1990s suggest, established monetary leaders can exert substantial power in the international monetary system. Others have described how monetary conservatism, particularly in the German case, deflected adjustment costs on to others.[63] Such power derives primarily from the way in which private-market agents favor the lead currency. Here, I focus on another kind of monetary power—the ability of the leader to depart from the first prerequisite of monetary leadership (the pursuit of a credibly conservative monetary policy) for what Eric Helleiner (chap. 4 in this volume) terms "extractive" purposes. What are the limits to this kind of monetary power?

Once a currency leader is entrenched, the policy requirements for sustaining such leadership are less onerous than the initial prerequisites and the potential for exercising coercive power over other actors is greater. As indicated earlier, this amounts to a form of monopoly power because it is costly for other actors to shift from the use of the established lead currency to an alternative. The costs of switching are especially high if there are large asymmetries in financial development that favor the currency leader. This consideration helps to explain why, despite the large fluctuations in the value of the dollar since 1973, there has been only a minor erosion of its position as the lead currency in the contemporary system. Network externalities compound the advantages that accrue to the lead currency, not least because its use by specialized private financial intermediaries is likely to deepen the existing cost advantages of transacting in this currency. Entrenched monetary leaders are able to depart from a current account surplus position and to borrow extensively and cheaply in their own currency, something Charles de Gaulle referred to as the

---

63. See, for example, Jean-Paul Fitoussi, Anthony B. Atkinson, Olivier E. Blanchard, and John S. Flemming, *Competitive Disinflation: The Mark and Budgetary Politics in Europe* (Oxford: Oxford University Press, 1993).

leader's "exorbitant privilege." This is a central aspect of international monetary power and is the other side of the coin of the "original sin" literature in economics, which considers the implications of the fact that most countries are able to borrow from international capital markets only in foreign currencies.[64] Consistent with the argument made here, this literature suggests that the handful of countries that enjoy the privilege of borrowing in their own currencies do so partly because of domestic institutions and economic strength and partly because market actors prefer to hold only a few major currencies in their asset portfolios.

Clearly, the extent of the leader's monopoly power depends on the degree of currency rivalry. The emergence of the U.S. dollar in the interwar period as a serious rival to sterling substantially limited the ability of British authorities to exploit the monopoly power that derived from sterling's international position. Indeed, what is striking about UK policy in the 1920s is the extent to which policy makers felt constrained by their need to maintain market confidence in the peg with gold. In a sense, market agents were constraining the leader more than they did other countries, although much of this boiled down to a deep ideological attachment to gold among British political and financial elites.[65] As it became clear that Britain's political and economic institutions could no longer deliver a credibly conservative macroeconomic policy after the stresses of two major wars, sterling's international position rapidly eroded vis-à-vis the dollar. Cultural factors slowed the decline: even in the mid-1960s, formally independent countries such as Australia continued to hold substantial sterling reserves, but this could not halt sterling's overall decline.

By contrast, there were no real rivals to the U.S. dollar in the 1960s and 1970s. This, the large U.S. economy's relatively low dependence on international trade, and the position of the United States as alliance leader increased the ability of U.S. policy makers to depart from fiscal and later monetary conservatism and to deflect and delay the related adjustment costs. Similarly, the essentially unrivalled position of the deutschmark within the EMS increased Germany's ability to depart from fiscal conservatism after 1990. However, given that the deutschmark was not a real rival to the dollar, the Bundesbank could not afford a loose monetary policy of the kind the U.S. Federal Reserve pursued in the 1970s.

In the long term, the leader's continued exploitation of its monopoly power is likely to produce countervailing responses. As C. Randall Henning argues (chap. 6 in this volume), EMU can be seen in part as a European response to the perceived mismanagement of the U.S. economy and the U.S. attempt to deflect adjustment costs on to others. Although the euro is not yet a serious rival to the dollar,[66] the continued exploitation by the United States of its dominant monetary position could

64. See Barry J. Eichengreen, Ricardo Hausmann and Ugo Panizza, "Currency Mismatches, Debt Intolerance and Original Sin: Why They Are Not the Same and Why It Matters," NBER Working Paper no. 10036, National Bureau of Economic Research, Washington, D.C., October 2003.

65. Barry J. Eichengreen and Peter Temin, "The Gold Standard and the Great Depression," NBER Working Paper no. 6060, National Bureau of Economic Research, Washington, D.C., June 1997.

66. Benjamin J. Cohen, "Global Currency Rivalry: Can the Euro Ever Challenge the Dollar?" *Journal of Common Market Studies* 41, no. 4 (2003): 575–95.

eventually make it so. The time is long past when the United States can use political linkage to force its major allies to maintain allegiance to the dollar. As we have seen, in the long run it is private-market agents who are most important in terms of the maintenance of a lead currency's status. Financial liberalization in the major countries since the 1970s, encouraged by the United States, has increased the options available to market agents and thereby reduced U.S. monopoly power. Since the 1979 shift back to U.S. monetary conservatism, there has been no abandonment of this policy stance.[67] In Europe in the early 1990s, market agents similarly looked for confirmation from the Bundesbank that its conservative monetary policy was not in question. Thus, in the longer run, the maintenance of currency leadership requires the center country to pursue reasonably conservative monetary policies, even if not as strictly as at the outset of a bid for currency leadership.

Monetary power is also likely to be constrained in the longer run by the normative and institutional underpinnings of leadership itself. U.S. monetary leadership after 1945 was founded on a broad-based solidarity of western nations during the Cold War, as well as the willingness of U.S. authorities to accept consensus language in the major postwar monetary and trade regimes and to manage disputes multilaterally. The implication of such U.S. leadership was clear to all because in playing this multilateral game the United States often found it had to foster followership by compromising on its initial demands. This also signaled to the followers that the United States would not overly exploit its enormous power.

The Nixon shocks of the early 1970s represented a clear step away from legitimate leadership based on persuasion within multilateral institutional frameworks toward hegemonic coercion, often undertaken outside the bounds of institutionally sanctioned practices. The acrimony that ensued over economic matters between the major countries reflected this shift. The United States blocked international monetary reform efforts in the 1970s and from the 1980s more actively used the IMF and World Bank to promote structural reform in the developing world. In the second half of the 1970s, the U.S. government showed a willingness to exploit, as it had never done before, the potentialities of the international role of the dollar, during the era of so-called "benign neglect." During 1977–79, the United States issued not-so-subtle threats to other G-7 countries that U.S. authorities would encourage further dollar depreciation if their partners failed to reflate their economies.[68] This threat, which fell clearly into the category of hegemonic coercion, was credible because of the sheer economic size of the United States, its relatively low trade dependence, and its ability to borrow enormous sums from abroad in its own currency, all of which meant that other economies lost more from dollar weakness than did the United States.

However, the very credibility of the U.S. threat further undermined the legitimacy of its monetary leadership in the eyes of major follower countries. The grow-

---

67. Since 2002, U.S. monetary policy has been exceptionally accommodative, but inflation remains very subdued.

68. Walter, *World Power and World Money*, 216–23.

ing reluctance of Germany and Japan to accede to U.S. pressure in a range of policy areas was a consequence. Perceived U.S. coerciveness boosted Germany's desire to create with its European partners a "zone of monetary stability" that would deepen the process of political integration in Europe.[69] In the first half of the 1980s, the United States borrowed enormous sums (in dollars) from Japanese investors, who subsequently experienced massive portfolio losses when the dollar depreciated against the yen and other currencies after 1985. Even greater losses accrued to Asian central banks in 2004–5 as their accumulated U.S. Treasury bond portfolios suffered from dollar depreciation. Moves toward closer monetary and financial cooperation in Asia, although as yet with little effect on the position of the dollar, could in the long run further reduce U.S. monetary power. The various signs from Asian governments in 2005 of their displeasure at dollar depreciation and open hints that they may reallocate their portfolios toward other currencies also suggest growing limits to U.S. monetary power.[70]

To summarize, the power that accrues to monetary leaders changes over time. It is very limited in the initial stages of a leadership bid, when the position of the currency depends on self-constraint that is transparently embedded in domestic institutions. The leader's power peaks when its currency is successfully entrenched at the top of the currency pyramid, creating a temptation to exploit the possibilities of its monetary power. In a third phase, monetary power declines when the leader persists in exploiting its monopoly power, thus encouraging the emergence of rival lead currencies and associated financial centers. If, as did the British in the twentieth century, the United States persists in exploiting its monopoly power, this is eventually likely to prove fatal to the maintenance of its leadership and power.

Conclusion

I have argued that monetary leadership requires a relatively (but not excessively) conservative macroeconomic policy from the leader. Many leading theories of international leadership have failed to recognize both this systemic asymmetry and its origins in domestic politics and institutions. The leader's conservative policy needs to be credible, which means firmly embedded in domestic political and institutional arrangements. Fundamental changes in the nature of this domestic institutional framework can eventually undermine the foundations of successful currency leadership, as in Britain after World War I. Particular kinds of domestic institutions, including limited government and pro-creditor legal frameworks, also helped to foster highly developed capital markets, themselves a prerequisite for currency leadership.

69. Kenneth Dyson, *Elusive Union: The Process of Economic and Monetary Union in Europe* (London: Longman, 1994), 303–4.

70. Of course, the danger in pursuing a strategy of reserve diversification is the possibility of precipitating a collapse of the dollar and, hence, further deterioration in the value of their existing monetary reserves. See "Moves to Calm Markets as Koizumi Comments Send Dollar Falling," http://www.FT.com (accessed March 11, 2005).

These preconditions of currency leadership are very difficult to manipulate, except in the long run. Currency leadership also creates its own self-sustaining market logic, a point further examined by David Andrews (chap. 5 in this volume). In sum, few states are ever in the position to successfully promote their currency abroad, let alone to become monetary leaders.

The policy credibility of the monetary leader provides incentives on the part of both public-sector and private-sector actors to follow. Such followership creates substantial potential benefits to the monetary leader, although there are limits on its ability to exploit these hegemonically in practice without undermining the very foundations of its leadership. The implication of my argument is that the extent of these limits depends on the degree of asymmetry of financial development in the world economy, the existence of potential rival lead currencies, the intellectual attachment of the leader's political elites to relative monetary conservatism, and its ability to use political linkage to ensure its continued leadership.

Does the advent of the euro create a new challenge to the primacy of the dollar that will reduce the ability of the United States to exploit its dominant position? Cohen has argued that the euro does not represent a serious challenge to the position of the dollar.[71] In contrast to the argument made here, he suggests that the monetary conservatism inherent in the constitution of EMU will limit returns on euro assets, reducing the attractiveness of the currency and offsetting the benefits of holding a hard currency. He also argues that the ambiguous division of policy responsibility between the European Central Bank and the Council of Ministers reduces the euro's credibility.

However, as we have seen, relative monetary conservatism is an important prerequisite in a potential monetary leader. Also, it may be debated how much low long-run growth in Europe is due to its monetary constitution and how much it is due to other factors, including inflexible factor and product markets.[72] After all, pre-1914 Britain did not have a pro-growth monetary constitution, and nor did West Germany after 1949, which enjoyed high growth for decades. Even when German growth slowed substantially after 1980, the deutschmark remained the lead currency within Europe. Furthermore, the nature of the U.S. Federal Reserve System is itself not entirely transparent and unambiguous; some find its governance structure "bizarre."[73]

Nevertheless, as Cohen and others suggest, a number of other factors work against the euro, including inertia in international financial markets and relatively low financial integration in Europe. So far, and in spite of the impressive growth of euro bond markets, there is little evidence of a dramatic shift against dollars in favor of euros either in international financial markets or in central bank reserves.[74] What Europe still lacks is a truly European euro-based integrated financial market

71. Cohen, "Global Currency Rivalry."

72. Ibid., 585. Later, Cohen accepts that nonmonetary factors do matter (587–88).

73. Faust, "Whom Can We Trust to Run the Fed?"

74. Cohen, "Global Currency Rivalry," 580; International Monetary Fund, *Annual Report* (Washington, D.C.: IMF, 2003), app. 1.

that can rival those of the United States; London's common law system and its newly transparent, credible monetary and financial regulatory framework provide it with substantial advantages over the rest of Europe in this regard. Even if the United Kingdom joins EMU, however, the segmentation of government bond markets in Europe will remain a major constraint on the euro's international role for the fore-seeable future and, hence, on Europe's ability to wield international monetary power beyond its borders.

In short, the relatively underdeveloped nature of financial markets in continental Europe generally—at least compared to those in the United States and United Kingdom—is a major and continuing obstacle to European monetary leadership. Although it is not the only such obstacle, it is the only one over which public authorities in European states have control. The euro area meets the economic criteria for Europe to assert international monetary leadership and enjoys a relatively conservative monetary policy framework—the first domestic prerequisite thereof. But the second domestic prerequisite for the realization of a global role—institutional arrangements that facilitate the emergence of highly developed financial markets—remain absent. As long as this is so, the dollar is likely to enjoy continued preeminence—despite the evident desire of both private- and public-sector actors for a more stable alternative.

CHAPTER FOUR

Below the State: Micro-Level Monetary Power

Eric Helleiner

The study of international monetary relations, whether conducted by economists or political scientists, has typically focused on the macro-level and especially on issues related to balance-of-payments disequilibria between states, as the preceding chapter suggests. These matters are unquestionably important. But the study of international monetary power must go well beyond this to consider a variety of phenomena at the micro-level—that is, issues that concern actors below the level of the state. As David Andrews puts it (chap. 1 in this volume), monetary relations can result in a "rearticulation" of these actors' interests and a "reconstruction" of their identities. Elsewhere I have argued that such transformations are significant in themselves;[1] but they can also influence power relations between states—the subject of this book. They therefore demand the close attention of even those scholars not normally inclined to look "below the state."

This chapter has three purposes: to outline some of the micro-level mechanisms by which monetary power is or can be exercised, to introduce a case study that illustrates some of these mechanisms, and to reflect on what sort of theoretical framework might best elucidate the indirect and sometimes even unintentional avenues of influence that these mechanisms entail. In addressing these three areas of concern, I touch on some macro-level mechanisms whereby monetary power can be exercised, with remarks on the capacity of states to extract wealth from one another and to impose their macroeconomic preferences abroad. My focus, however, is not on these matters but on micro-level aspects of monetary relations between states. I

For their support, I am grateful to the Social Sciences and Humanities Research Council of Canada and the Canada Research Chair program. I also thank Jeffrey Chwieroth, Randy Germain, Joseph Jupille, Kathleen McNamara, Thomas Willett, and all the participants in this volume, particularly David Andrews, for their helpful comments.

1. Eric Helleiner, *The Making of National Money: Territorial Currencies in Historical Perspective* (Ithaca: Cornell University Press, 2003).

therefore draw attention to the means by which states are sometimes able to shape the institutions of financial regulation beyond their jurisdiction; the ways in which some states play a privileged role in international financial crisis management; and, more broadly, the capacity of international monetary relations to influence economic geography and even social identities.

The theoretical discussion that I undertake concerns structural power, a concept addressed by a number of authors who have commented on international monetary affairs but especially by Susan Strange. The importance of examining structural power, I argue, is that it widens our sense of how monetary power is exercised and what it can accomplish. I therefore begin my remarks with a critical review and reconsideration of this literature. I then turn to its past applications to the study of international monetary relations and suggest how these might be expanded. I conclude with a look at informal dollarization outside the United States as a demonstration of the points that I am making.

Structural Power and International Relations Theory

What exactly is structural power? A number of leading thinkers who have written about international relations have made reference to the significance of structural forms of power, especially with reference to the international monetary realm. Three in particular bear mentioning. Benjamin Cohen was the first to discuss the concept in the context of international monetary relations, when in his 1977 seminal work *Organizing the World's Money* he made a distinction between what he called "process power" and "structure power" in international monetary relations.[2] In her various writings from the early 1980s onward, Susan Strange picked up this distinction between two kinds of monetary power, arguing that "structural power" was becoming more important than what she called "relational power."[3] The concept of structural power also made an appearance in Jonathan Kirshner's important 1995 work *Currency and Coercion*, where he argued that dominant states derive both "overt" and "structural" power from the currency blocs they lead. He echoed Strange's view of the importance of the latter, arguing that "the opportunity for structural benefits . . . is what motivates states to create monetary systems."[4]

2. Benjamin Cohen, *Organizing the World's Money* (New York: Basic Books, 1977), 53–77.

3. See especially Susan Strange, "Still an Extraordinary Power: America's Role in a Global Monetary System," in *The Political Economy of International and Domestic Monetary Relations*, ed. Raymond E. Lombra and Willard E. Witte, 73–93 (Ames: Iowa State University, 1982); *Casino Capitalism* (Oxford: Blackwell, 1986); "The Persistent Myth of Lost Hegemony," *International Organization* 41, no. 4 (1987): 551–74; *States and Markets* (London: Pinter Publishers, 1988); "The Future of the American Empire," *Journal of International Affairs* 42, no. 1 (1988): 1–17; "Toward a Theory of Transnational Empire," in *Global Changes and Theoretical Challenges*, ed. James N. Rosenau and Ernst Otto Czempiel, 161–193 (Lexington: Lexington Books, 1989); "Finance, Information and Power," *Review of International Studies* 16 (1990): 259–74; *Mad Money* (Ann Arbor: University of Michigan Press, 1998).

4. Jonathan Kirshner, *Currency and Coercion: The Political Economy of International Monetary Power* (Princeton: Princeton University Press, 1995), 267.

Because the concept of structural power was most prominent in Strange's writings, I begin with her views on the subject. The analysis of power—and the distinction between relational and structural power, in particular—was at the center of most of Strange's theoretical writings after the early 1980s about the global political economy. She argued that scholars of international relations had devoted too much attention to relational power, which she described as "the ability of A to get B by coercion or persuasion to do what B would not otherwise do."[5] In her view, structural power was much more important in the contemporary world than this conception allowed. She described structural power as:

> the power to shape and determine the structures of the global political economy within which other states, their political institutions, their economic enterprises, and (not least) their scientists and other professional people have to operate; structural power, in short, confers the power to decide how things shall be done, the power to shape frameworks within which states relate to each other, relate to people, or relate to corporate enterprises.[6]

Strange's concept of structural power has been criticized for its lack of precision.[7] What specific causal mechanisms account for the outcomes she ascribed to structural power? Relational power refers to outcomes influenced by an application of direct pressure or threat of direct pressure. In the case of structural power, however, Strange suggested that the causal mechanism was more indirect. In her words,

> the possessor is able to change the range of choices open to others, without apparently putting pressure directly on them to take one decision or to make one choice rather than others. Such power is less "visible." The range of options open to the others will be extended by giving them opportunities they would not otherwise have had. And it may be restricted by imposing costs or risks upon them larger than they would otherwise have faced, thus making it less easy to make some choices while making it more easy to make others.[8]

Stefano Guzzini has usefully noted how Strange, in fact, suggested two distinct causal mechanisms by which structural power is exercised in this indirect manner.[9]

5. Strange, "Toward a Theory of Transnational Empire," 165.

6. Strange, *States and Markets*, 24–25. As Susan Strange notes, in *The Retreat of the State: The Diffusion of Power in the World Economy* (Cambridge, UK: Cambridge University Press, 1996), 19, the concept bears some similarity to Joseph Nye's concept of "soft power" in his *Bound to Lead: The Changing Nature of American Power* (New York: Basic Books, 1990).

7. Robert Keohane, "Foreword," in *Strange Power: Shaping the Parameters of International Relations and International Political Economy*, ed. Thomas C. Lawton, James N. Rosenau, and Amy C. Verdun, ix–xv (Aldershot, UK: Ashgate, 2000); Ronen Palan, "Susan Strange 1923–1998: A Great International Relations Theorist," *Review of International Political Economy* 6, no. 2 (1999): 130.

8. Strange, *States and Markets*, 31.

9. Stefano Guzzini, "Structural Power: The Limits of Neorealist Power Analysis," *International Organization* 47, no. 3 (1993): 443–78; "Strange's Oscillating Realism: Opposing the Ideal—and the Apparent" in *Strange Power: Shaping the Parameters of International Relations and International Political Economy*, ed. Thomas C. Lawton, James N. Rosenau, and Amy C. Verdun, 215–28 (Aldershot, UK: Ashgate, 2000).

First, a dominant state may influence other states' behavior by actively altering or shaping the practices and institutions of the global political economy within which they operate.[10] This indirect institutional power—to use Guzzini's term—involves the intentional manipulation of the rules of the game by states through specific decisions or even what Strange called "non-decisions." At the same time, Strange was keen to point out that she was concerned with "more than the power to set the agenda of discussion or to design (in American academic language) the international regimes of rules and customs that are supposed to govern international economic relations"[11]—in other words, arrangements among the states themselves. Although such international regimes are significant, the global economy is governed, in her view, not just by states but also by other various arrangements established by nonstate authorities (especially private corporations) and by the operation of market forces. Because these arrangements have become more important in the contemporary age, she argued that power within the global political economy was increasingly held by those states best able to alter and shape those private institutions and practices as well.

The second way in which structural power can be exercised is what Guzzini calls "non-intentional power." As Strange put it, structural power "need not be confined to outcomes consciously or deliberately sought for."[12] Because of its dominant position, a state can influence outcomes "involuntarily and unintentionally" simply through its unilateral actions or even by the way it has organized the global political economy.[13] In Strange's words, "Power can be effectively exercised by 'being there', without intending the creation or exploitation of privilege or the transfer of costs or risks from oneself to others, for instance."[14] Guzzini notes that international relations scholars who embrace an agency-driven conception of power—particularly those of a realist persuasion—have often neglected this form of power. But he points out that this neglect "leaves the analysis with a specific blind spot, namely, the tacit power of the strong." Ignoring this form of influence can bias the study of power by limiting attention to the intentional exercise of power by a dominant actor. By contrast, the study of nonintentional power examines structural power from the "receiving side."[15]

It is worth taking a moment to discuss how the concepts presented by Strange and elaborated on by Guzzini relate to the discussion of power presented by Andrews (chap. 1 in this volume), particularly because of the potential confusion over different uses of the term relational power. When Andrews notes that power is understood throughout this volume as a relational property, he simply means that *A*'s

---

10. For example, note that Strange's analysis of the monetary realm made reference to the "financial structure," defined as "the sum of all the arrangements governing the availability of credit plus all the factors determining the terms on which currencies are exchanged for one another," *States and Markets*, 90.

11. Ibid., 25.

12. Strange, *Retreat of the State*, 26

13. Strange, "Still an Extraordinary Power," 77.

14. Strange, *Retreat of the State*, 26.

15. Guzzini, "Structural Power," 461.

relationship with B is making B behave in certain ways, even if A did not intend to exert this power. This is a broader meaning for the term relational power than Strange intended and even overlaps with her notion of structural power, particularly in its acceptance of the idea of nonintentional power. But the extent of this overlap should not be overstated.

Strange emphasized that her central goal was to develop a conception of power as control over *structures* instead of control over *other states*.[16] She was, in other words, explicitly trying to move away from a conception of power conceived in terms of direct relationships among states. Of course, the exercise of structural power by state A can indirectly influence the behavior of state B, as Guzzini explains, by controlling the structures within which the latter exists. But this was not the central point of Strange's analysis. Instead, Strange was inclined to define power *not* in terms of the ability of state A to influence state B's behavior but rather in terms of the ability of state A to influence outcomes more generally within the global political economy in ways congruent with its preferences.[17] In other words, the potential targets of state A's power include not just (or even primarily) state B but instead various nonstate actors and market forces. Indeed, if the behavior of these nonstate actors and market forces could be influenced in ways that serve state A's preferences without influencing state B whatsoever, Strange was nevertheless satisfied that this constituted a successful exercise of structural power.

Because the focus of this book is the study of monetary power in the context of interstate relations, this very broad conception of structural power is not employed here.[18] Rather, structural power is discussed only in terms of state's ability to alter the behavior of other states through indirect means, by controlling the structures within which they exist. Likewise, to avoid terminological confusion I employ the term *direct power* when referring to what Strange called *relational power*.

Structural Power and the Study of International Monetary Relations

How does Strange's conception of structural power compare to the use of this term by Cohen and Kirshner? Neither of these authors discussed the meaning of structural power in as much detail as Strange did, but their writings suggest some similar thinking. Cohen, for example, defined structural power as "the ability to gain by rewriting the rules of the game," whereas he saw "process power" as "the ability to

---

16. See, for example, Strange, *Retreat of the State*, 26.

17. See, for example, ibid., 17.

18. I am also restricting my analysis of structural power to that held by states. Some may see this restriction as unjustly downplaying the novelty of Strange's approach. For example, structural power can also be held by nonstate actors, as Strange and others have pointed out; see, for example, Stephen Gill and David Law, "Global Hegemony and the Structural Power of Capital," *International Studies Quarterly* 33, no. 4 (1989): 475–99. For a discussion of the tension within Strange's thought itself on some of these issues, see Guzzini, "Strange's Oscillating Realism."

gain under the prevailing rules of the game." Although this phrasing seems to emphasize primarily the causal mechanism of "indirect institutional power," Cohen also made clear that he embraced the idea of nonintentional power: "[power] need not be exercised with conscious intent; the behavior of others or the outcome of events can be controlled or influenced simply as a by-product of 'powerful' acts (or potential acts)."[19]

Likewise, most of Kirshner's analysis of international monetary power in *Currency and Coercion* focuses on "direct power." This, he argues, can be exerted in three ways: currency manipulation (involving attacks on the stability and value of a foreign currency), systemic disruption, and the fostering and exploitation of monetary dependence. He mentions structural power in his discussion of monetary dependence, noting that the leading state of a currency bloc derives not just "overt" power but also a less visible form of influence that is derived "from the structure of the system."[20] Overt power is exercised directly, through the threat of "expulsion" from a monetary bloc or through "enforcement" of the bloc's rules (e.g., altering the availability of the dominant state's currency to the target state). But aspects of monetary power related to structure are exercised indirectly, in ways that I describe in some detail later in this chapter. In brief, for Kirshner structural power refers not just to the manipulation of the rules of the system but also to the dependence that is cultivated through "the simple act of participation in a monetary system."[21]

Although Kirshner's conception of structural power is similar to that of Strange in certain respects, he deliberately narrows his analysis to examine only cases in which monetary power is consciously exercised. In other words, he does not examine the nonintentional dimensions of structural power that so interested Strange; and this focus on intentionality (or monetary statecraft, as Andrews puts it in chap. 1) leads him to worry more than Strange did about the measurability of structural forms of power. Kirshner notes that structural forms of influence "are exerted invisibly, which makes it difficult to tell if there is an influence attempt in effect."[22] This concern is notably absent from Strange's writings because in her view the exercise of power takes place independently of the question of intentionality. Because of her broader conception of structural power, she was primarily concerned with whether outcomes in the global political economy reflect the preferences of the dominant state.

This approach has its limitations; after all, outcomes may reflect a state's preferences for reasons unrelated to either the conscious or unconscious exercise of power. Moreover, Strange's approach is at points inconsistent with the narrower conception of power at the center of this book, which understands power in a more strictly state-to-state sense (even if the mechanisms for such influence can be indirect). Notwithstanding these points, Strange shares with Cohen and Kirshner a broadly similar conception of the distinctive meaning of structural power in the context of

---

19. Cohen, *Organizing the World's Money*, 54, 56.
20. Kirshner, *Currency and Coercion*, 117.
21. Ibid., 268.
22. Ibid., 243.

interstate relations. Each argues that structural power is exercised indirectly by influencing the environment within which other states operate. This indirect influence, in turn, can take place in one of two ways. The first involves an intentional and active manipulation of the rules of the game by the dominant state. The second—embraced by Strange and Cohen, but not as clearly adopted by Kirshner—does not require intentionality or agency on the part of the dominant state, but instead results from the prevailing institutions and practices of the international monetary system.

Macro-Level Monetary Applications

Structural power analysis has most commonly been applied to the macro-level on international monetary relations. For example, Cohen, Strange, and Kirshner are all interested in how the dollar's global role enhances the ability of the United States to extract wealth from foreigners. When foreigners hold dollars, they provide the equivalent of an interest-free loan to the United States, thus easing the ability of Washington to finance external payments deficits and contributing to what Cohen (chap. 2 in this volume) calls the Power to Delay. This capability, in Strange's words, "may well be the most significant attribute of power in the international monetary system."[23] Kirshner likewise examines "the use of the rules and consequences of the system to extract wealth from the member states" of currency areas, and he examines cases ranging from U.S. policy in the early 1970s to British policy toward sterling bloc countries during and after World War II.[24]

Foreigners who agree to hold dollars also become vulnerable to U.S. decisions to depreciate the currency in which it borrowed. The decision to shut the gold window in 1971 was one such instance, and Strange argued that for this very reason the incident signaled the power—not the weakness—of the United States. As she put it, "the US government was exercising the unconstrained right to print money that others could not (save at unacceptable cost) refuse to accept."[25] A decade and a half later, Japanese investors also experienced this vulnerability to U.S. dollar depreciation during the 1985–87 period. To be sure, there are limits to the exercise of this kind of indirect structural power; foreigners will eventually react to dollar depreciation by dumping their dollar holdings, as happened briefly in 1979 and 1987. But the process of creating attractive alternative world currencies in which to hold assets—challenging U.S. structural power in this realm—has been very slow, as the analysis by C. Randall Henning (chap. 6 in this volume) suggests.

In a related fashion, the dollar's central role has enabled the United States to project its macroeconomic preferences indirectly worldwide. In *Casino Capitalism*, Strange put this case in the following way: "when US domestic monetary policy changed direction, and when interest rates in the United States responded to

---

23. Strange, "Still an Extraordinary Power," 81.
24. Kirshner, *Currency and Coercion*, 117.
25. Strange, "Persistent Myth of Lost Hegemony," 569.

changes of policy, other states had no choice but to adjust their own interest rates and their domestic policies to such changes, whereas it never happened the other way around."[26] One of her favorite examples involved the U.S. decision to combat domestic inflation by hiking interest rates in the late 1970s, a move that prompted a worldwide shift toward restrictive monetary policy.[27] A key reason that U.S. monetary policy had this global influence was that the United States retained a unique capacity to attract internationally mobile financial capital. This "pulling power" over footloose global funds is linked partly to the unparalleled depth and openness of U.S. financial markets, as Andrew Walter (chap. 3 in this volume) explains, but also to the dollar's international role.

More generally, structural power analysis helps elucidate how it is that the United States has been able to prompt foreign governments to assume the burden of adjustment to U.S. payments imbalances. This Power to Deflect (to use Cohen's phrase) has been exercised partly in a direct fashion, via international diplomacy and pressure. But it has also been exercised indirectly, by talking down the dollar's value. As Henning discusses (chap. 6 in this volume), the use of this indirect exchange-rate weapon has altered incentives facing foreign governments in ways that encourage them to embrace the macroeconomic outcomes preferred by U.S. policy makers.

Micro-Level Applications

As the preceding discussion suggests, structural power can be a useful concept in addressing important aspects of international monetary relations at the macro-level. Each of the examples cited here concerns the ability of the United States to influence the behavior of foreigners, not directly through the exercise of coercion or force but indirectly by controlling and shaping the monetary environment in which they operate. The fact that Washington issued and managed a currency widely used by others enabled the United States to change the range of choices others faced without directly applying pressure on them.

But structural power analysis need not be limited to these sorts of macro-level considerations. Indeed, attention to the concept of structural power can help elucidate aspects of international monetary power that might otherwise be ignored. These neglected aspects of international monetary power include many—perhaps even most—of the micro-level considerations that characterize international monetary affairs, including especially the practices and institutions associated with money and finance at both the domestic and international levels.

What are those micro-level considerations? To begin with, the dollar's central global role has given the United States indirect power to influence regulatory trends and crisis management in international financial markets. On the regulatory front, Strange argued that the emergence of more liberal and deregulated global financial markets since the 1970s was largely a product of various U.S. decisions and "non-

---

26. Strange, *Casino Capitalism*, 22.
27. See, for example, ibid., 55.

decisions." Because of the dominant position of the U.S. dollar in the markets, the United States had considerable power to slow down or even reverse this process, a power it chose not to exercise. Strange argued that this U.S. policy stance, in combination with its own domestic deregulation and liberalization moves, had the effect of indirectly prompting foreign states, often reluctantly, to follow the U.S. regulatory lead because of their fear of losing financial business and capital to liberal and deregulated U.S. dollar markets. Although this indirect U.S. role of influencing global regulatory trends was often unintentional, she suggested that it also sometimes reflected a conscious (even if not always widely shared) recognition of the benefits that might accrue to the United States from the dominant role of U.S. financial markets and financial institutions within the newly liberalized global financial markets.[28]

In addition, Strange argued that the dollar's worldwide role ensured that the United States remained the key international lender-of-last-resort during financial crises. She highlighted how the United States played a lead role in determining the outcome of the debt crisis of the early 1980s partly for this structural reason: "it possessed two weapons more powerful than those of any other government: it could make advances in dollars to meet an emergency; and it could twist the arms of the largest and most influential banks [i.e., those in the U.S.] in the system to follow its example with renewed medium-term credit."[29] In this way, the global role of the U.S. banking sector reinforced the global role of the dollar, ensuring that U.S. decisions about whether to provide lender-of-last-resort lending to private institutions played a decisive role in shaping the global financial environment within which foreign states operated during the crisis. This, in turn, altered the incentives those states faced in ways that prompted them to accept approaches to the resolution of these crises that the United States favored.[30]

Strange thus identified important micro-level considerations in her analysis of international monetary relations. Kirshner's discussion, by contrast, is both narrower and broader. It is narrower in that his focus on how monetary power is used to "advance security-related or other non-economic goals"[31] does not prompt him to address the ways in which the issuing of a key currency can generate structural power relating to macroeconomic preferences or financial regulation and crisis management. But, in other respects, Kirshner's analysis helps to deepen the structural approach advocated by Strange.

In particular, in addition to his attention to wealth extraction, Kirshner identifies "entrapment," or "the transformation of interests that results from participation in

28. See, especially, Strange, *Casino Capitalism*.

29. Strange, "Persistent Myth of Lost Hegemony," 569.

30. Strange's example of international lender-of-last-resort lending is one that may, in some instances, straddle the concept of relational and structural forms of power because direct pressure can certainly be applied on foreign states in conjunction with such lending. The utility of the structural power concept is most evident when lender-of-last-resort activities extend to private institutions in global financial markets.

31. Kirshner, *Currency and Coercion*, 4.

a currency system," as a mechanism for the indirect exercise of monetary power.[32] His analysis highlights how membership in a currency bloc diverts trade and strengthens private-sector coalitions with close economic ties to the dominant state. Participation in a currency area also ensures that member governments acquire an interest in the stability and value of the dominant state's currency. These developments reinforce the dependence of the subordinate state on the dominant state in ways that are difficult to measure but are nonetheless highly significant.[33] Indeed, Kirshner argues that the goal of entrapment has been the most important reason why currency blocs have been created by dominant states in the past, such as colonial Britain and France, as well more recently by states such as Germany during the 1930s.[34]

Kirshner's discussion of entrapment highlights two broader analytical points. The first is that currency relations contribute to state power by influencing economic geography. When Kirshner notes that a currency bloc can alter trade patterns to foster dependency, he is calling attention to the fact that currency arrangements alter transaction costs. A country's fixed exchange rate vis-à-vis a dominant power's currency can facilitate cross-border economic transactions by eliminating the costs associated with exchange-rate volatility. If the country goes further and actually adopts the dominant state's currency—thus eliminating even the costs associated with currency exchange—recent analyses by Andrew Rose suggest that the implications for trade patterns may be even more significant.[35] The resulting reorientation of a country's economic geography may not only reinforce the dependency of the subordinate state on the dominant one but may also facilitate trade and investment flows to and from the subordinate state that directly benefit the dominant state. In these instances, the dominant state achieves the desired outcomes, not through an exercise of direct coercive power but by controlling the spatial dimensions of the environment within which they operate.

This important domain of structural power in the monetary realm has often attracted the attention of state authorities. During the age of imperialism of the late nineteenth century and the first half of the twentieth century, the desire to influence economic geography provided a key rationale for the dramatic monetary reforms launched in colonized regions. Most imperial powers completely transformed the colonial monetary environment by demonetizing precolonial currencies and introducing new currencies whose values were tied tightly to that of the imperial power (and in some cases were the same as that of the imperial power). These reforms were designed to support the imperial goal of constructing export-oriented colonial economies that could supply commodities to the imperial center. They did this not just by eliminating exchange-rate risk between colonies and the home country—an outcome that also encouraged private banks, companies, and individuals in many colo-

---

32. Ibid., 118.
33. Ibid., 167, 268.
34. Ibid., 169, 249, 267.
35. See, for example, Andrew Rose, "One Money, One Market: Estimating the Effect of Common Currency on Trade," *Economic Policy* 15, no. 30 (2000): 7–33.

nial regions to export savings and liquid funds to financial markets in the imperial power. The elimination of precolonial currencies was also designed to undermine precolonial commercial circuits and to force local inhabitants to join the colonial economy as wage laborers in colonial enterprises, producers of cash crops for export, and payers of taxes to the colonial state. Given these goals, it is not surprisingly that this transformation of the monetary rules of the game often prompted enormous resistance among the colonized.[36]

Equally important is Kirshner's observation that participation in a currency bloc encourages member governments and societal groups within their countries to take an interest in the stability and value of the dominant state's currency. This is particularly true if the dominant state's currency has been adopted as their domestic currency. Indeed, in this instance, the entire population of these countries suddenly find themselves with an important stake in the management of that currency. Like it or not, they are forced to recognize that the value and use of their money is now dependent on the actions of the dominant state that issues and manages the money. This dependence, in turn, is likely to encourage a certain identification of local interests with those of the dominant state.

Participation in a currency bloc may also foster closer identification with the dominant state in other ways that Cohen has identified in his more recent writings. When he was writing in 1977, Cohen argued that structure and process power were relevant to only two aspects of monetary relations: balance-of-payments adjustment and the creation of international liquidity.[37] More recently, however, Cohen has widened his focus (while dropping the distinction between structure and process power), arguing that currency arrangements influence state power in four ways: seigniorage, macroeconomic management, "insulation" (a concept that he draws from Kirshner's notion of monetary dependence, especially as it relates to "enforcement"), and symbolism.[38] The first three concern issues we have already identified, but the fourth raises a mechanism that involves much more than the concept of entrapment. It is associated with the broader influence of currency to sway identities.

Currencies have often been used historically to bolster state power in a symbolic manner. Because coins and banknotes are "among the most mass-produced objects in the world," the imagery placed on them offers what Virginia Hewitt calls "an unparalleled opportunity for officially-sanctioned propaganda, to color the recipient's view."[39] The fact that money is encountered so regularly in the context of daily routines only contributes to the potential force of imagery on money. More generally, because money has long been seen as a key symbol of sovereignty, the issuer of a currency often derives symbolic authority from this function.[40] Structural power in the

---

36. Eric Helleiner, *Making of National Money*, 163–85.

37. Cohen, *Organizing the World's Money*, 57.

38. See especially Benjamin Cohen, *The Geography of Money* (Ithaca: Cornell University Press, 1998).

39. Virginia Hewitt, *Beauty and the Banknote: Images of Women on Paper* (London: British Museum Press, 1994), 11.

40. In the context of his discussion of currency manipulation, Kirshner also notes, in *Currency and Coercion*, that the stability of currency is linked to national honor and prestige (11–12).

monetary realm may thus enable a dominant state to influence the symbolic environment within which others operate in these ways.

This goal was prominent in the age of imperialism. For example, some members of the U.S. Congress at the turn of the last century argued that the dollar should be introduced into newly acquired colonies as a way of teaching "the lessons of the flag and impress upon [locals] the power and glory of the Republic."[41] Similarly, Hopkins notes that in Africa "[m]oney was not only a means of assisting commercial transactions but also a medium of values: accepting colonial currencies was a symbol of submission."[42] Kirshner also points out that Japan introduced distinct currencies into the parts of China it occupied during the 1930s partly as a means of delegitimizing the Chinese government by removing this symbol of its sovereignty.[43] Many imperial powers also saw their control of the imagery on colonial currencies as an opportunity to influence the identities of the colonized. Both Wambui Mwangi and Virginia Hewitt, for example, highlight very effectively how the imagery on colonial notes was often designed to reinforce colonial ideologies of conquest and cultural superiority in various ways.[44]

I have suggested elsewhere that the link between currency structures and identities need not be restricted to the sense of a common economic interest in a currency's value or even to these larger symbolic issues.[45] In addition, currency use can be linked to a deeper intracommunity trust that has important consequences for identities. Likewise, the use of a common money may foster a sense of community because money acts, in ways similar to language, as an elemental medium of social communication. When people share a common currency, their sense of common identity may also be fostered by the fact that they experience monetary phenomena together.

These kinds of relationships between identities and the use of money deserve much more study than they have so far received. Indeed, the topic is one that ought to generate keen interest among scholars working in the constructivist theoretical tradition. These relationships call attention to a point long recognized by sociologists and anthropologists: if we want to explore how currency structures influence power, we must embrace a wider lens that sees money not just as an economic phenomenon but also as a cultural and sociological one.[46] Money is, after all, deeply and

41. Quoted in Edwin Kemmerer, *Modern Currency Reforms* (New York: Macmillan, 1916), 303.

42. A. G. Hopkins, "Review of Money Matters: Instability, Values and Social Payments in the Modern History of West African Communities," *International Journal of African Historical Studies* 29, no. 3 (1997): 583–85, quotation on 584.

43. Kirshner, *Currency and Coercion*, 62.

44. Wambui Mwangi, "The Lion, the Native and the Coffee Plant: Political Imagery and the Ambiguous Art of Currency Design in Colonial Kenya," *Geopolitics* 7, no. 1 (2002): 31–62; Virginia Hewitt, "A Distant View: Imagery and Imagination in the Paper Currency of the British Empire, 1800–1960," in *Nation-States and Money*, ed. Emily Gilbert and Eric Helleiner, 97–116 (London: Routledge, 1999).

45. Eric Helleiner, "National Currencies and National Identities," *American Behavioral Scientist* 41, no. 10 (1998), 1409–36; *Making of National Money*, chap. 5.

46. See, for example, Viviana Zelizer, *The Social Meaning of Money* (Basic Books: New York, 1994); David Akin and Joel Robbins, eds., *Money and Modernity: State and Local Currencies in Melanesia* (Pittsburgh: University of Pittsburgh Press, 1999).

Table 4.1 Examples of macro-level and micro-level powers

	Aspect of monetary power	Primary mechanisms
Macro-level	Extraction of wealth	Seignorage; devaluation/ depreciation of currency
	Projection of macroeconomic preferences	"Pulling power" in global financial markets; use of exchange-rate weapon
Micro-level	Influence over financial regulation in other states	Regulation of financial markets employing core currency
	Influence over international financial crisis management	Public lender-of-last-resort activities; influence over private institutions lending in the core currency
	Reshaping of economic geography	Altering transaction costs to foster economic links with core economy
	Formation of identities	Creation of a common interest in value and stability of core currency; symbolic role of money; shared trust within the community using and issuing core currency; common "economic language"; collective monetary experiences

intricately embedded in culture and society as one of the basic structures of everyday life.[47]

In short, international monetary relations can influence policy outcomes at both the macro-level and micro-level, as table 4.1 summarizes. Furthermore, the concept of structural power opens the door to understanding the mechanisms associated with each of these manifestations of monetary power. In the section that follows, I seek to demonstrate the utility of such an analysis—and to underline how even the chief advocate of structural power analysis failed to grasp its full potential.

Dollarization and U.S. Structural Power

As we have seen, Susan Strange argued that the concept of structural power is particularly useful in highlighting the enduring international monetary power of the United States. But I suggest that her thesis could be developed more fully. We have already seen that she did not devote attention to the spatial and ideational signifi-

---

47. Fernand Braudel, *The Structures of Everyday Life* (London: Fontana, 1985).

cance of the dollar's international role. An equally important limitation was her neglect of the phenomenon of informal dollarization.

At the core of Strange's thesis about the growing importance of structural power was her belief that all states are losing power to global market forces and various nonstate authorities. Given this belief, it is odd that Strange's writings about the international role of the dollar were rather conventional. When she discussed the dollar's importance within the global political economy, she focused primarily on its prominence in the foreign currency reserves of states, in international financial markets, and in international trade. She did not devote much attention to one of the most interesting ways in which many poorer states are losing power in the monetary realm: the fact that the dollar is increasingly used *within* their domestic monetary systems as a store of value, unit of account, and even medium of exchange. In many countries where this informal dollarization has been very extensive (e.g., in Latin America), the U.S. currency now makes up an important part of the domestic money supply.[48]

As Cohen has pointed out, informal dollarization is a largely market-driven process that is linked to a deeper deterritorialization of monetary structures encouraged by financial globalization.[49] Individuals in poorer countries have turned to the use of the dollar as a way of insulating themselves from domestic inflationary conditions and broader domestic economic and political uncertainty. Some governments have attempted to stop the trend with anti-inflationary programs and regulatory means. But this has proven difficult in contexts where the state's credibility is weak and its capacity to regulate and influence the activities of its citizens is not high. The globalization of finance has further undermined these initiatives by making it easier for domestic citizens to move their wealth into dollar-based financial instruments offshore. Indeed, massive capital flight of this kind has often forced governments to quickly back down from "de-dollarization" initiatives.

In the context of this deterritorialization of currencies, Cohen suggests that the contemporary world monetary system is, in fact, best thought of as a kind of currency pyramid in which the U.S. dollar sits as the "top" currency whose authoritative domain is very wide and no longer corresponds with territorial borders. He argues that the dominant position of the dollar within this transformed monetary order has important implications for the distribution of power within the global political economy, implications that have not been adequately appreciated by international political economy scholars. In addition to augmenting the power of markets vis-à-vis states, informal dollarization has bolstered the power of the United States vis-à-vis other states.

Cohen's analysis of the significance of informal dollarization reinforces Strange's broader argument about the enduring role of U.S. power in the world monetary system. Indeed, his description of the deterritorialized authoritative domain of the U.S. dollar is quite reminiscent of a point Strange often made—that the United States

---

48. Cohen, *Geography of Money.*
49. Ibid.

increasingly resembles a new kind of nonterritorial empire.[50] This nonterritorial empire rested, in her view, on the structural power of the United States. Cohen does not use the distinction between direct and structural power when discussing the ways in which dollarization has bolstered U.S. power. Let me suggest, however, that the study of informal dollarization provides an important example of the point Strange made about the contemporary significance of U.S. structural power.

Although the literature about informal dollarization is now quite large, scholarly analyses have been dominated by economists who have been less interested in its power implications. Both Cohen and Kirshner have, however, briefly addressed the subject, with each highlighting how the United States has a new ability to directly coerce dollarized countries by controlling access to dollars. They both cite the case of Panama, which found its access to dollar resources cut off by the United States as part of a sanctions program directed against Manuel Noriega's rule in the late 1980s. As Kirshner notes, this case is a good example of how monetary dependence can leave a state vulnerable to the direct power of enforcement.[51]

Although this episode was important, such direct and overt exercise of monetary power by the United States in a dollarized state has few parallels; the more important implications of dollarization for U.S. power involve the ongoing exercise of structural power across the six areas summarized in table 4.1. Cohen, for example, mentions how the dollar's use abroad has strengthened U.S. power in a macroeconomic sense and also in terms of its ability to earn seigniorage revenue.[52] He also highlights how dollarization may influence identities abroad at a symbolic level. In his words, the dollar's global role becomes "an important source of status and prestige," whereas the governments of the countries experiencing dollarization "are apt not to command much respect" because the currency they issue provides citizens with "a daily reminder of inadequacy and impotence."[53] Cohen also suggests briefly that dollarization may influence identities in a more concrete sense because "the more a foreign currency is used domestically in lieu of national money, the less the citizens will feel inherently connected to the state or part of the same social entity."[54] This suggestion is very interesting because it raises the point about entrapment that Kirshner mentioned—that holding a foreign currency may generate a strong interest in the stability and value of that currency and, thus, bring about a closer identification with the state that issues and manages it. It also highlights the broader sociological point that users of dollars in effect join a wider dollar-based trust community and find themselves sharing collective monetary experiences with other holders of dollars rather than with their fellow citizens who still use the national currency.

These points are particularly important when we recognize that dollarization is

50. See, for example, Strange, "Future of the American Empire."
51. Cohen, *Geography of Money*, 44–46, 126–28; Kirshner, *Currency and Coercion*, 158–66.
52. Cohen, *Geography of Money*. See also Kenneth Jameson, "Dollar Bloc Dependency in Latin America: Beyond Bretton Woods," *International Studies Quarterly* 34, no. 4 (1990), 519–41.
53. Quotes from Cohen, *Geography of Money*, 120, 121.
54. Ibid., 120.

generally experienced very unevenly in class terms across Latin America and elsewhere. In most countries, the wealthy elite have dollarized much more extensively than the poor. As a result, the two groups increasingly operate in two distinct, although interconnected, monetary universes. The broader sociological implications of this situation have received very little attention in existing scholarly literature. One exception, however, is a study by the anthropologist Alaina Lemon, who examines the sociocultural implications of dollarization in Russia during the first half of the 1990s. At that time, Russia had experienced considerable dollarization, and Lemon notes that this monetary phenomenon reinforced social divisions within the country. Elites with dollar holdings did not, for example, experience the inflation of the ruble to nearly the same extent as the rest of the population. They also had much greater access to foreign goods and private stores that would accept payment only in dollars. Indeed, she notes that "journalists coined the term *currency apartheid* to label ways in which public space was being separated into 'ruble' and 'dollar' sides, for instance, in the two separate dining rooms in the Moscow Pizza Hut." More generally, she observes that dollars were seen "as a passport to restricted or faraway exchange."[55]

These observations about how dollarization was linked to social division and the broader internationalization of Russian elites relate in an interesting way to a broader argument that Strange made about the nature of the nonterritorial empire of the United States. She drew a parallel to the Roman Empire, in which "citizenship was not a matter of domicile and . . . there were gradations of civil and political rights and responsibilities, ranging from slaves to senators, which did not depend on what we, today, understand by 'nationality', indicated by possession or non-possession of a passport." Similarly, she argued that participation in the cultural and financial dimensions of the contemporary U.S. empire depends not on passports but on such things as competence in English, involvement with U.S.-based professional organizations, and "possession and use of US dollars and dollar-denomination assets." As she put it, "in financial and cultural matters, the distinction between first-class, passport-holding citizens and second-class, non-passport-holding participants is increasingly blurred. The peripheral allies have been unconsciously recruited into the American Empire."[56]

In addition to influencing extraction, macroeconomic preferences, and identities, the analysis I presented earlier suggests that informal dollarization may also bolster U.S. structural power in two other areas: the changing nature of economic geography and the financial environment of dollarized countries. Concerning the former, dollarization lowers the transaction costs associated with commerce with the United States and thus encourages market actors in these countries to cultivate closer economic ties with the United States. This may have fostered not only the kind of entrapment that Kirshner identifies but also specific trade and investment flows that benefit the United States.

55. Alaina Lemon, "'Your Eyes and Green Like Dollars': Counterfeit Cash, National Substance, and Currency Apartheid in 1990s Russia," *Cultural Anthropology* 13, no. 1 (1998), 22–55, quotations on 41, 45.

56. Strange, "Future of the American Empire," 11.

As to the financial environment of these countries, dollarization has strengthened the ability of the United States to project its regulatory preferences in the financial sector. For example, by imposing regulations relating to the control of money laundering on users of U.S.-based dollar-clearing networks, the United States can indirectly pressure dollarized countries to follow its regulatory lead.[57] Some analysts have also noted that dollarization has left U.S. banks with a competitive advantage in the local financial system because of their privileged access to the Federal Reserve's lender-of-last-resort lending and discount activities.[58]

The significance of this last point was highlighted historically in Cuba when it was a U.S. protectorate during the early twentieth century. Like many other Caribbean-basin countries that fell under the direct and indirect influence of the United States during this period, Cuba's domestic monetary system became increasingly dollarized during the first two decades of the twentieth century. When a financial crisis struck in 1920–21, Cuban-owned banks collapsed because they had no access to the lender-of-last-resort facilities of the U.S. central bank. U.S. banks then quickly emerged in a dominant position in the Cuban financial system. In this way, the United States exerted a major influence over the Cuban financial system simply by what Strange calls a "non-decision"—that is, by not providing lender-of-last-resort support to Cuban banks. Interestingly, after this crisis, the U.S. Federal Reserve Bank of Atlanta (as well as that of Boston, between 1923 and 1926) established an agency in Cuba to carry out lender-of-last-resort functions.[59]

In sum, the study of informal dollarization reinforces Strange's general thesis about the enduring power of the United States in the international monetary system. Dollarization bolsters the power of the United States not just because the door is opened for it to exert a kind of direct form of coercion, Panama-style. More significant (if less visible) is the structural form of power that accrues to the United States in the six areas noted previously and especially in the micro-level issues that are rarely addressed in conventional analyses.

Conclusion

Informal dollarization appears to be recreating the kind of monetary dependence that characterized the era of colonial currency blocs.[60] This is not taking place within the context of the kinds of formal empires that existed in the first half of the twentieth century; indeed, Washington has played little direct role in promoting dol-

57. See, for example, Eric Helleiner, "The Politics of Global Financial Regulation: Lessons from the Fight against Money Laundering," in *International Capital Markets: Systems in Transition,* ed. John Eatwell and Lance Taylor, 177–206 (Oxford: Oxford University Press, 2002).

58. See, for example, Benjamin Cohen, "US Policy on Dollarization: A Political Analysis," *Geopolitics* 7, no. 1 (2002), 63–84.

59. Henry Wallich, *Monetary Problems of an Export Economy: The Cuban Experience 1914–1947* (Cambridge, Mass.: Harvard University Press, 1950), 69; Eric Helleiner, "Dollarization Diplomacy: US Policy Towards Latin America Coming Full Circle?" *Review of International Political Economy* 10, no. 3 (2003), 406–29.

60. See, for example, Jameson, "Dollar Bloc Dependency in Latin America."

larization abroad. Nevertheless, the United States has profited from this development; and one of the best ways of understanding the benefits that accrue to the United States as a result of dollarization is by applying, and extending, the concept of structural power.

Structural power is a form of monetary power that is exercised indirectly—and sometimes even unintentionally—through the shaping and controlling of the monetary environment within which others must operate. This environment is not limited to the macro-level, where most analyses of international monetary relations begin and end, but extends to the micro-level as well—below the state—including the ability of currency relations to affect domestic financial regulation, international financial crisis management, economic geography, and identity formation. As we have seen, attention to how a dominant state can shape these elements of the international monetary environment provides important insights into the nature of U.S. monetary power today.

Although the concept of structural power contributes to our understanding of international monetary power in these ways, its importance should not be overstated. As Strange, Cohen, and Kirshner have each highlighted, the structural power of the United States, like that of all other states, is increasingly constrained by global market pressures and nonstate actors. Any analysis of U.S. structural power today must therefore be qualified. A major portion of U.S. power consists of its ability to influence global structures; and although this ability is significant, it is not unlimited.

Likewise, because the exercise of structural power relies on subordinate states' remaining dependent on the currency that the dominant state controls, the existing distribution of structural power is not immutable. If subordinate states throw off their monetary dependence, they can free themselves from this form of structural power. The prospects for this kind of exit strategy will obviously increase when there is more than one viable world currency. It may also be encouraged if the dominant state begins to exploit its dominant monetary position excessively, either in a direct manner or indirectly—for example, by extracting additional resources through substantially depreciating its currency.[61]

Finally, I note that despite its obvious attractiveness, the concept of structural power in the monetary realm also has some important analytical limitations. It is primarily useful in addressing the issues of how monetary power is expressed and what it can accomplish; it is less helpful for analyzing the sources of monetary power. To understand this latter issue, Strange suggested—but never discussed in any depth—that we need to explore how a state's structural power in the financial realm may be reinforced or undermined by its structural power in other realms such as security, production, and knowledge. Structural power in each of these areas was, in her view, "supported, joined to and held up by the other three."[62] Equally impor-

61. See for example Kirshner, *Currency and Coercion*, 119, 168–69, 249, 267; Eric Helleiner, "Still an Extraordinary Power, but for How Much Longer?" in *Strange Power: Shaping the Parameters of International Relations and International Political Economy*, ed. Thomas C. Lawton, James N. Rosenau, and Amy C. Verdun, 229–48 (Aldershot, UK: Ashgate, 2000).

62. Strange, *States and Markets*, 26. In this regard, recall again the broad definition of the *financial structure* that Strange provides (see note 10).

tant, the relationship between structural power and more direct forms of power also needs to be examined. The former is sometimes highly dependent on the latter; the colonial currency blocs that provided imperial powers with structural power, for example, were created and sustained only with the highly coercive power of the colonial state. In contrast, U.S. structural power deriving from informal dollarization, for example, has resulted largely from market forces. The relationship between structural and more direct forms of power is thus complicated and requires greater analytical attention than it has thus far received.

CHAPTER FIVE

Monetary Policy Coordination and Hierarchy

David M. Andrews

Invoking a metaphor from family therapy, David Lake describes hierarchy as "one of the 'dead horses' plaguing the study and practice of international politics. It is a fact of international life, but we refuse to recognize it. Indeed, for much of the last fifty years, we have refused to talk about it, and now, after decades of trying to forget, we have even lost the language to describe it."[1] In this chapter, I try to recover some of that language, particularly with regard to the study of monetary policy coordination but with more general applications as well.[2]

To do so, I begin with two observations. First, formal negotiations aimed at coordinating monetary policies are relatively rare. This is true whether one is speaking of ad hoc arrangements (such as the Bonn summit of 1978, or the Plaza or Louvre accords of the 1980s) or of bargaining within formal institutions (such as the Bretton Woods system or the European Monetary System). Although the literature tends to dwell on these instances of state-to-state negotiations, most of the time macroeconomic policy coordination is not the subject of official discussions. Compare, in this respect, trade, where formal bilateral and/or multilateral negotiations have been an almost continuous feature of the international system for over one hundred years.

I am grateful to the contributors to this project and to the participants at the Florence workshop for their comments on this chapter.

1. David A. Lake, "The New Sovereignty in International Relations," *International Studies Review* 5, no. 3 (2003): 303–23, quotation from 303. Lake is characterizing the mainstream study of international relations in the United States; attention to international hierarchy has of course been a perennial focus of both radical scholars and non-American observers.

2. Although rare, analysis of hierarchy in international monetary affairs has by no means been nonexistent. Of particular note are two formulations, Susan Strange's political theory of international currencies and Benjamin Cohen's notion of the currency pyramid. Susan Strange, *Sterling and British Policy: A Political Study of an International Currency in Decline* (London: Oxford University Press, 1971), 2–40; Benjamin Cohen, *The Geography of Money* (Ithaca: Cornell University Press, 1998), especially 92–118.

The second observation is that a substantial degree of monetary policy coordination results anyway—for example, between Austria and Germany for the quarter century prior to the introduction of the euro. Why is this? Because monetary policy coordination is a domain in which the weak typically accommodate the policies of the strong without receiving reciprocal concessions. Indeed, one of the defining features of strength in this important dimension of international monetary affairs is the capacity to remain indifferent to the policy preferences of others. Because this is so, responsibility for undertaking the domestic policy adaptations necessary to promote international policy coordination tends not to be shared.[3] Again, compare this with other areas of international economic activity, and certainly trade relations, where the principle of reciprocity is well entrenched not only as a behavioral norm but as a practical fact of life. A trade negotiator who is unprepared to make tactical concessions is unlikely to secure many of her objectives. Not so, however, when it comes to international monetary policy coordination.

Monetary policy coordination takes place primarily on the basis of passive leadership by the strong—sometimes called "benign neglect"—and unilateral adaptation by the weak. This constitutes a hierarchical state of affairs—that is to say, a state of affairs in which power asymmetries are both pronounced and persistent, resulting in a social division of labor that is equally pronounced and persistent.[4] This condition is rarely acknowledged in either the policy world or the academy; the resulting hierarchy therefore remains informal. But its informality does not mean that monetary hierarchy is unreal or insignificant. Quite the contrary: as this chapter demonstrates, the hierarchical characteristics of international policy coordination efforts are momentous and pervasive.

Acknowledging the presence and importance of hierarchy in monetary policy coordination requires revisiting one of the core concepts in the study of international relations—cooperation.[5] Before doing so, I examine more closely the relative dearth

3. Because this chapter engages several different scholarly traditions, a terminological problem arises. The international cooperation literature, as well as many scholars of domestic policy processes, use *adjustment* interchangeably with *adaptation* to mean a change of policy. But *adjustment* has a technical meaning in the economics literature, where *real adjustment* refers to the mutual reallocation of resources necessary to eliminate a payments imbalance; this can take place through either a change in domestic policies or a change in the exchange rate (see the discussion by Cohen, chap. 2 in this volume). To limit confusion, I generally reserve *adjustment* to instances in which the subject matter is real adjustment, referring to more general changes in domestic policy as *adaptation;* but I make no effort to alter the language of other scholars whose work I quote or paraphrase, many of whom use the term *adjustment* more broadly.

4. Compare the discussion of anarchy and hierarchy in Kenneth Waltz, *Theory of International Politics* (New York: McGraw-Hill, 1979), 114–16.

5. Helen Milner provides an authoritative survey of mainstream approaches to this subject in "International Theories of Cooperation among Nations: Strengths and Weaknesses," *World Politics* 44, no. 3 (1992): 466–96. Subsequent critiques of this mainstream consensus include Stephen D. Krasner, "Global Communications and National Power: Life on the Pareto Frontier," *World Politics* 43, no. 3 (April 1991), 336–66; James D. Fearon, "Bargaining, Enforcement, and International Cooperation," *International Organization* 52, no. 2 (April 1998), 269–303; Thomas Oatley and Robert Nabors, "Redistributive Cooperation: Market Failure, Wealth Transfers, and the Basle Accord," *International Organization* 52, no. 1 (winter 1998), 35–54; Lloyd Gruber, *Ruling the World: Power Politics and the Rise of Supranational Organizations* (Princeton: Princeton University Press, 2000).

of formal monetary negotiations accompanied by an abundance of de facto coordination. I discuss why it is that monetary policy coordination efforts tend to assume an exceedingly hierarchical form despite diplomatic routines emphasizing the norms of sovereign equality. I then critically review the literature on international cooperation and conclude by discussing the role of power in bringing about monetary coordination.

Procedural and Substantive Coordination

Before discussing my empirical claims about policy coordination, some definition of the concept is in order. In principle, policy coordination might mean either of two different things: policies that are mutually established (co-ordained) or policies that are mutually appropriate (according to some set of welfare criteria). The first refers to process, the second to substance, and these are quite distinct. A jigsaw puzzle provides a useful metaphor. Did several players participate in its assembly, and what was the nature of their interaction? These are questions about procedural coordination. Do the pieces go together well? Do they fit? These are questions about substantive coordination.

Distinguishing between procedural and substantive coordination—between the act of coordinating and the state of being coordinate[6]—is critical to recovering a language for the analysis of hierarchy. In fact, it is a critical task for policy analysis more generally. Why? Because the mutual establishment of policy (procedural coordination) sometimes fails to produce mutually appropriate policies (substantive coordination), and mutually appropriate policies sometimes occur without procedural coordination. Our understanding of important aspects of international relations will deepen to the extent we keep this distinction in mind.

Why might procedural coordination fail to yield substantive coordination? To begin with, the objectives of the co-ordaining authorities may differ from the welfare criteria employed to evaluate the resulting policies.[7] This is the essence of the time-inconsistency problem, whereby political authorities with short-term time horizons enact policies yielding quick benefits but resulting in substantial longer-term costs.[8] In addition, procedural coordination might fail to result in substantive coordination because of model failure. In such cases authorities with righteous intentions embark on a course of action that fails to produce the desired results because they have mis-

6. These are the two primary meanings of *coordination* offered by *The American Heritage Dictionary,* 4th ed. (2000).

7. For example, Martin Feldstein argues that, as a general matter, what I call procedural coordination can reduce overall economic welfare by allowing governments to postpone reforms. "International Economic Cooperation: Introduction," in *International Economic Cooperation,* ed. Martin Feldstein, 1–10 (Chicago: University of Chicago Press for the National Bureau of Economic Research, 1988).

8. The classic source on this subject is Finn E. Kydland and Edward Prescott, "Rules Rather than Discretion: The Inconsistency of Optimal Plans," *Journal of Political Economy* 85, no. 3 (1977): 473–91. For an argument about a similar phenomenon (the political-business cycle), see Edward Tufte, *Political Control of the Economy* (Princeton: Princeton University Press, 1980).

understood some element of the problem.[9] For example, if my five-year-old and three-year-old sons jointly choose which clothes to wear, those choices are by definition procedurally coordinated; but whether the resulting outfits are substantively coordinated is a matter of taste.[10] Finally, policies might remain uncoordinated because of insufficient effort, on the part of one or more parties, to implement agreed policy changes. Regardless of the source of the disjunction, procedural coordination plainly does not guarantee substantive coordination.

Conversely, the existence of substantive coordination need not imply that procedural coordination has taken place. In fact, Robert Keohane's tripartite formulation of harmony, cooperation, and discord relies on this distinction. According to this rubric, policies are harmonious when each actor's independent choices are regarded by others as facilitating the attainment of their goals; as a result, substantive coordination is a serendipitous outcome. In such cases, cooperation—which Keohane defines in procedural terms (as "a process of policy coordination")—is not required.[11]

In short, procedural coordination is neither a sufficient nor a necessary condition of substantive coordination. Given the indeterminate relationship between these two concepts and that either one could be reasonably understood as policy coordination, it is little wonder that confusion ensues in discussions of the same; hence the need for scholarly conventions.

Although individual practice varies, the general convention in economics has been to prefer the procedural definition over its substantive variant. Thus for example Ralph Bryant writes that "coordination involves *jointly designed mutual adjustments* of national policies. In clear-cut cases of coordination, bargaining occurs and governments agree to behave differently from the ways they would have behaved without the agreement."[12]

In political science, the story is somewhat more complicated. An influential definition offered by Charles Lindblom mixes elements of process and substance as fol-

---

9. Alternatively, the model may have been appropriate when adopted but subsequent changes in the operating environment may have rendered it invalid. Note that the definition of model failure I employ here, in which actors perform in a manner consistent with their causal beliefs about the necessary conditions to obtain a given set of results but these beliefs are mistaken, differs from standard academic accounts of model uncertainty. For discussions of model uncertainty as applied to international monetary affairs, see Keisuke Iida, *International Monetary Cooperation among the United States, Japan, and Germany* (Boston: Kluwer Academic, 1999); Thomas D. Willett, "Developments in the Political Economy of Policy Coordination," *Open Economies Review* 10 (1999): 221–53. On the role of causal beliefs in the policy-making process more generally, see Robert O. Keohane and Judith Goldstein, *Ideas and Foreign Policy: Beliefs, Institutions, and Political Change* (Ithaca: Cornell University Press, 1993).

10. In this analogy, *taste* corresponds to the choice of welfare criteria. My boys may employ different criteria than their parents, or they may attempt to fulfill their parents' criteria without success; in either case, procedural coordination fails to yield substantive coordination (as judged by their parents).

11. Robert O. Keohane, *After Hegemony: Cooperation and Discord in the World Political Economy* (Princeton: Princeton University Press, 1984, reissued in 2005 with a new preface by the author), 51–55. Keohane describes cooperation in terms of "a process of policy coordination" (51, 52). For a summary of key passages on this subject, see note 21.

12. Ralph C. Bryant, *International Coordination of National Stabilization Policies* (Washington, D.C.: Brookings Institution, 1995), xxiv (emphasis added).

lows: "a set of decisions is coordinated if adjustments have been made in them [a procedural qualification] such that the adverse consequences of any one decision for other decisions are to a degree and in some frequency avoided, reduced, or counterbalanced or overweighed [a substantive qualification]."[13] Still, this definition—the second of two offered by Lindblom for the concept of coordination in his 1965 study of policy adjustment—places relatively greater emphasis on process than does its predecessor.[14] In his discussion of policy coordination, Keohane relies on Lindblom's later definition, thus emphasizing the procedural element; but, lest any doubt remain, he insists in subsequent passages that he means "a process of policy coordination."[15]

In so doing, of course, Keohane implicitly acknowledges that coordination might be conceived in substantive terms as well. Indeed, vexing problems result from coordination's dual meaning in the English lexicon. For example, in the ensuing discussion, when Keohane asks "whether actors' policies automatically facilitate the attainment of others' goals," he is posing a question about substantive, not procedural, coordination. Likewise his description of a condition in which "each actors' policies (pursued without regard for the interests of others) are regarded by others as facilitating the attainment of their goals" is purely substantive.[16] Similarly, Bryant acknowledges that the "basic rationale for coordination" (or at least for "activist coordination") is policy optimization—a substantive outcome—and this is the criterion by which coordination should be judged.[17] Notwithstanding these potential ambiguities, both Bryant and Keohane, and the disciplines they represent, tend to favor a procedural understanding of coordination.[18]

Closely linked to coordination is the concept of cooperation. For Bryant, and for most international economists, cooperation is, like coordination, understood in a procedural sense but in broader and less demanding terms. The term's meaning encompasses the mutual exchange of policy information, including information about policy intentions, as explained in this passage:

> "Cooperation" is best used as an umbrella term for the entire spectrum of interactions among national governments designed to deal with the arbitrage pressures and cross-border spillovers among national economies. "Consultation," "mutual recogni-

13. Charles Lindblom, *The Intelligence of Democracy: Decision Making through Mutual Adjustment* (New York: The Free Press, 1965), 227. (This concept is first introduced on p. 154 and then restated.)

14. Early in his study, Lindblom provides an initial or "tentative" definition of *coordination* as follows: "a set of interdependent decisions is coordinated if each decision is adapted to the others in such a way that for each adjusted decision, the adjustment is thought to be better than no adjustment in the eyes of at least one decision maker." Ibid., 24. He restates this definition on pp. 153–54 immediately before introducing its (relatively) procedural variant.

15. Keohane, *After Hegemony*, 51, 52.

16. Ibid., 51, 52, 53.

17. Bryant, *International Coordination of National Stabilization Policies*, 35–45; quotations on 35.

18. Milner, in "International Theories of Cooperation," cites Keohane prominently before writing that "policy coordination . . . implies that the policies of each state have been adjusted to reduce their negative consequences for the other states" (467). This definition again combines procedural and substantive elements, but with a continued emphasis on process.

tion," various forms of "coordination," and "explicit harmonization" are varieties of intergovernmental cooperation, each involving some element of management of the interactions among nations.[19]

For Lindblom, by contrast, cooperation (or "cooperative discussion") is an exceedingly narrow concept, limited to instances when actors' underlying goals were not at odds and, hence, the "techniques of mutual adjustment" are not required.[20] Keohane turns this distinction on its head: all instances of policy adjustment are termed cooperative.[21] Helen Milner, although describing Keohane's work as the basis of "a consensus on a definition of cooperation," nevertheless refines that definition considerably, describing (for example) unilateral policy adjustment as an alternative to cooperation.[22]

I return to these rival conceptions of cooperation later in this chapter.[23] But with this discussion as background, we can now return to my central empirical claims. By saying that there has been a great deal of monetary policy coordination without a great deal of formal negotiation, what I mean is that a great deal of substantive coordination has occurred without a correspondingly great deal of procedural coordination.[24] My argument is that, at least in many instances, monetary policies are mutually appropriate without having been mutually determined. The remainder of this section substantiates and qualifies this assertion.

---

19. Bryant, *International Coordination of National Stabilization Policies*, 6.

20. "In the face of conflicts among their actual or intended decisions, decision makers might enter into a cooperative discussion of their common problems on the supposition that there are agreed criteria sufficient to determine upon investigation the proper course of action for each of them. . . . Given the assumption that there is an agreed criterion sufficient for the resolution of their problem, it is clear that they cooperatively investigate their problem rather than bargain or negotiate with one another or employ any of the other techniques of mutual adjustment." Lindblom, *Intelligence of Democracy*, 28. Central to the prospects for cooperative discussion is the absence of what Lindblom calls "partisans," who do not agree to submit their actions to such criteria (28–32).

21. For Keohane, "cooperation occurs when actors adjust their behavior to the actual or anticipated preferences of others, through a process of policy coordination." This contrasts with harmony, or "a situation in which actors' policies (pursued in their own self-interest without regard for others) *automatically* facilitate the attainment of others goals." Discord, "a situation in which governments regard each others' policies as hindering the attainment of their goals, and hold each other responsible for these constraints," results when harmony does not obtain and adjustments are either not made or are insufficient. Keohane, *After Hegemony*, 51–52 (emphasis in original).

22. Milner, "International Theories of Cooperation: Strengths and Weaknesses;" "a consensus" on p. 467, unilateralism cited as an example of "what is not cooperation" on p. 468. For more on unilateralism cited as an example of "what is not cooperation," see note 69.

23. *Cooperation* also has a technical meaning in the public choice literature, referring to circumstances under which agreements are subject to binding third-party enforcement. Because this definition does not correspond either to conventional meanings of the term or to typical uses in either economics or political science, I do not discuss it further here.

24. More generally, when I refer to *coordination* (the noun) without the use of a modifier I mean substantive coordination, whereas *coordinate* (the verb) without modification means procedural coordination.

The Paucity of Formal Negotiations

To limit payments imbalances, states need coordinated policies, at least to some degree;[25] and the demand for substantive coordination is especially intense when capital is mobile.[26] But this demand is rarely vocalized, at least in state-to-state negotiations. As a result, formal negotiations intended to limit payments imbalances or to agree how to adjust to them are relatively rare.

Of course such negotiations sometimes do occur, and when they do they are often important, as several of this volume's contributors document. Nevertheless, the focus of formal monetary negotiations within the global and regional forums generally has to do with matters other than policy coordination per se. For example, discussions about the terms and availability of balance-of-payments financing are hardy perennials in the International Monetary Fund (IMF) and used to take place regularly in the European Monetary System (EMS) as well. But payments financing is a substitute for policy coordination and for the real adjustments it entails. These subjects tend to lurk in the background, like the dead horse in Lake's analogy; it is easier by far to discuss symptom management than to address the root causes of payments imbalances.[27]

Thus, instances of state-to-state negotiations regarding policy coordination, although sometimes significant, tend to be few and far between. For example, C. Randall Henning (chap. 6 in this volume) identifies five crisis periods in monetary relations among the United States, Japan, and Europe; in sum, these periods amount to somewhat less than half of the thirty-four years since the closing of the gold window in 1971. But formal negotiations—that is, meetings between official representatives of these states where the order of business was agreeing to change domestic policies in order to enhance international coordination—took place during only a tiny fraction of that span. Much more characteristic of these crisis periods, Henning explains, was the use of various techniques—most notably the "exchange-rate weapon"—to pressure partners into making policy changes *without* the benefit of formal negotiations or as a prelude to official meetings that were typically brief and decisive (even if the decision was to do nothing). Compare this situation once again with trade negotiations, a protracted process characterized by the repeated exchange of official position papers and formal proposals over a period of many years.

The same reluctance to negotiate policy coordination exists at the regional level. Canadian authorities do not call for periodic meetings with their U.S. counterparts

25. Robert Mundell, *International Economics* (New York: Macmillan, 1968), is the classic reference.

26. David M. Andrews, "Capital Mobility and State Autonomy: Towards a Structural Theory of International Monetary Relations," *International Studies Quarterly* 38, no. 2 (1994): 193–218; Michael C. Webb, *The Political Economy of Policy Coordination: International Adjustment since 1945* (Ithaca: Cornell University Press, 1995).

27. Likewise, although international organizations such as the IMF, the Bank for International Settlements, and the Organization for Economic Cooperation and Development frequently issue policy recommendations for their member states, these are generally not evidence of authoritative negotiations to coordinate policies. More typically, they reflect frustration that such negotiations are not taking place.

to discuss monetary policy coordination; indeed, as Louis Pauly (chap. 9 in this volume) underlines, they seek to avoid such meetings if at all possible. Likewise, French monetary authorities rarely insisted on interviews with their German colleagues during the days of the EMS. The most noteworthy exception, *la grande gaffe* (discussed by Andrew Walter, chap. 3 in this volume), suggests why this rule prevailed: the French were humiliated. National authorities typically avoid negotiations of this sort precisely because they are likely to be a source of embarrassment for all concerned—the strong because of their strength, the weak because of their weakness—especially in the face of diplomatic norms that insist on formal equality among states.

Meanwhile, the academic literature on monetary policy coordination, especially in political science, tends to dwell on the creation and role of formal regimes governing monetary relations.[28] Attention is therefore focused on arrangements such as the Bretton Woods agreement and the founding of the EMS—and with good reason, as these institutions provide the ground rules for subsequent negotiations over many important matters.[29] But both Bretton Woods and the EMS were conspicuous for failing to specify adjustment responsibilities. For example, officials at the Bundesbank made it clear that the deutschmark's participation in the exchange-rate mechanism of the EMS was contingent on the absence of adjustment responsibilities for West Germany.[30] Within both these regimes, informal (and distinctly hierarchical) practices developed that did not correspond in the least to the symmetry in their formal rules; and potential conversations about coordinating policy generally did not take place precisely because their outcomes were understood to be substantially preordained.

The Abundance of Coordination

Although the procedural coordination of monetary policy is unusual, a great deal of substantive coordination results anyway. Why is this? Substantive coordination—the pursuit of mutually appropriate monetary policies—can result either from harmonious choices arrived at independently by multiple national authorities or by policy adaptations on the part of at least some states. Over the past thirty years, conditions have favored the increased occurrence of both these outcomes.

Harmony, although still rare, is more likely when there are widely shared changes in officials' causal beliefs, as when many national monetary policy makers began to discount the apparent attractiveness of inflationary policies.[31] Meanwhile, policy adaptation is more likely when increases in international capital mobility systematically punish some policies while rewarding others; this pattern, too, was evident.[32]

28. For example, see Benjamin J. Cohen, "Balance-of-Payments Financing: Evolution of a Regime," in *International Regimes,* ed. Stephen Krasner, 315–36 (Ithaca: Cornell University Press, 1983).

29. Scott Cooper (chap. 8 in this volume) is particularly clear on this point.

30. See the discussion in C. Randall Henning, *Currencies and Politics in the United States, Germany, and Japan* (Washington, D.C.: Institute for International Economics, 1994), especially 187–89.

31. See, for example, Kathleen R. McNamara, *The Currency of Ideas: Monetary Politics in the European Union* (Ithaca: Cornell University Press, 1998).

32. Andrews, "Capital Mobility and State Autonomy."

Strikingly, neither of these outcomes is dependent on procedural coordination, with leaders striking deals aimed at reducing payments imbalances (or other goals), reminding us that the mutual establishment of policies is but one of several possible sources of substantive coordination.

In point of fact, however, all three of these factors—ideational change, structural change, and increased efforts at procedural coordination—have been in play during recent decades. As previously noted, disinflationary policies became popular at the same time that the costs of pursuing uncoordinated policies rose; it is little wonder, then, that low-inflation targets became the focal points of substantive coordination. But procedural coordination, although still rare, became relatively more common as well. Indeed, there was far more effort to co-ordain policies during the 1980s and 1990s—a period bemoaned by many observers for the dearth of cooperative behavior in international monetary relations—than there had been during the heyday of the Bretton Woods system.[33] In that earlier era, cooperation consisted largely of agreeing to new schemes for financing payments deficits; but, as capital became more mobile, this form of symptom management became less efficacious. Political authorities therefore became more inclined to contemplate, and sometimes even to adopt, measures aimed at improving the mutual suitability of their policies. This change has been evident both globally (as with the Bonn Summit, the Plaza Agreement, and the Louvre Accord) and at the European level (especially after the dramatic reversal of French economic policy in 1982–83). True, this increased willingness to contemplate domestic policy adaptation was most evident in monetary followers, not leaders; and it is also true that this later period experienced exchange-rate movements that were both more frequent and more severe than those of the 1950s and 1960s. But these occasional crises came about despite greater efforts at policy coordination, not because of their absence. Indeed, it was the threat of increased instability—due to heightened financial integration—that prompted greater attention to coordinating policies.[34]

Still, this increase in procedural policy coordination is purely relative: the mutual establishment of policy remains a rare phenomenon. Although a great deal of substantive coordination takes place, it typically does so in highly asymmetric fashion and in the absence of procedural coordination—that is, reciprocated policy changes. And attention to reciprocity, or its absence, is essential to the study of hierarchy, just as it is to power analysis more generally.

Coordination versus Convergence

When distinguishing between procedural and substantive coordination, it is also important to differentiate between substantive coordination and policy convergence. Generally, policy convergence (which implies sameness) can indeed be taken

33. A point emphasized by Webb, *Political Economy of Policy Coordination* (e.g., 1–11).

34. David M. Andrews and Thomas D. Willett, "Financial Interdependence and the State: International Monetary Relations at Century's End," *International Organization* 51, no. 3 (summer 1997): 479–511, especially 484–96.

as an initial approximation of substantive coordination (which denotes mutual suit-ability).[35] But what mutual suitability means in practice depends on context, in terms of both the objectives of governments and the conditions under which they act on those objectives.[36]

To illustrate this point, recall that states participating in the exchange-rate mech-anism (ERM) of the EMS during the foreign-exchange crises of 1992 and 1993 and experiencing speculative outflows of capital needed to raise domestic interest rates in order to maintain their exchange-rate pegs to the deutschmark. In fact, many of them needed to raise interest rates to levels far surpassing those in Germany.[37] This constituted an extreme instance of a more general phenomenon that Fritz Machlup once called "compensatory corrections."[38] Machlup's term refers to policies de-signed to reduce the immediate demand for policy change without engaging in real adjustment—in other words, without effecting a marginal reallocation of resources. In the case of the ERM crisis, then, interest rates in the Federal Republic's partners diverged from German policy not as a display of policy independence but, ironically enough, in order to validate the exchange-rate regime. By contrast, monetary au-thorities in the United Kingdom demonstrated their policy independence by *refus-ing* to raise interest rates in order to defend sterling's deutschmark parity. Somewhat paradoxically, the result was that UK interest rates were (at least temporarily) more convergent with German rates than were those of several of the states remaining within the ERM.

Policy within the ERM was therefore temporarily divergent, but it was a case of what might be deemed "compensatory divergence" because its purpose was specif-ically to promote substantive coordination, understood here in terms of limiting payments imbalances and stabilizing mutual exchange rates. As a consequence, temporary policy divergence was in many instances positively correlated with com-mitment to the ERM. This should serve as a warning of the difficulties associated

35. As I do in David M. Andrews, "Capital Mobility and Monetary Adjustment in Western Europe," *Policy Sciences* 27, no. 4 (December 1994): 425–55.

36. As Bryant notes, "the differences between coordination and harmonization [his term for conver-gence] are fundamental. Normally, one would *not* expect coordinated national monetary and fiscal poli-cies to be harmonized. For example, national governments would not necessarily adjust policies in the same directions, with every government contracting or every government expanding. Heterogeneity might well prevail even for the hypothetical case of all governments undertaking 'optimal' coordination." *International Coordination of National Stabilization Policies,* 37 (emphasis in original).

37. This was especially evident in of some of the smaller European economies. For general discus-sions, see Group of Ten, *International Capital Movements and Foreign Exchange Markets* (Basel, Switzer-land: Bank for International Settlements, 1993); International Monetary Fund, *International Capital Markets: Part I. Exchange Rate Management and International Capital Flows* (Washington, D.C.: IMF, 1993); International Monetary Fund, *World Economic Outlook* (Washington, D.C.: IMF, 1993). For a po-litical account of these developments, see David M. Andrews, "European Monetary Diplomacy and the Rolling Crisis of 1992–1993," in *The State of the European Union,* Vol. 3, ed. Carolyn Rhodes and Sonia Mazey, 159–76 (Boulder: Lynne Rienner, 1995).

38. Fritz Machlup, "Adjustment, Compensatory Correction, and Financing of Imbalances in Inter-national Payments," in *Trade, Growth, and the Balance of Payments: Essays in Honor of Gottfried Haber-ler,* ed. Robert E. Baldwin, Richard E. Caves, Harry G. Johnson, and Peter B. Kenen, 185–213 (Chicago: Rand McNally and Company, 1965).

with statistical analyses of monetary policy independence.[39] Although policy convergence is often a useful initial approximation of coordination, the terms are not synonymous; treating them as such can be misleading. Returning to the metaphor of the jigsaw puzzle, the puzzle's pieces are coordinated when they go together well, not when they are identical to one another (except under restrictive assumptions). Analogously, coordination implies convergence only under similarly restrictive conditions.

In sum, monetary policies that are merely similar (or, in other words, convergent) may or may not be coordinated—that is, well suited to one another—given the purpose at hand. Context and intent are critical. As Clifford Geertz reminds us, despite little physical differentiation between a wink and a blink, there is a world of difference in meaning.[40] For the power analyst, monetary policy must be evaluated in terms of intent, even if this is difficult to ascertain, if we are to make sense of its political meaning and not simply ascribe policy behavior to the equivalent of physical reflex.[41] Why did policy makers adopt particular policies under particular circumstances? What did they perceive to be their alternatives? What did they believe would be the consequences of their actions and of other actions that they might have undertaken? Absent the consideration of these and like questions, power analysis is not merely hamstrung; it is impossible.

Bargaining over Policy Coordination

Having established that substantive coordination of monetary policies often—even typically—takes place without the benefit of procedural coordination, we can now examine why this situation arises. The chief sources of this curious outcome are found in the demand for policy coordination, which tends to be at least mildly asymmetrical, and in the strategic interactions that result from efforts to satisfy those demands, which tend to be highly asymmetrical. These outcomes derive from fairly inflexible variables and, hence, tend to be stable over time. As a result, hierarchy— a state of affairs in which power asymmetries are pronounced and persistent, reshaping the social division of labor accordingly—is particularly decided in the field of monetary relations.

39. The distinction between policy divergence and policy independence may help explain why Andrew Rose finds a weak empirical relationship between policy divergence, capital mobility, and exchange-rate volatility. Andrew Rose, "Explaining Exchange Rate Volatility: An Empirical Analysis of 'the Holy Trinity' of Monetary Independence, Fixed Exchange Rates, and Capital Mobility," *Journal of International Money and Finance* 15, no. 6 (December 1996): 925–45.

40. Clifford Geertz, *The Interpretation of Cultures: Selected Essays* (New York: Basic Books, 1973), 6–7. Keohane also invokes Geertz, arguing that "each act of cooperation or discord . . . must therefore be interpreted as embedded within a chain of such acts and their successive cognitive and institutional residues." *After Hegemony,* 56.

41. Hence, the construction of indifference curves (or reaction functions) based on actors' revealed preferences cannot be an uncritical exercise for the power analyst because one of the manifestations of power is a disjunction between underlying preferences and observed behavior.

Negotiating Dynamics: Money versus Trade

Like other forms of interaction, international monetary relations create potential rewards for joint action as well as potential costs for failing to act (whether jointly or singly).[42] These potential costs and benefits are likely to vary across parties, an observation that lies at the heart of multiple theories of negotiation.[43] But negotiations regarding international policy coordination have certain distinctive characteristics as well—most notably that the strong are often able to accomplish their objectives simply by failing to act.[44]

Stated more formally, the outside option—the alternative to a negotiated agreement—is not only usually acceptable to the stronger party in negotiations regarding policy coordination, it is often desirable. This is entirely different from the negotiating dynamic that prevails in many other realms of international bargaining, including trade negotiations.[45] As mentioned earlier, when a state negotiates access to another state's markets, typically some form of reciprocity is required; weak parties in trade negotiations do not typically respond to recalcitrance on the part of their stronger partners by unilaterally eliminating tariff and nontariff barriers to trade. Quite the opposite, in fact—many of the weakest (and poorest) participants in the international trading system also have the highest barriers to foreign goods and services. Although this outcome frustrates many international economists, who are persuaded that such behavior is self-defeating, it no doubt also frustrates the national authorities of rich countries who desire access to these markets.

But, although neither weak nor strong actors can accomplish their international trade objectives—to gain access to one another's markets—on the basis of unilateral changes to their own domestic policies, the same is not true of interstate monetary policy coordination. As long as *some* party to those relations regards the costs of policy discord as high, this relatively vulnerable actor will often conclude that subordinating internal policies to external circumstances is preferable to relying on

42. Milner regards the existence of mutual benefits as one of two defining elements of cooperation; see "International Theories of Cooperation," 467–68.

43. See, for example, Howard Raiffa, *The Art and Science of Negotiation* (Cambridge, Mass.: Harvard University Press, 1982); David A. Lax and James K. Sebenius, *The Manager as Negotiator: Bargaining for Cooperation and Competitive Gain* (New York: Free Press, 1986); Richard J. Zeckhauser, Ralph L. Keeney, and James K. Sebenius, eds., *Wise Choices: Decisions, Games and Negotiations* (Boston: Harvard Business School Press, 1996). For applications to both trade and monetary negotiations, see John S. Odell, *Negotiating the World Economy* (Ithaca: Cornell University Press, 2000).

44. Gruber, in *Ruling the World*, makes a different but related argument, maintaining that the attractiveness of the "go it alone" option explains bargaining dynamics in EMU and the North American Free Trade Agreement (NAFTA). See as well the discussion of agenda setting in Oatley and Nabors, "Redistributive Cooperation."

45. Previous work has compared the different domestic political dynamics of money and trade; see, for example, Stephen D. Krasner, "United States Commercial and Monetary Policy: Unravelling the Paradox of External Strength and Internal Weakness," in *Between Power and Plenty: Foreign Economic Policies of Advanced Industrialized States*, ed. Peter J. Katzenstein, 51–87 (Madison: University of Wisconsin Press, 1978); Joanne S. Gowa, "Public Goods and Political Institutions: Trade and Monetary Policy Processes in the United States," *International Organization* 42, no. 1 (winter 1988), 15–32. Here I engage a different question: the differing characteristics of interstate relations in these two fields.

negotiated reciprocity. The outcome will be the coordination of policies, albeit achieved through highly asymmetrical policy adaptation—that is, substantive coordination without procedural coordination.[46]

Asymmetrical Demand for Monetary Policy Coordination

The roots of asymmetrical policy adaptation are to be found in cross-national differences in the demand for substantive policy coordination. Because states differ in their assessments of the benefits of coordinated policies, and of the costs of acting to coordinate policies, the propensity of national authorities to accommodate the policies of their partners differs across states. In a well-known treatment of this problem, Keohane and Joseph Nye focus attention on the extent to which such differing assessments result in asymmetric interdependencies.[47] The literature on optimal currency areas, although framed differently—focusing on welfare rather than power considerations—draws attention to similar concerns. The central conclusion of that literature is that national monetary authorities rationally differ both in the degree of their attentiveness to particular exchange rates and in their capacity to influence those exchange rates without interfering with other important policy objectives. In particular, authorities from relatively large and closed economies are likely to draw considerably different conclusions about the costs and benefits of adapting their domestic policies to conditions elsewhere than are authorities from relatively small and open economies.[48]

Of course economic size is not the only determinant of these differing assessments. Benjamin Cohen argues (chap. 2 in this volume) that states vary both in their

46. Lindblom, in *Intelligence of Democracy*, 66–68, uses *symmetrical* to mean that policy adaptation is mutual and reciprocated, regardless of the exact distribution of associated costs. By contrast, I reserve that term for those instances when the distribution of costs is at least roughly equal; hence, by *asymmetrical policy adaptation* I mean that the distribution of costs is severely skewed, with unilateral subordination to another state's policies being the most extreme example thereof.

47. "We must also be careful not to define interdependence entirely in terms of situations of *evenly balanced* mutual dependence. It is *asymmetries* in dependence that are most likely to provide sources of influence for actors in their dealings with one another. Less dependent actors can often use the interdependent relationship as a source of power in bargaining over an issue and perhaps to affect other issues. . . . And that is where the heart of the political bargaining process of interdependence lies." Robert Keohane and Joseph Nye, *Power and Interdependence: World Politics in Transition* (Boston: Little, Brown and Company, 1977), 10–11 (emphasis in original).

48. See, for example, Robert Mundell, "A Theory of Optimum Currency Areas," *American Economic Review* 51, no. 4 (1961): 657–65; Ronald McKinnon, "Optimum Currency Areas," *American Economic Review* 53, no. 4 (1963): 717–25; Peter Kenen, "The Theory of Optimum Currency Areas: An Eclectic View," in *Monetary Problems of the International Economy*, ed. Robert Mundell and Alexander Swoboda, 41–60 (Chicago: University of Chicago Press, 1969). For a review of this literature, see Clas Wihlborg and Thomas D. Willett, "Optimum Currency Areas Revisited," in *Financial Regulation and Monetary Arrangements after 1992*, ed. Clas Wihlborg, Michele Fratianni, and Thomas Willett, 279–97 (Amsterdam: North Holland, 1991). For some interesting recent revisions of this approach, see, for example, Jeffrey A. Frankel and Andrew K. Rose, "The Endogeneity of the Optimum Currency Area Criteria," *Economic Journal* 108, no. 449 (July 1998): 1009–25; Peter B. Kenen, "Currency Unions and Policy Domains," in *Governing the World's Money*, ed. David M. Andrews, C. Randall Henning, and Louis W. Pauly, 78–104 (Ithaca: Cornell University Press, 2002).

Power to Deflect the transitional costs of real economic adjustment (depending primarily on their relative economic characteristics) and in their Power to Delay the continuing costs of such adjustment (depending primarily on their relative financial characteristics). These varying capacities to avoid the burden of adjustment help explain why national authorities are likely to perceive the costs of policy discord—the absence of substantively coordinated policies—quite differently. National authorities from a state that is easily able to finance the payments imbalance generated by policy discord are likely to regard those imbalances with relative equanimity. So too are authorities from a state that is generally able to pass the transitional costs of adjustment on to its economic partners (the Power to Deflect).

Indeed, the Power to Deflect the transitional costs of adjustment hinges on cross-national differences in the costs of policy discord as compared with the costs of unilaterally adapting policy to produce substantive coordination. Relative indifference to the possibility of monetary policy discord results in a strong bargaining position in negotiations, whether actual or potential, over international policy coordination. After all, deflecting adjustment's transitional costs means that they must be absorbed by some other party. Parties that are better prepared to endure discord's consequences will often be able to avoid those consequences, either altogether or in part, simply by inaction, thereby obliging their more vulnerable partners to adapt their policies instead. This is what I mean by *passive leadership*.

Of course, this does not mean that monetary leaders must regard policy discord as being without cost. But because states vary substantially in the range of outcomes to which they are indifferent and because international monetary relations are strategic in nature (exchange rates being mutual phenomena), variation in vulnerability normally translates into bargaining power. Such calculations are necessarily contingent, leaving extensive room for posturing, bluffing, and collusion—the essence of negotiation.[49] Nevertheless, the room for creative solutions to the underlying problem should not be overestimated. For example, because the chief variables identified by optimum-currency-area theorists as being crucial to informing national monetary authorities' sensitivity to exchange-rate movements are fairly easily surmised by officials from neighboring states, the prospects appear dim for bamboozling one's economic partners in discussions about the desirability of policy coordination.[50]

Given these characteristics of negotiations regarding policy coordination, defection is a dominant strategy for relatively strong bargaining partners. To illustrate, consider a static model of bilateral bargaining—tacit or voiced—over the same. Assuming that their preferences are not harmonious, authorities from each of two

---

49. Indeed, sincerity provides no assurance of mutual accommodation. In an examination of multilateral bargaining situations under incomplete information with strategic characteristics similar to those examined here, Roger Myerson concludes, in "Incentive Compatibility and the Bargaining Problem," *Econometrica* 47, no. 1 (1979): 61–74, that honest revelation of private information by individual bargainers—for example, the sharing of national economic data—is incompatible with Pareto efficient outcomes.

50. Nevertheless, the subjective element of these assessments remains important. Contemporary perceptions (rather than ex post appraisals) must inform ex ante analysis of bargaining power. Although contemporaneous perceptions may subsequently prove inaccurate, the result of information updating will be to change future, not present, bargaining positions.

Table 5.1 Bargaining over policy coordination[a]

		Country Y	
		Adapt	Neglect
Country X	Adapt	A	B
	Neglect	C	D

[a]A, mutual (shared) adaptation; B and C, unilateral (unshared) adaptation; D, mutual neglect

countries, X and Y, must decide whether to make the changes in their domestic policies ("adapt" or "neglect") that are necessary to achieve substantive coordination. If both states undertake these changes, the result is shared policy adaptation (A); if either state engages in such actions without reciprocity from its partner, the result is unilateral adaptation (B and C); if neither state adapts its policies, the result is mutual neglect (D). This is depicted in table 5.1.[51]

Let us assume, as is not unreasonable, that both countries would prefer that the other bear the full costs of producing substantive coordination—that is, X's ideal point is C and Y's ideal point is B. Regardless of the remaining structure of their preferences, shared policy adaptation (A) cannot represent a Nash equilibrium.[52] This is true even if both parties prefer shared adaptation to mutual neglect and, indeed, if mutual neglect is the least desired outcome for both parties.

For example, in the variant of the latter case that is most plausibly associated with shared adaptation—in which preferences correspond to those typically associated with the governments of small, open, and highly interdependent economies, each deeply vulnerable to movements in their mutual exchange rate—the payoff structure in table 5.2 results. Note that both B and C (instances of unilateral adaptation) represent Nash equilibrium outcomes. Outcome A (shared adaptation) is highly unstable, with both players sorely tempted to defect first.

In principle, this problem can be resolved if mutual adaptation is an explicit feature of the policy regime and if this rule can be enforced—in other words, if the center state or policy leader has explicit obligations to share the burden of policy adaptation and if defection from those obligations is regarded as costly. Historically, the commitment of U.S. authorities to maintain the domestic price of gold at $35 per ounce under the Bretton Woods regime was intended to serve as such a constraint. But the United States eventually renounced this obligation, suggesting that regime rules (like national policy) can be adapted as cost-benefit analyses change.[53]

51. By *shared adaptation,* I mean that all parties make significant (not merely token) changes to their domestic policies. Of course, asymmetrical outcomes are still possible when costs are shared; but asymmetry, and hence hierarchy, will be most extreme when they are not. See in this regard note 46.

52. Indeed, this statement would be true even if only one party had as its ideal point unilateral adaptation by its partner.

53. I provide a discussion of this regime shift in chapter 1. For an examination of U.S. policy makers' changing views of the Bretton Woods system that makes good use of primary sources, see Francis J.

Table 5.2 Payoff table when mutual neglect is the least desired outcome for both countries

		Country Y: B > A > C > D	
		Adapt	Neglect
Country X:	Adapt	3,3	2,4
C > A > B > D	Neglect	4,2	1,1

Likewise, heightened attention to the possible gains from future interactions—a lengthened "shadow of the future"—might result in shared adaptation as a stable outcome.[54] But it bears mentioning that even in the institutional environment generally regarded as best suited to outcomes of this kind—the former European Community (now European Union)—Germany's partners could persuade the Bundesbank neither to commit to mutual adaptation during the negotiations to found the EMS nor to share the burden of policy adaptation thereafter.[55]

In short, the barriers to mutual policy adaptation in the field of monetary coordination are profound. Indeed, if mutual adaptation does not arise in the absence of formal negotiations, it is unlikely to take place because of them. States that are capable even on occasion of indifference to policy discord will generally find adapting their domestic policies to accommodate joint goals an extremely onerous task; the costs will be high and the perceived benefits low. Coordination among such parties is more likely to result either from one state's yielding to its (even marginally) stronger partner or from the temporary and felicitous harmonization of policy preferences than from negotiated reciprocal concessions.

Policy Coordination among Multiple Actors

To summarize the discussion thus far, cross-national differences in the demand for policy coordination can be significant. But because unilateral adaptation on the part of the (relatively) weak can produce substantive coordination, even mild asymmetries in the demand for coordination can result in exaggerated asymmetries in the satisfaction of those demands. This is especially true if multiple actors are involved.[56] Under those circumstances, decisions by authorities representing rela-

Gavin, *Gold, Dollars, and Power: The Politics of International Monetary Relations, 1959–1971* (Chapel Hill: University of North Carolina Press, 2004).

54. Kenneth Oye, "Explaining Cooperation under Anarchy: Hypotheses and Strategies," *World Politics* 38, no. 1 (October 1985): 1–24.

55. See note 30.

56. For formal examinations of the dynamics resulting from the presence of multiple actors, see Koichi Hamada, "Alternative Exchange Rates Systems and the Interdependence of Monetary Systems," in *National Monetary Policies and the International Financial System*, ed. Robert Z. Aliber, 13–33 (Chicago: University of Chicago Press, 1974); K. Hamada, "A Strategic Analysis of Monetary Independence," *Journal of Political Economy* 84, no. 4 (August 1976): 677–700; Michael Artis and Sylvia Ostry, *International Economic Policy Coordination*, Chatham House Papers (London: Royal Institute of International Affairs, 1986); and, more recently, Iida, *International Monetary Cooperation*.

tively weak states can help tip the balance between larger economic partners—partners who might otherwise be fairly evenly balanced in terms of their vulnerability to policy discord.

This insight helps account for why France and West Germany—two states with economies of roughly the same economic size prior to German unification—ended up in a completely asymmetrical monetary relationship, with substantive coordination of their policies entirely dependent on adaptation by the French. The decision by Austrian authorities to peg the schilling to the deutschmark—a policy of "autonomous solidarity" with the Bundesbank, as described by Louis Pauly (chap. 9 in this volume)—had repercussions beyond the Austro-German relationship; it pressured Swiss authorities to pay heightened attention to the Swiss franc–deutschmark exchange rate, inasmuch as this now influenced Swiss trade not only with Germany but with neighboring Austria as well. A similar dynamic emerged to Germany's north, where Holland's decision to shadow the deutschmark helped pressure Belgium eventually to do the same. As a result, French monetary authorities in due course found themselves negotiating with German counterparts who established policy—effectively if not officially—over a much wider economic zone than merely the German national economy. Not surprisingly, German officials were relatively indifferent to movements in the bilateral rate of the deutschmark and the French franc because these were much more disruptive to the French—who risked exchange-rate instability with all these trading partners—than they were to the Germans.[57]

The implications of this analysis for monetary cooperation are discussed in the next section. But the preceding discussion should suffice to demonstrate two points. First, the distribution of the costs of policy adaptation normally reflects relative indifference to the consequences of policy discord. Monetary leadership is therefore characteristically passive, meaning that leaders typically allow their followers to make the policy changes necessary for substantive coordination to result. Absent some formal or informal agreement to subvert this outcome, even mildly asymmetric monetary interdependence can lead almost inexorably to highly asymmetrical policy adaptation.

Second, by shaping weaker states' choices, the capacity of stronger states to act relatively independently renders the monetary environment still more permissive for themselves. This outcome may be sought after or it may arise spontaneously.[58] In either event, relative autonomy begets external influence, which in turn begets enhanced autonomy.

57. Of course, the emergence of Germany in the 1970s and 1980s as a regional monetary leader is not completely explained by these strategic interactions among states; the independence of the Bundesbank and price stability of the deutschmark are part of the story as well. But it is noteworthy that Germany emerged as a monetary leader in the 1930s as well, when its governance arrangements and inflation performance were quite different.

58. On the sometimes unintended benefits of monetary leadership, see Eric Helleiner's discussion of structural power (chap. 4 in this volume). On the conscious pursuit of monetary leadership, see the discussions of monetary dependence by Jonathan Kirshner (chap. 7 in this volume) and of statecraft within currency areas by Scott Cooper (chap. 8 in this volume).

Cooperation Redux

We return now to our discussion of the meaning of cooperation in the international relations literature. The concept has an interesting genesis, deriving initially—as does so much of the international relations theory developed by U.S. scholars—from the study of U.S. politics.

An important point of departure was Charles Lindblom's previously mentioned study, whose revealing subtitle was *Decision Making through Mutual Adjustment*. In this work, Lindblom sought to demonstrate that procedural coordination could result without requiring central coordinators, central planning, or centralized authority; this, in his view, was the intelligence of democracy.[59] The intellectual problem Lindblom faced was to account for how partisans—whom he defined as individuals unwilling to engage in cooperative discussion—might nevertheless participate fruitfully in the policy-making process.[60] Grappling with this problem, he developed a complex typology of the forms that coordination might assume through what he called "partisan mutual adjustment." Lindblom identified twelve forms that such adjustment could assume, three of "adaptive adjustment" and nine of "manipulated adjustment."[61] In addition, and critically for our purposes, Lindblom identified "one final closely related alternative method by which coordination among political leaders could be achieved," namely cooperative discussion.[62] In other words, Lindblom explicitly defined *cooperative discussion* as an alternative to partisan mutual adjustment, precisely because his definition of cooperative discussion relied on the absence of partisans as he understood them.

Writing twenty years later, Keohane faced a quite different challenge: to carve out a space for the study of international cooperation in the face of hostile developments in both the policy and academic worlds.[63] In responding to that challenge, Keohane found Lindblom's study of mutual adjustment quite helpful; he discusses it at some length and cites Lindblom as the source for his definition of coordination.[64] But in

---

59. "A simple idea is elaborated in this book: that people can coordinate with each other without anyone's coordinating them, without a dominant common purpose, and without rules that fully prescribe their relationship to each another." Lindblom, *Intelligence of Democracy*, 3.

60. See note 20.

61. Lindblom, *Intelligence of Democracy*, 35–84, with a tabular summary on 63. There is also a preliminary discussion on 32–34. In developing this typology, Lindblom explicitly differentiated between what he termed "unilateral" and "symmetric" adjustments, which could be achieved via either "partisan discussion," "bargaining," or "reciprocity."

62. Ibid., 28.

63. In policy terms, Keohane published *After Hegemony* at a time when the institutions of international cooperation, especially in economic affairs, appeared under severe stress. Meanwhile, in the academy the concept of complex interdependence that Keohane had advanced in the 1970s (together with his collaborator Joseph Nye) threatened to be eclipsed by an increasing scholarly emphasis on the distribution of power, both in the burgeoning scholarship on hegemonic stability theory as pioneered by Stephen Krasner (although Keohane, interestingly enough, coined the term) and in structural realism as advanced by Kenneth Waltz. Stephen Krasner, "State Power and the Structure of International Trade," *World Politics* 28, no. 3 (April 1976): 317–43; Kenneth Waltz, *Theory of International Politics*.

64. Keohane, *After Hegemony*, 51–53.

doing so, and in making "a process of policy coordination" central to his definition of cooperation, Keohane faced a conundrum: although Lindblom adopted an extremely restrictive definition of cooperation, Keohane sought the opposite outcome.

In the event, Keohane decided to define cooperation very broadly, effectively including not only cooperative discussion but all modes of what Lindblom called partisan mutual adjustment.[65] This served as a useful corrective to then-prevailing intellectual currents and helped spark a resurgence of academic interest in international cooperation.[66] But, in adopting such an expansive definition, cooperation was deprived of much of its commonsense meaning. For one thing, unilateral adaptation was subsumed in the term.[67] As a result, although cooperation could be distinguished from harmony and discord, it could no longer be distinguished from benign neglect (or passive leadership, as previously described) or even from malign exploitation.[68]

Milner, in a sympathetic review, recognized these problems but sought to resolve them by retaining Keohane's core formulation while qualifying it in various ways. In her interpretation, cooperation could be tacit, negotiated, or even imposed, but it definitely could not be unilateral (hence ruling out passivity, or what she called "inactivity," on the part of policy leaders).[69] Instead, cooperation "entails mutual policy adjustments so that all sides end up better off than they would otherwise be." This requirement extends even to instances when cooperation is imposed: "if the stronger party also adjusts its own policies and attempts to realize mutual gains, [then and only then] cooperation has occurred."[70]

These amendments were sensible and helped to restore some of the conventional meaning of *cooperation*—joint effort toward a common goal—to academic dis-

65. See note 21.

66. Of course, Keohane was not alone in this effort; Robert Axelrod published *The Evolution of Cooperation* (New York: Basic Books, 1985) in the same year that *After Hegemony* appeared, Stephen Krasner had edited the special issue of *International Organization* on international regimes in 1982, and *World Politics* would soon publish a special issue on cooperation under anarchy (edited by Kenneth Oye) in 1985. Still, *After Hegemony* played a major role in advancing international cooperation as a central concern of the study of international relations.

67. "The policy coordination that leads to cooperation need not involve bargaining or negotiation at all. What Lindblom calls 'adaptive' as opposed to 'manipulative' adjustment can take place: one country may shift its policy in the direction of another's preferences without regard for the effect of its action on the other state, defer to the other country, or partially shift its policy in order to avoid adverse consequences for its partner." Keohane, *After Hegemony*, 52.

68. "Cooperation [in contrast to harmony] is highly political: somehow, patterns of behavior must be altered. This change may be accomplished through negative as well as positive inducements. . . . Under a variety of conditions strategies that involve threats and punishments as well as promises and rewards are more effective in attaining cooperative outcomes than those that rely entirely on persuasion and the force of good example. . . . Cooperation therefore does not imply an absence of conflict. On the contrary, it is typically mixed with conflict and reflects partially successful efforts to overcome conflict, real or potential." Keohane, *After Hegemony*, 53–54.

69. "Unilateral behavior, in which actors do not take account of the effects of their actions on others, and also inactivity are alternatives to cooperation." Milner, "International Theories of Cooperation among Nations," 468; for the discussion of tacit, negotiated, and imposed forms of cooperation, see p. 469.

70. Ibid., 468, 469.

course. But at the same time, such refinements deeply compromised the tripartite universe of policy harmony, cooperation, and discord introduced by Keohane. In the absence of harmony, discord could be avoided not only by cooperation but by various "alternatives to cooperation," to use Milner's phrase.[71] In other words, there is an entire class of international policy interactions that is neither harmonious, cooperative, nor discordant. And it is this class of activity that is central to understanding hierarchy.[72]

Constructing Policy Coordination

If substantive coordination does not emerge spontaneously, then it must be constructed; otherwise, discord will result. Coordination can be constructed cooperatively—that is, on the basis of joint effort—but the preceding analysis suggests that this is a highly unlikely outcome in international monetary relations. Instead, much coordination is constructed more or less unilaterally, on the basis of policy *subordination*, simply because the weaker party to the interaction considers discord to be excessively costly. Policy subordination, like adaptations that are imposed by the strong on the weak but that do not serve the latter's interests, may indeed result in substantive coordination. But in such instances coordination is definitely not cooperative in the commonsense meaning of the term.

To better understand the different ways in which policy coordination can be constructed, consider a stylized world in which international policy interactions can be characterized in terms of just two considerations: the extent to which policies are mutually consistent (that is, the degree to which substantive coordination obtains) and the role played by domestic policy adjustments in achieving this consistency. The resulting interactions are depicted in figure 5.1.

Note that this depiction captures Keohane's central insight that coordination either can arise spontaneously when autonomously chosen policies felicitously coincide (what Keohane terms harmony) or it can be constructed.[73] Constructed coordination always requires that some state adapt its domestic policies; but this adaptation can assume either of two general forms, as indicated by the shaded boxes in figure 5.1.

---

71. Ibid., 468.

72. Keohane engaged the difficult issue of choice under political constraint on pp. 70–73 of *After Hegemony*, including problems associated with the notion of voluntary action. The concerns raised in these pages, however, are not reflected in the earlier, definitional section on harmony, cooperation, and discord (pp. 51–55) that proved so influential. See in this regard note 73.

73. Keohane plainly considered the distinction between harmony and cooperation—one basis on which coordination can be constructed—the key to his typology. "Cooperation must be distinguished from harmony. . . . Harmony and cooperation are not usually distinguished form one another so clearly. Yet, in the study of world politics, they should be. . . . Defining cooperation in contrast to harmony should, I hope, lead readers with a Realist orientation to take cooperation in world politics seriously rather than to dismiss it out of hand." *After Hegemony*, 51, 53, 55. When he revisited the subject in 2005, Keohane again emphasized this distinction as "the central theoretical argument of the book" ("Preface to the 2005 Edition," x).

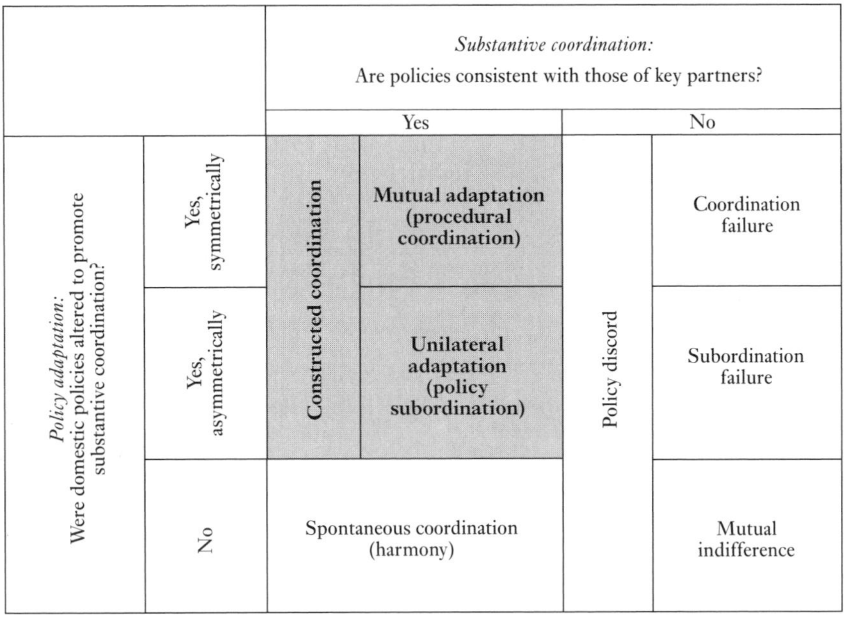

		Substantive coordination: Are policies consistent with those of key partners?			
			Yes		No
Policy adaptation: Were domestic policies altered to promote substantive coordination?	Yes, symmetrically	Constructed coordination	**Mutual adaptation (procedural coordination)**	Policy discord	Coordination failure
	Yes, asymmetrically		**Unilateral adaptation (policy subordination)**		Subordination failure
	No		Spontaneous coordination (harmony)		Mutual indifference

Figure 5.1 International policy interactions.

Substantive coordination can be constructed on the basis of shared effort; in other words, policy can be mutually adapted or, as I put it earlier, co-ordained. Indeed, this is the definition of procedural coordination introduced at the beginning of this chapter. Procedural coordination is what many international relations theorists appear to have in mind when they speak of cooperation—although I would argue, following the conventions of economics, that this is probably better thought of as a particular instance of a broader category of cooperative behaviors.[74] But substantive coordination can also be constructed on the basis of unilateral (or essentially unilateral) adaptation by monetary followers to passive policy leaders. Here, policy is not co-ordained; it is instead established hierarchically because the follower's policy is subordinated to that of the leader.[75]

This way of conceptualizing international policy interactions also underlines the distinction among three very different forms of discord or, in other words, the absence of substantive policy coordination. *Coordination failure*, shorthand for a failure of procedural coordination efforts to produce mutual consistency, occurs when states undertake to adapt their policies jointly (at least at the margins) in order to produce greater mutual consistency but fail to achieve their objectives. This might arise because of insufficient effort, model failure, changing circumstances, or some

74. See note 19 and the associated discussion in the text.
75. This corresponds to cells B and C in table 5.1. See as well the discussion in note 46.

other reason altogether. The point is that there is genuine dissatisfaction on the part of at least some governments at the resulting state of affairs: efforts have been expended to coordinate policies, and the hoped-for results have failed to materialize. This was the case, for example, in the wake of the 1978 Bonn summit, when a change in economic circumstances—the second oil shock—suddenly raised the costs of the fiscal expansion to which both Japan and Germany had agreed, leaving policy makers quite upset.[76]

Similarly, *subordination failure* refers to a failure of unilateral adaptation efforts to produce substantive coordination. In this case, too, there is dissatisfaction with the result, although that unhappiness is likely to be concentrated in the state or states that undertook unreciprocated alterations to their domestic policies, not in the impassive policy leader. This was the case during the ERM crisis, when—despite momentarily (and only marginally) reducing interest rates in September 1992—German authorities mostly contented themselves with expressions of concern while monetary policy in many of their closest trading partners was in a shambles.

But policy discord can also arise because of *mutual indifference,* suggesting an entirely different state of affairs. Here policies are mutually inconsistent with respect to some broadly shared objective, but no party cares enough about this to rectify the situation. In fact, mutual indifference was the sought-after outcome for at least for some of the promoters of the shift to flexible exchange rates in the early 1970s: states would be able to pursue policies of their choosing without having to worry excessively about either external context or consequences.[77] This would indeed constitute discord of a sort, in the sense that autonomously chosen policies failed to coincide and, hence, substantive coordination failed to obtain. But the politics of the resulting situation are completely different from those of coordination or subordination failures because no state feels sufficiently aggrieved to act in order to change the situation.

Although the shift to flexible exchange rates did not result in enhanced monetary independence for all parties, it certainly did increase U.S. autonomy; more recently, the introduction of the euro has helped participating states achieve some of the same benefits. Monetary relations between the United States and the eurozone therefore have been and will likely remain, at least most of the time, an example of genuine and sustained mutual indifference. The Atlantic partners are not completely indif-

76. See the account in Henning, *Currencies and Politics,* 129–32, 189–90.

77. During the late 1960s and early 1970s, advocates of a shift to flexible rates, or at least some of them, suggested that exchange-rate movements would typically be smooth instead of violent, of modest proportions, and correspond to underlying economic fundamentals; furthermore, trade relations would endure the shift to floating rates because specialized currency contracts allowed both exporters and importers to hedge against the risks posed by these limited rate movements. The result would therefore be a world in which national authorities would be at substantially greater liberty to pursue policies corresponding to diverse domestic preferences, without respect (or at least without undue attention) to external circumstances. For a survey of the early views of academic economists on the desirability of floating rates, see the discussion in Thomas D. Willett, *Floating Exchange Rates and International Monetary Reform* (Washington, D.C.: American Enterprise Institute for Public Policy Research, 1977), 15–22; for Willett's assessment of how those views held up in the face of events, see pp. 32–41.

ferent to changes in the exchange rate between the euro and the dollar; but, notwithstanding periodic mutual recrimination, typically neither side will be prepared to alter domestic policy in order to influence this value.[78]

In short, although the depiction of international policy interactions in figure 5.1 fails to capture all the nuance of Lindblom's typology, it nevertheless expands quite significantly the conceptual universe offered by standard accounts. It acknowledges that hierarchical relationships exist and the role these can play in constructing policy coordination. It also recognizes that policy discord can assume a variety of forms, a distinction that has not received sufficient theoretical attention.

Conclusion

When substantive coordination does not emerge spontaneously, it can be constructed, either cooperatively—that is, on the basis of joint effort toward a common goal—or unilaterally, as one or more actors simply accommodate their partners' policies. The latter is a hierarchical outcome; it is also the form that monetary policy coordination generally assumes. Without attention to this class of policy interaction, power—and hierarchy—disappear from the analysis because they have been excluded from the inquiry; all instances of policy adaptation become instances of cooperation because no alternatives are seriously entertained.

Of course, unilateral adaptation by weak (but sovereign) negotiating partners is not the only form that hierarchy can assume.[79] In the preceding discussion, political control over domestic policy has been presumed to remain in the hands of national officials; this is not always the case.[80] Nevertheless, the assumption of internal sovereignty addresses the experience of most of the world's political communities, now that formal empire has become passé, and the resulting analysis helps illuminate an important class of policy interactions that conventional accounts of international cooperation otherwise risks ignoring. "Autonomous solidarity" may seem a paradoxical appellation, but it is not a wholly misleading designation for Austria's pre-EMU monetary regime: national authorities did autonomously choose to subordinate domestic monetary policy to the Bundesbank. They did so because this decision seemed the best available strategy for achieving Austria's nationally conceived policy goals.

The Austrian monetary policy regime, although extreme, is suggestive of a more general feature of policy coordination efforts. I began this chapter by noting that a

78. See David M. Andrews, "Comments," in *EMU Rules: The Political and Economic Consequences of European Monetary Integration,* ed. Francisco Torres, Amy Verdun, Chiara Zilioli, and Hubert Zimmermann, 311–313 (Baden-Baden: Nomos Verlagsgesellschaft, 2005).

79. For a provocative discussion of different forms of hierarchy, see Lake, "New Sovereignty in International Relations," 309–15.

80. Although I disagree with Milner that cooperation can be imposed ("International Theories of Cooperation among Nations," 469), there is no doubt that coordination can be. Such imposition is indeed one of the central characteristics of formal empire.

great deal of substantive monetary policy coordination takes place without a correspondingly great deal of formal interstate negotiation of the same. Such negotiations, this chapter has argued, are typically unnecessary because of the effectiveness of market forces in persuading authorities in follower states to engage in unilateral policy adaptations without insisting on reciprocity from their policy leaders. Put differently, when it comes to monetary policy coordination, hegemony's first face is rarely visible because its second face generally suffices.[81]

Finally, monetary hierarchy need not be malign.[82] The United States provided important public goods to the international community under the Bretton Woods regime, especially in its early years, and many of Germany's EMS partners used a peg to the deutschmark as a means of achieving disinflations that they both desired and felt incapable of producing otherwise. Indeed, monetary hierarchy can even be "cooperative," at least in the broad sense employed by international economists. But monetary hierarchy cannot be symmetrical; by definition, the burden of domestic policy adaptation is not equally shared. What Thucydides said of international politics generally is especially true of efforts to coordinate monetary policy: the strong do what they can while the weak suffer what they must.[83]

81. Scott James and David Lake, "The Second Face of Hegemony: Britain's Repeal of the Corn Laws and the American Walker Tariff of 1846," *International Organization* 43, no. 1 (1989): 1–30, especially 3–9.

82. Andrew Walter (chap. 3 in this volume) likewise emphasizes that monetary leadership can be either benign or exploitive. For a more general statement along these lines, see Duncan Snidal, "The Limits of Hegemonic Stability Theory," *International Organization* 39, no. 4 (autumn 1985), 579–614.

83. Thucydides, *The Peloponnesian War*, trans. by Richard Crawley (New York: E. P. Dutton, 1926), 394.

PART THREE

Monetary Statecraft

The Exchange-Rate Weapon
and Macroeconomic Conflict

C. Randall Henning

Monetary statecraft, understood as efforts to influence the policies of other states by manipulating monetary conditions, has been a recurring feature of the global economy since World War II. At critical moments over the last four decades, the United States has exploited the vulnerability of countries in Europe and East Asia to changes in their currencies' exchange rates vis-à-vis the dollar in an effort to extract policy adjustments from their governments and central banks. More successful in some episodes than in others, this "exchange-rate weapon" has played a central role in international conflicts over balance-of-payments adjustment. This instrument of leverage is critical to explaining the behavior of governments and central banks and the distribution of the costs of adjustment among conflicting states. When collective management of the international monetary system has been required, currency coercion has often underpinned agreements among the larger players.

The exchange-rate weapon—a concept that I have developed elsewhere and elaborate here—can take two forms, one passive and the other active.[1] U.S. officials can

The author is grateful to Clas Wihlborg, Benjamin J. Cohen, Robert Hancke, Eric Helleiner, Louis W. Pauly, David M. Andrews, Jonathan Kirshner, Matthias Kaelberer, Saori Katada, and Thomas D. Willett for comments on previous drafts, as well as to Youliana Ivanova for superb research assistance.

1. My earlier treatments of the exchange-rate weapon include C. Randall Henning, *Macroeconomic Diplomacy in the 1980s: Domestic Politics and International Conflict among the United States Japan, and Europe*, Atlantic Paper, no. 65 (London: Croom Helm for the Atlantic Institute for International Affairs, 1987): 1–4, 30–39; "Europäishe Währungsunion und die Vereinigten Staaten," in *Europa auf dem Weg zur Währungunion,* ed. Manfred Weber, 317–40 (Darmstadt: Wissenschaftliche Buchgesellschaft, 1991); "Systemic Conflict and Regional Monetary Integration: The Case of Europe," *International Organization* 52, no. 3 (summer 1998): 537–73. Cases of deployment of this weapon are treated in I. M. Destler and C. Randall Henning, *Dollar Politics: Exchange Rate Policymaking in the United States* (Washington, D.C.: Institute for International Economics, 1989), 50–56; Robert D. Putnam and C. Randall Henning, "The Bonn Summit of 1978: A Case Study in Coordination," in *Can Nations Agree? Issues in International Economic Cooperation,* Richard N. Cooper, Barry Eichengreen, Robert D. Putnam, C. Randall Hen-

allow the exchange rate to shift, perhaps even overshoot, in the knowledge that a partner country is more vulnerable and thus subject to incentives to adjust its fiscal or monetary policy. U.S. authorities can also actively encourage a shift in the rate to induce a shift in a partner's macroeconomic policy. The two forms are deliberate, often coincide empirically, and have similar effects, namely the encouragement of domestic policy change on the part of partners. When successful, they can both delay the continuing costs and deflect the transitional costs of adjustment, in the terminology advanced by Benjamin J. Cohen (chap. 2 in this volume).

By deflecting and deferring adjustment costs, deployment of the exchange-rate weapon has helped to sustain political support for open trade and investment policy in the United States at junctures when that support has been in jeopardy. However, this leverage has also generated resentment on the part of foreign partners, who consequently developed defenses against currency coercion. Both unilateral and regional in nature, these countermeasures contributed substantially to altering the international terrain over which balance-of-payments conflicts will be fought in the future.

This chapter provides an overview of the conceptual foundations of the exchange-rate weapon and then surveys the use of this instrument of international monetary statecraft since the dissolution of the Bretton Woods regime. I then address the countermeasures pursued by Europe, Japan, and East Asia and the resulting changes in the structure of international monetary relations. The chapter concludes by evaluating the limits of the weapon's effectiveness in light of structural shift.

The Exchange-Rate Weapon: Concepts and Mechanisms

The exchange-rate weapon becomes particularly relevant when current account imbalances become unsustainable and conflict erupts among key states over remedial action. In this situation, each country individually faces three basic choices: (1) persuade other states to change their macroeconomic policy, (2) accept a change in the mutual exchange rate, and (3) alter its own monetary and/or fiscal policies.[2] The hi-

---

ning, and Gerald Holtham (Washington, D.C.: Brookings Institution, 1989), 49–53, 82–84. Other authors who examine the concept include Eric Helleiner, *States and the Re-emergence of Global Finance: From Bretton Woods to the 1990s* (Ithaca: Cornell University Press, 1994); Jonathan Kirshner, *Currency and Coercion: The Political Economy of International Monetary Power* (Princeton: Princeton University Press, 1995); Michael Webb, *The Political Economy of Policy Coordination: International Adjustment since 1945* (Ithaca: Cornell University Press, 1995); Keisuke Iida, *International Monetary Cooperation among the United States, Japan, and Germany* (Boston: Kluwer Academic Publishers, 1999).

2. The extent to which these choices are alternatives is partial because changes in macroeconomic policy might well effect adjustment through changes in the exchange rate. The extent to which adjustment is effected through expenditure switching (exchange rate) versus expenditure changing (aggregate income) depends on the particular economic circumstances, including size, openness, and capital mobility. The steepness of the trade-off between choices is specified by the particular open economy model that applies under the circumstances. Under most conditions, however, both expenditure switching and expenditure changing will apply and there will thus be scope for trading off changes in macroeconomic policy for changes in the exchange rate in securing adjustment.

erarchy of each government's preferences is generally as just presented: each prefers the others to adjust their policies and is averse to changing its own, with a shift in the exchange rate lying between these two alternatives. Because states generally confront partners with the same preference ordering, a change in the exchange rate is generally the solution of least resistance.

When negotiating, or groping, toward a solution to the adjustment problem, however, governments can trade off one type of solution for another, choosing a mix. Anticipating a large and painful appreciation of the currency, for example, a government might ease monetary policy, thereby selecting a combination of currency appreciation and policy change. But the trade-off between solutions will differ across countries, with some governments more fearful of exchange-rate movements and willing to limit them with shifts in monetary and fiscal policy. Aware of the greater vulnerability of others, some countries might countenance or encourage exchange-rate movements in the hope of inducing policy adjustments on the part of their partners. The use of the exchange rate by one state to secure policy change on the part of another defines the concept.

Causal Mechanisms

When two states conflict over macroeconomic and exchange-rate policies, macroeconomic effects are transmitted from the large, dominant state to its smaller partners. When capital mobility is high, the transmission of macroeconomic effects occurs under both fixed and flexible exchanges rates and in the cases of both monetary and fiscal policy. The case of monetary policy under flexible exchange rates could be an exception, depending on other conditions.[3] Generally, however, flexible exchange rates do not fully insulate countries from policy shocks abroad in the presence of high capital mobility.[4]

These cross-border transmission effects create domestic economic and political pressure within other countries for policy adjustment. In this way, a larger and more powerful state can alter the payoffs to existing policy settings in its smaller and weaker partners and thereby force a reconsideration of macroeconomic policies and domestic political agreements that underpin them, inducing policy change.

---

3. On the differences among econometric models on this point, see Ralph C. Bryant, Dale Henderson, Gerald Holtham, Peter Hooper, and Steven Symansky, *Empirical Macroeconomics for Interdependent Economies* (Washington, D.C.: Brookings Institution, 1988).

4. This is the subject of an extensive literature in open economy macroeconomics. Richard E. Caves, Jeffrey A. Frankel, and Ronald W. Jones, *World Trade and Payments: An Introduction,* 9th ed. (Boston: Addison-Wesley, 2002); and Maurice Obstfeld and Kenneth Rogoff, *Foundations of International Macroeconomics* (Cambridge, Mass.: MIT Press, 1982), for example, present textbook treatments of standard theories of open economy macroeconomics. The academic literature on the international transmission of national macroeconomic policies, particularly as it relates to coordination, is reviewed by Ralph C. Bryant, *International Coordination of National Stabilization Policies* (Washington: D.C.: Brookings Institution, 1995); Torsten Persson and Guido Tabellini, "Double-Edged Incentives: Institutions and Policy Coordination," in *Handbook of International Economics,* ed. Gene M. Grossman and Kenneth Rogoff (Amsterdam: Elsevier, 1995), 1973–2030; among others.

Consider the example of a large country embarking on a fiscal stimulus under flexible exchange rates in an environment of high capital mobility. As the fiscal expansion is transmitted abroad, the small country experiences an increase in prices, employment, and income. The existing policies of the small country have targeted a combination of inflation, employment, and growth that was considered optimal by its government. The transmission effects strengthen an incentive for the small country to tighten policy (avoiding inflation) while easing a constraint (avoiding unemployment). If the existing policy is not changed in the face of the stimulus from abroad, it will contribute to an overshooting of the targets for inflation, employment, and growth. In this way, the fiscal stimulus in the large country creates economic pressures for a tightening of macroeconomic policy in the small country.[5]

The strength of these pressures rises as we consider three additional factors. First, until now we have assumed that the large country generally neglects the policies of others and the external consequences of its own policies (as discussed by David M. Andrews, chap. 5 in this volume). Such a country, however, rather than being simply passive or indifferent, might deliberately attempt to induce a change of policy in the smaller country in order to ease its own balance-of-payments constraint. Aggressive policies such as these give rise to international policy conflict.

Second, we have also assumed until now that the exchange rate is completely endogenous to the open economy macroeconomic model and the transmission process. However, governments and central banks can influence the exchange rate to varying degrees without changing monetary and fiscal policy through, for example, declarations, signaling, and foreign-exchange intervention. Less vulnerable to precipitous exchange-rate swings and prolonged exchange-rate misalignments because its economy is more closed, among other factors, the large country might well employ exchange-rate policy in its effort to extract policy adjustment from the small state.

The scope of government capacity to affect exchange rates without altering underlying policies (monetary, fiscal, or structural) is widely disputed. Economists' models of exchange-rate determination are notoriously weak, depriving analysts of reliable counterfactuals against which to measure the effects of government action in foreign-exchange markets. The professional consensus on the effectiveness of intervention, for example, has swung back and forth over the decades. The availability of daily intervention data over the last ten years has improved these studies. More recent studies have also addressed more sophisticated questions, differentiating the circumstances under which intervention is and is not likely to be effective. As a result of this evolution, these more recent studies generally find intervention to be more effective than did studies conducted during the 1980s.[6] Experience with mas-

5. Martin Feldstein, "US Budget Deficits and the European Economies: Resolving the Political Economy Puzzle," *American Economic Review* 76, no. 2 (May 1986): 342–46; Henning, *Macroeconomic Diplomacy in the 1980s*, 21–23.

6. For a review, see Lucio Sarno and Mark P. Taylor, "Official Intervention in the Foreign Exchange Market: Is It Effective and, If So, How Does It Work?" *Journal of Economic Literature* 39, no. 3 (2001): 839–68. Ramana Ramaswamy and Hossein Samiei, "The Yen-Dollar Rate: Have Interventions Mattered?" in *Japan's Lost Decade: Policies for Economic Revival*, ed. Tim Callen and Jonathan D. Ostry, 224–

sive Chinese and Japanese interventions during 2002–4 suggests they can indeed be effective with and without capital controls. Extended discussion is beyond the scope of this paper. Suffice it to say that government action can be successful under a variety of circumstances, such as when it is publicly announced, conducted jointly by two or more central banks, consistent with the underlying fundamentals, and the exchange rate is far from equilibrium.[7]

The conditions that create scope for intervention to be at least partially effective also create scope for other, more subtle instruments. In the presence of high capital mobility, flexible exchange rates are often driven by herd behavior and expectations, and are thus frequently disconnected from the underlying economic fundamentals. In addition, the foreign-exchange markets often exhibit multiple equilibria. When private expectations are easily swayed, governments are more likely to be able to induce a shift from one equilibrium to another. Particularly when the rate moves far from equilibrium, governments might well coordinate the expectations of private participants by articulating an emerging consensus on the direction of movement.[8]

Government officials can influence these expectations, depending on market sentiment, by signaling their desire for a stronger, weaker, or stable currency; foreswearing intervention; and intervening. Under some market conditions, such as a profound current account imbalance, a "no comment" in the face of a significant exchange-rate movement can be interpreted by the market as a clear signal of approval. Conflict over trade policy and market access can enhance the markets' sensitivity to official statements. Thus, even if U.S. policy makers have only partial influence over the exchange rate, that influence can be substantial at particular junctures.

Third, we have not yet referred to the international roles of currencies, the importance of which is emphasized by Cohen (chap. 2 in this volume). When a large share of international trade is invoiced in the currency of the large country—the most prominent example being the pricing of oil in dollars—a depreciation affects

---

50 (Washington, D.C.: International Monetary Fund, 2003), find intervention specifically in the yen-dollar market to be reasonably effective.

7. See Pietro Catte, Giampaolo Galli, and Salvatore Rebecchini, "Concerted Interventions and the Dollar: An Analysis of Daily Data," in *The International Monetary System*, ed. Peter B. Kenen, Francesco Papadia, and Fabrizio Saccomanni (Cambridge, UK: Cambridge University Press, 1994), 201–49; Kathryn M. Dominguez and Jeffrey A. Frankel, *Does Foreign Exchange Intervention Work?* (Washington, D.C.: Institute for International Economics, 1993); John Williamson, *Exchange Rate Regimes for Emerging Markets: Reviving the Intermediate Option*, Policy Analyses in International Economics no. 60 (Washington, D.C.: Institute for International Economics, 2000); Sarno and Taylor, "Official Intervention"; Takatoshi Ito, "Is Foreign Exchange Intervention Effective?: The Japanese Experiences in the 1990s," NBER Working Paper no. 8914, National Bureau of Economic Research, Cambridge, Mass., 2002; Mark Taylor, "Is Official Exchange Rate Intervention Effective?" CEPR Discussion Papers no. 3758, Centre for Economic Policy Research, London, 2003; Christopher Kubelec, "Intervention When Misalignments Are Large," paper presented at the conference of the Institute for International Economics, Dollar Adjustment: How Far? Against What?, Washington, D.C., May 2004. Marcel Fratzscher, "Communication and Exchange Rate Policy," ECB Working Paper Series no. 363, European Central Bank, Frankfurt, 2004; and Hans Genberg and Alexander Swoboda, "Exchange-Rate Regimes: Does What Countries Say Matter?" paper presented to the conference of the International Monetary Fund, Mussa Fest, Washington, D.C., June 2004, find official declarations to be significantly effective.

8. Taylor, "Is Official Exchange Rate Intervention Effective?"

the small state beyond the extent of its trade with its large partner. When foreign investors accept financial assets denominated in the large country's currency, they facilitate the financing of current account deficits and enable the large country to deflect the exchange-rate risks associated with foreign borrowing. When, under conditions of fixed exchange rates, foreign central banks hold the large country's currency in reserves, the monetary policy of the large country dominates monetary conditions of the system as a whole. The role of the currency, in sum, magnifies the asymmetry in macroeconomic interdependence between the large and small state.

Consider now the small state's response to the pressures for policy change by referring again to the case of a large country's fiscal stimulus under flexible exchange rates. Preconflict policy settings presumably represent a bargain that satisfies a governing majority within the target state. The economic pressures arising from the stimulus abroad satisfy demands for jobs and growth but aggravate fear of inflation and its consequences, altering the political demands on the policy-making process. Because macroeconomic policies are set through an elaborate architecture of political and governmental institutions, the politics of renegotiating the original bargain in order to adjust policy are unlikely to be smooth. Moreover, domestic bargains, carefully and delicately crafted, often have broader purposes than simply attaining the macroeconomic targets; these might include the satisfaction of key constituency demands, pursuit of ideological priorities, and fulfillment of election promises. Any decision to tighten fiscal policy, for example, would have to specify the particular spending programs to be cut or the particular taxes to be raised. The adjustment of macroeconomic policy will therefore probably be fraught with domestic political conflict and, therefore, resisted.

Assumptions and Preconditions

The ability of one state to use the exchange rate as a tool in international conflict over adjustment and macroeconomic policy hinges on a number of conditions and assumptions. These include (1) asymmetry in the size and openness of the states concerned, (2) asymmetry in the domestic political influence of traded- and non-traded-goods sectors, and (3) global macroeconomic conditions.

The first assumption, asymmetry in size and openness, has already been made explicit. A pair of countries of equal size and openness would have more equal vulnerability to exchange-rate change than a pair composed of one large closed economy and one small open economy. As the exchange rate shifts, two equally large economies experience effects that are roughly equal in magnitude, although opposite in sign. Differences in economic conditions (recession versus overheating), flexibility of domestic prices and wages, and domestic political bias (toward trade versus nontraded sectors) might still impart differences in sensitivity to exchange-rate change. But the scope for the use of the exchange rate as a tool in conflict is circumscribed in the presence of symmetry. Given the differences between the United States and its partners during the second half of the twentieth century, the assumption of asymmetry is historically realistic.

The magnitude of the effects of an exchange-rate change is also equal, in principle, in the traded- and nontraded-goods sectors within each country. By reducing the price of traded goods, for example, an appreciation of the currency hinders traded-goods producers and benefits traded-goods purchasers, principally the non-traded-goods sector. If the political power of the traded and nontraded sectors were equal, there would be little reason to expect policy outcomes to favor one over the other. There would be little reason to expect that central banks would ease monetary policy, for example, to blunt an appreciation of the currency if the interests of both sectors weighed equally on the policy process.

But there are a number of reasons to believe that the political power of traded and nontraded sectors is in fact not equal.[9] To begin with, because the nontraded sector is usually the larger of the two, while the economic effects are roughly equal, firms and workers in the traded-goods sector feel the effects with greater intensity than those in the nontraded sector. In addition, owing to differences in the organization of firms and workers in these sectors for political action, the traded sector may have more sway over policy than the nontraded sector. Manufacturing constitutes a large share of the traded sector and is often well represented in the policy process. Its general dominance of trade also imparts greater homogeneity of interests to that sector compared to the nontraded sector. Critically, moreover, the links between manufacturing and the banking system in bank-dominated systems consolidate the interests of the two sectors and confer access to government financial agencies that determine exchange-rate policy.[10] Again, the assumption of asymmetrical political influence of the traded- and nontraded-goods sectors appears realistic for a large number of countries during the second half of the twentieth century.

The potency of the exchange rate as a tool for inducing policy change also hinges on the international macroeconomic environment and the particular conditions in the target. When governments are primarily concerned about restraining generally high inflation, they are more averse to the depreciation of their currencies than when prices are generally stable. When governments are primarily concerned with avoiding deflation, they are more averse to the appreciation of their currencies than when prices are generally stable. The effectiveness of the exchange-rate weapon is thus likely to depend on both the inflationary (or deflationary) conditions and the direction of the exchange-rate shift called for by the particular adjustment problem.

Because the availability and potency of the exchange-rate weapon hinges on these conditions and assumptions, the tool is not consistently available even to large closed states. However, the junctures at which this lever becomes available tend to be formative episodes in international economic relations. The resolution of macroeconomic conflict involves political choices with continuing effects that give rise to path

9. On the ramifications of the distinction between traded and nontraded goods for the political economy of exchange-rate policy see, among others, Jeffry A. Frieden, "Invested Interests: The Politics of National Economic Policies in a World of Global Finance," *International Organization* 45, no. 4 (autumn, 1991): 425–51; C. Randall Henning, *Currencies and Politics in the United States, Germany, and Japan* (Washington, D.C.: Institute for International Economics, 1994); James I. Walsh, *European Monetary Integration and Domestic Politics: Britain, France and Italy* (Boulder: Lynne Rienner, 2000); Lawrence J. Broz and Jeffry Frieden, "The Political Economy of International Monetary Relations," *Annual Review of Political Science* 4 (June 2001): 317–43.

10. Henning, *Currencies and Politics;* Walsh, *European Monetary Integration and Domestic Politics.*

dependency. During the crises of the early 1970s, late 1970s, and mid-1980s, for example, U.S. administrations confronted strong protectionist pressures that were defused in part by the use of the exchange rate to secure adjustment. Had the U.S. Treasury simply let market forces bring adjustment in their own good time, and in their own good measure, U.S. trade policy could well have been overwhelmed by domestic protectionism and taken a turn toward closure, or at least considerably slower liberalization, with effects for years to come.

This example raises two additional points worthy of mention. First, domestic politics, and in particular the struggle over the openness of international economic policy (with respect to trade, investment, etc.), has been at the root of the motivations of the United States in using the exchange-rate weapon. Historically, U.S. administrations and congresses have tended to resort to manipulating the dollar when the trade deficit was large and in the midst of resulting conflict over adjustment. Pressure for macroeconomic expansion on the part of other states was an explicit part of the strategy, in several cases, of maintaining open policies in international economics. Deflecting the responsibility for adjustment was considered crucial for maintaining a coalition of politically active societal interests in favor of openness and further liberalization. Thus, it was considered politically necessary to adopt coercive methods to extract policy concessions on the part of others or at least to attempt to extract them.

Second, the exchange-rate weapon also tends to be deployed not only in the presence of adjustment conflict but also during conflicts over trade policy. Threats to close the U.S. market, or part of it, and to raise the cost of access (tariffs) are additional arrows in the quiver of administrations confronting balance-of-payments problems, and they reinforce the exchange-rate instrument. Serious threats over trade policy tend to alert foreign-exchange markets to the policies and preferences of the antagonists. To the extent that they provide information about the intensity with which the U.S. government is likely to pursue adjustment on the part of others, trade threats can affect foreign-exchange markets directly, at least in the short term, or can sensitize them to officials' declarations about rates and intervention.

The empirical coincidence of exchange-rate and trade coercion creates an explanatory problem in some cases. In the language of an econometrician, if we were to regress adjustment outcomes on both, we would encounter multicollinearity—that is, it would be difficult to disentangle the independent effects of each on observed outcomes. However, for purposes of prediction, it may not be necessary to separate the effects of the two factors—provided they continue to coincide in the future. More generally, trade and exchange-rate coercion should be considered together because there are interaction effects between them.

History

Over the last half century, international monetary relations have exhibited distinct cycles, each containing a period of relative harmony, followed by heightened conflict over adjustment and then some degree of cooperation. Because U.S. payments difficulties lie at the heart of each conflict episode, these cycles also correspond to shifts in U.S. international economic policy between neglect and activism.[11] With the international system now in the midst of the fifth adjustment conflict since the 1960s, these cycles are an entrenched feature of global political economy. Each cycle can be identified by its phase of acute tension: (1) the breakdown of the Bretton Woods regime in the early 1970s; (2) conflicts over world reflation that were resolved at the Bonn summit of 1978; (3) hostility in the mid-1980s, at the center of which stood the Plaza and Louvre accords; (4) recession and recovery in the early and mid-1990s; and (5) the present adjustment dispute.[12]

During each cycle, U.S. administrations pressed European and Japanese governments and/or central banks for expansionary measures and often actively encouraged a depreciation of the dollar.[13] The United States used the exchange-rate weapon with more success in some episodes, such as 1971–73, 1977–78, and 1985–87, than in others, such as during the 1990s. Each of these episodes, which are summarized briefly next, highlights strategic considerations in monetary statecraft. Specifically, the wielder of the exchange-rate weapon confronts a trade-off between securing adjustment on favorable terms in the short term and creating incentives for the targets to insulate themselves against future episodes of monetary coercion over the long term.

The First Episode (1971–1973)

Confronted with payments imbalances that had become chronic by the late 1960s (although small by present standards), the Bretton Woods regime would have required agreement on fundamental adjustments of macroeconomic policy to be preserved.[14] Unable to reach agreement on this politically charged question, for reasons

11. Benjamin J. Cohen, "An Explosion in the Kitchen? Economic Relations with Other Advanced Industrial States," in *Eagle Defiant: United States Foreign Policy in the 1980s,* ed. Kenneth A. Oye, Robert J. Lieber, and Donald Rothchild (Boston: Little, Brown, 1983), 105–30; C. Fred Bergsten, "America's Unilateralism," in *Conditions for Partnership in International Economic Management,* C. Fred Bergsten, Etienne Davignon, and Isamu Miyazaki, Report to the Trilateral Commission 32 (New York: Trilateral Commission, 1986), 3–14; Henning, *Currencies and Politics.*

12. There were certainly adjustment conflicts between the United States and its major economic partners during the fixed-rate Bretton Woods era as well, but these did not involve use of the exchange-rate weapon as I develop the concept here.

13. Relatively recent overviews of episodes of policy coordination can be found in Iida, *International Monetary Cooperation;* Laurence H. Meyer, Brian M. Doyle, Joseph E. Gagnon, and Dale W. Henderson, "International Coordination of Macroeconomic Policies: Still Alive in the New Millennium?" International Finance Discussion Papers no. 723, Board of Governors of the Federal Reserve System, Washington, D.C., April 2002; David M. Andrews, C. Randall Henning, and Louis W. Pauly, eds., *Governing the World's Money* (Ithaca: Cornell University Press, 2002); Edwin M. Truman, "A Critical Review of Coordination Efforts in the Past," paper presented to the Kiel week conference, Macroeconomic Policies in the World Economy, June 2003.

14. Classic references include John S. Odell, *International Monetary Policy: Markets, Power, and Ideas as Sources of Change* (Princeton: Princeton University Press, 1982); Joanne Gowa, *Closing the Gold Window: Domestic Politics and the End of Bretton Woods* (Ithaca: Cornell University Press, 1983); Robert

well-documented in the literature on this episode, the United States suspended gold convertibility and imposed a 10 percent surcharge on imports in August 1971—measures known in Japan as the "Nixon Shock." After a brief floatation of the dollar, the G-10's Smithsonian Agreement repegged it to the yen at a level 17 percent below the Bretton Woods parity, to the deutschmark at about 14 percent below, and to the British pound and French franc at about 9 percent below. These rates proved to be unsustainable by early 1973, when the currencies were permanently floated.

Because U.S. macroeconomic autonomy was never seriously constrained by the Bretton Woods regime, it would be an overstatement to suggest that the shift to floating rates unshackled the United States from its "constraints." Federal Reserve Board Chairman Arthur Burns explicitly stated in early 1973 that monetary policy would not be tightened to preserve the revised parities. The fundamental cause of the regime's collapse was that the United States refused to submit to those constraints or, more judgmentally, to "play by its rules." However, the shift to floating rates did expand the range of options available to U.S. exchange-rate policy and unshackled the exchange-rate weapon.

Although greater exchange-rate flexibility afforded an opportunity to others to halt the "importation" of U.S. inflation, most governments did not take advantage of it. Japanese Prime Minister Kakuei Tanaka engineered an extraordinary expansion using both monetary and fiscal policy during the early 1970s in an effort to maintain the Smithsonian parity and offset the contractionary effects of the yen appreciation. That policy response produced not only high growth but also hoarding of several commodities and double-digit inflation in Japan. At the same time, partly attributable to the 1973–74 oil shock, Japan's external surplus temporarily evaporated.[15] European governments also generally responded with expansionary policies, although there was considerable dispersion among them. Germany was the least accommodating; it eased monetary and fiscal policy in 1972, tightened both in 1973, eased fiscal policy early in 1974, and then monetary policy in late 1974.[16] With

---

Solomon, *The International Monetary System, 1945–1981,* rev. ed. (New York: Harper & Row, 1982); Paul A. Volcker and Toyoo Gyohten, *Changing Fortunes: The World's Money and the Threat to American Leadership* (New York: Times Books, 1992); Benjamin J. Cohen, *Organizing the World's Money: The Political Economy of International Monetary Relations* (New York: Basic Books, 1977); John Williamson, *The Failure of World Monetary Reform, 1971–1974* (New York: New York University Press, 1977); Otmar Emminger, "The D-mark in the Conflict between Internal and External Equilibrium, 1948–75," in Princeton Essays in International Finance no. 122, Princeton University International Finance Section, Princeton, N.J., June 1977; Gunter D. Baer and Tommaso Padoa-Schioppa, "The Werner Report Revisited," in *Delors Report,* 53–60 (Luxembourg: Office of Official Publications of the European Community, 1989); C. Fred Bergsten, *The Dilemmas of the Dollar: The Economics and Politics of United States International Economic Policy* (New York: New York University Press, 1975).

15. Gardner Ackley and Hiromitsu Ishi, "Fiscal, Monetary and Related Policies," in *Asia's New Giant: How the Japanese Economy Works,* ed. Hugh Patrick and Henry Rosovsky, 153–247 (Washington, D.C.: Brookings Institution, 1976); Ryutaro Komiya and Miyako Suda, *Japan's Foreign Exchange Policy: 1971–82* (Sydney: Allen & Unwin, 1991); Robert C. Angel, *Explaining Economic Policy Failure: Japan in the 1969–1971 International Monetary Crisis* (New York: Columbia University Press, 1991).

16. See, for example, Stanley W. Black, *Floating Exchange Rates and National Economic Policy* (New Haven: Yale University Press, 1977).

the partial exception of Germany, therefore, policy changes within most European countries and Japan contributed to the substantial correction in the U.S. current account position.

U.S. officials did not exactly encourage the weakness of their currency in order to secure adjustment on the part of foreign partners during this episode. When domestic macroeconomic choices placed downward pressure on the dollar, however, they did precious little to support it themselves. They bargained aggressively for larger rather than smaller devaluations, coercing partners into agreeing to larger parity changes than these governments would have preferred, and accepted substantial depreciation after the switch to floating rates. In doing so, U.S. officials were acutely conscious that the devaluations and depreciation of the dollar created substantial incentives for Europeans and Japanese officials to deliver expansionary policies.

The Second Episode (1977–1978)

U.S. policy makers deployed the dollar weapon more actively during the 1977–78 conflict. Because economic recovery in the United States preceded that in Europe and Japan, a substantial U.S. current account deficit reemerged in 1977. The Jimmy Carter administration responded by advocating the "locomotive theory," under which the surplus countries would stimulate their economies to restore robust growth not only for themselves but also for the world economy more broadly. Both Japan and Germany, the countries to which this strategy was primarily directed, resisted this advice. U.S. authorities let it be known that they would be content to allow the dollar to depreciate against the surplus-country currencies in the absence of macroeconomic stimuli.[17] The subsequent appreciation of the yen and deutschmark reduced the U.S. current account surplus, dampened growth and inflation prospects in Japan and Germany, and placed formidable domestic political pressure on these governments to provide the stimulus demanded by U.S. officials.

The government of Prime Minister Takeo Fukuda therefore agreed to a fiscal stimulus, first in an agreement between U.S. Trade Representative Robert Strauss and Japanese economic Ambassador Nobuhiko Ushiba in early 1978 and subsequently among the heads of government themselves at the Bonn Summit in July. German Chancellor Helmut Schmidt also acceded to expansionary fiscal policy at the summit as part of a package of mutual concessions.[18] Although controversial, these policy adjustments, coupled with the second oil shock, eliminated the Japanese and German current account surpluses in 1979 and 1980. During this episode, as during the early 1970s, the exchange rate proved to be a powerful weapon in the

17. Stephen D. Cohen and Ronald L. Meltzer, *US International Economic Policy in Action* (New York: Praeger, 1982).

18. I. M. Destler and Hisao Mitsuyu, "Locomotives on Different Tracks: Macroeconomic Diplomacy, 1977–1979," in *Coping with US-Japanese Economic Conflicts*, ed. I. M. Destler and Hideo Sato, 243–70 (Lexington: Lexington Books, 1982); Putnam and Henning, "The Bonn Summit of 1978," 12–140.

hands of U.S. officials trying to extract macroeconomic policy change from foreign governments.

The Third Episode (mid-1980s)

The second Ronald Reagan administration again benefited from the exchange rate as an inducement for macroeconomic stimulus abroad and the reduction of current account imbalances. During the first half of the 1980s, the first Reagan administration and Japanese governments largely ignored the extraordinary appreciation of the dollar and record current account imbalances.[19] This laissez-faire stance proved to be unsustainable in the face of mounting protectionist pressure in the U.S. Congress, which boiled over in summer 1985. In the Plaza accord in September, the United States and Japan agreed with their European partners in the Group of Five to intervene in the foreign-exchange market to appreciate the yen and deutschmark against the dollar to redress the payments imbalance. Mutual agreement on this strategy proved to be ephemeral, however, and the United States again began "talking down" the dollar further in order to encourage stimuli to domestic demand in Japan and Germany. Unprecedented appreciations of the yen and mark occurred, prompting calls from within these countries' private sectors for expansionary measures to offset the contractionary effect.

U.S. support for exchange-rate stability, in conjunction with European and Japanese policy accommodations, were the essence of the resulting bargain struck at the Louvre in February 1987. Rather than providing a strong fiscal stimulus, however, the Japanese government chose to boost domestic demand primarily by substituting a dramatic monetary expansion.[20] For their part, the German government and Bundesbank responded with a mix of fiscal and monetary stimulus.[21] This combination of exchange-rate movement and macroeconomic policy change helped reduce the U.S. current account deficit during 1988–91 to low levels.

The Fourth Episode (mid-1990s)

The subsequent episode, by contrast, suggests a significant weakening of the influence of the exchange-rate weapon. The U.S. economy experienced a recession in

19. The exchange-rate weapon also played a critical role in the standoff between the first Reagan administration and the François Mitterrand government during 1981–83. See Jeffrey Sachs and Charles Wyplosz, "The Economic Consequences of President Mitterrand," *Economic Policy* 1, no. 2 (April 1986): 261–306; Henning, *Macroeconomic Diplomacy in the 1980s;* Michael Loriaux, *France after Hegemony: International Change and Financial Reform* (Ithaca: Cornell University Press, 1991); John B. Goodman, *Monetary Sovereignty: The Politics of Central Banking in Western Europe* (Ithaca: Cornell University Press, 1992); Christian de Boissieu and Jean Pisani-Ferry, "The Political Economy of French Economic Policy in the Perspective of EMU," in *Forging an Integrated Europe,* ed. Barry Eichengreen and Jeffry Frieden, 49–89 (Ann Arbor: Michigan University Press, 1998). This episode suggests that the United States could employ such coercion in the absence of a current account adjustment problem and, depending on the economic circumstances, could deploy both appreciation and depreciation coercively.

20. Yoichi Funabashi, *Managing the Dollar: From the Plaza to the Louvre* (Washington, D.C.: Institute for International Economics, 1988); Henning, *Currencies and Politics.*

21. Henning, *Currencies and Politics,* 203–8.

1991 and a slow recovery in 1992, with a delayed response in the labor market.[22] When Bill Clinton became president in January 1993, his administration encountered a global pattern of staggered business cycles similar to that confronted by the early Carter administration: the U.S. economy was beginning to recover while those of Europe and Japan lagged behind, poised for export-led growth at the expense of the U.S. current account position. Japan became the particular focus of the administration's attention, as President Clinton and Treasury Secretary Lloyd Bentsen signaled the desirability of yen appreciation. The Japanese currency quickly moved to the 100 level against the dollar briefly in summer 1993 and reached an all-time high of 80 to the dollar in mid-1995.

The Japanese response contrasts with earlier episodes, however. Although successive governments introduced a number of supplemental budgets during 1993–95 and exchange rates might have played a role in prompting one of these (the 1995 supplemental), the expansionary content of these budgets was frequently less than advertised. Stimuli were also retracted at critical points, such as in 1996, aborting a promising recovery. Over the decade as a whole, Japanese fiscal policy was not particularly responsive to exchange-rate pressure, nor was it managed in a fashion as to produce a sustained recovery.[23] In the second half of the 1990s, robust U.S. growth eased concern about the current account position.

Countermeasures and Structural Shift

As with other forms of coercion, the deployment of the exchange-rate weapon generates defensive countermeasures on the part of the targets. The cumulative effect of such countermeasures over time, along with the progressive internationalization of the U.S. economy, has shifted the structure of global monetary relations.[24] Struc-

---

22. During 1991 and 1992, the George H. W. Bush administration objected to the tightening of European monetary policy in the wake of German unification and, belatedly, to the restrictiveness of the convergence criteria embodied in the Maastricht treaty sections on monetary union. Exchange-rate coercion did not come into play on this occasion, however, notwithstanding a neglectful posture on the part of the Treasury secretary and White House.

23. On the variability of the effectiveness of foreign pressure on Japan across different issue areas, see Leonard J. Schoppa, *Bargaining with Japan: What American Pressure Can and Cannot Do* (New York: Columbia University Press, 1997); "Two-Level Games and Bargaining Outcomes: Why Gaiatsu Succeeds in Japan in Some Cases but Not Others," *International Organization* 47, no. 3 (1993): 353–86. C. Randall Henning, "Japan's Resistance to Macroeconomic Gaiatsu," American University and Institute for International Economics, Washington, D.C., June 2003, addresses the particular question of the role of the exchange-rate coercion in the 1990s.

24. *Structure* in this sense refers to the distribution of power assets in the international system and thus coincides with its traditional use by international relations scholars, within the realist tradition in particular. Determined by the size, openness, and vulnerability of states, structure confers on some states the ability to use the exchange rate as an instrument of coercion. Eric Helleiner's discussion of *structural power,* by which he means the ability to alter the behavior of others indirectly by controlling the monetary environment within which they operate, is broader but compatible with the sense in which *structure* is used here. Indeed, Helleiner specifically cites the exchange-rate weapon as a macro-level example of the exercise of structural power.

tural shift, in turn, reduces the ability of the United States to use the exchange-rate weapon effectively. We review these changes before turning to the fifth (and current) episode of macroeconomic conflict.

Europe

The postwar cycles of policy conflict and cooperation greatly assisted the process of European monetary integration.[25] Forward progress in regional monetary cooperation was very closely associated with periods of transatlantic conflict over adjustment and exchanges rates, including use of the exchange-rate weapon. Periods of calm in transatlantic monetary relations, by contrast, were followed by partial backsliding in European monetary integration.

When, over the decades, the members of the Community were divided over or uncertain about exchange-rate stabilization, global monetary and exchange-rate instability helped to nudge the most reticent among them along the path toward regional integration. Although systemic instability created incentives for all European states to augment regional cooperation, it placed particularly strong pressure on the "outliers"—France in 1973, Germany in 1978, France in 1983, and Germany in 1987, for example[26]—contributing to intraregional accommodation. France gradually relinquished its attachment to monetary autonomy and accepted a price-stability orientation. The Bundesbank, hostile to the European Monetary System (EMS) at the time of the system's creation, became a defender of the system by the mid-1980s, and Germany gambled on the durability of the stability orientation of its partners when concluding the Maastricht treaty. Although U.S.-generated disturbances did not extinguish intra-European disputes, in short they did increase the payoff to European monetary integration.

Since Europe's commitment to form a monetary union became clear in the 1990s, one big question facing transatlantic relations has been whether the euro area might act as a counterweight to the United States and the dollar in the international monetary system. The European Commission, in a major report on Economic and Monetary Union (EMU) in 1990, explicitly argued that greater symmetry in the international monetary system—read less U.S. dominance—would contribute to better macroeconomic policy outcomes in this way.[27]

Indeed, the formation of the euro area in January 1999 created, in one fell swoop, a new monetary region of roughly equivalent weight to the United States. The GDP of the euro area is about three-fourths that of the United States, its external trade is

---

25. This theme is developed in Henning, "Systemic Conflict and Regional Monetary Integration," on which this and the following paragraph draw. See, as well, Loriaux, *France after Hegemony;* Kenneth Dyson, *Elusive Union: The Process of Economic and Monetary Union in Europe* (London: Longman, 1994); Peter H. Loedel, "Enhancing Europe's International Monetary Power," in *The State of the European Union: Vol. 4, Deepening and Widening,* ed. Pierre-Henri Laurent and Marc Marasceau, 243–62 (Boulder: Lynne Reinner, 1997).

26. See, as well, Loriaux, *France after Hegemony,* 248–52, 260–64.

27. European Commission, "One Market, One Money," *European Economy* 44 (October 1990).

comparable, and the euro area population exceeds that of the United States. The euro area thus carries far more weight than any other partner of the United States since World War II. With new members of the European Union anxious to join, the euro area's relative position is likely to increase rather than decline in the future. Although the euro certainly has some distance to go before it rivals the dollar as an international currency, the establishment of the monetary union makes a challenge to its hegemony possible. Should the euro area develop and implement external monetary policy in a deliberate, proactive, and assertive fashion, it could throw its own weight around in international monetary affairs.[28]

The creation of the euro area also rendered Europe less susceptible to pressure from the United States for policy change and to fluctuations in the U.S. dollar. Reduced susceptibility derives from several factors, including the elimination of the "wedge effect," by which fluctuations of the dollar affected European currencies asymmetrically; modest diversion of European trade to other members of the euro area; denomination of a larger share of European trade in European currency; and denomination of a larger share of European international financial assets in euros as opposed to dollars.[29] In each of these ways, the euro area reaps benefits from EMU in terms of insulation from the dollar.

The completion of EMU is therefore the most profound transformation of the structure of international monetary relations since the 1960s, or perhaps even since the Bretton Woods conference of 1944. It has succeeded in large measure because the United States induced European states to cooperate by neglecting the stability of the international monetary system at critical junctures and by exploiting the asymmetry in vulnerability to exchange-rate changes on several occasions since the late 1950s.[30] EMU thus demonstrates that, over the long run, even the structure of the system can respond to the policy behavior of the dominant state.

Japan and East Asia

While Western European states were pursuing monetary integration, Japan, by contrast, lacked a plausible regional partner. With more limited options, Japan relied principally on unilateral measures to blunt the impact of the strong yen. Over time, however, U.S. actions with respect to Korean, Taiwanese, and Chinese ex-

---

28. C. Randall Henning, "US-EU Relations after the Inception of the Monetary Union: Cooperation or Rivalry?" in *Transatlantic Perspectives on the Euro*, C. Randall Henning and Pier Carlo Padoan, 5–64 (Washington, D.C.: Brookings Institution, 2000); C. Randall Henning and Sophie Meunier, "United Against the United States?: The European Union as International Actor in Trade and Finance," in *The State of the European Union: Vol. 7, With US or against US? European Trends in American Perspective*, ed. Nicolas Jabko and Craig Parsons, 75-102 (New York: Oxford University Press, 2005).

29. See European Commission, *Quarterly Report on the Euro Area* (Brussels: European Commission, 2003).

30. This chapter is not a normative assessment of the economic merits of U.S. policy. Sometimes the use of the exchange-rate weapon was appropriate and at other times it was not; but such normative questions are separate from the causes, mechanisms, and consequences of the exchange-rate weapon.

change-rate policies and the Asian financial crisis of 1997–98 contributed a strong impetus for a regional movement.

Conflicts between the United States and Japan in the 1990s differed from earlier episodes in that Japan was less responsive to U.S. pressure for fiscal reflation.[31] In particular, Japan was less responsive to the exchange rate as a weapon of macroeconomic conflict. Internal adaptation to the strong yen and direct investment abroad rendered many Japanese companies that had previously been susceptible to currency appreciation considerably less vulnerable. Greater distance between banks and industrial corporations weakened the coalition favoring a stable, competitive currency value. These changes in the Japanese economy resulted in different private preferences with respect to exchange-rate policy. Less vulnerable to yen appreciation, private actors petitioned less for intervention to weaken the currency or for fiscal stimuli to offset the contractionary effects. In addition, domestic political realignment and electoral reform afforded less latitude for party and cabinet officials to satisfy external pressure in the 1990s. Meanwhile, U.S. threats over trade policy declined after 1995, easing upward pressure on the yen. Changes in the Japanese political economy, driven by previous exposures to yen appreciations, had deprived the exchange-rate weapon of much of its potency.

This is not to say that the exchange-rate weapon has lost all potency, nor does the Japanese experience of the 1990s suggest that the exchange-rate weapon would be ineffective if applied to other countries. To the contrary, many states are still vulnerable to currency shifts vis-à-vis the dollar, as suggested by continued large foreign-exchange interventions, especially in East Asia. Were these countries to become the target of exchange-rate pressure, trade threats, and moral suasion, they might well alter their macroeconomic policies.

With respect to Japan, however, the 1990s demonstrate that the exchange-rate weapon was sometimes irrelevant because the yen was moving in the wrong direction (as in 1998) and sometimes unusable because, owing to financial fragility and deflation in the target, recession undermined the desired external adjustment. And even at those moments when the exchange-rate weapon was both relevant and usable, the yen would have needed to move farther than in the past to induce significant policy adjustments.

The investments of Japanese multinational corporations elsewhere in Asia, spawned in large measure by yen appreciation, effectively regionalized the adjustment problem. Owing to regional corporate networks,[32] as well as to progressive

---

31. See Yoshiko Kojo, "Japan's Changing Attitude toward Adjusting Its Current Account Surplus: The Strong Yen and Macroeconomic Policy in the 1990s," in *New Perspectives on US-Japan Relations,* ed. Gerald L. Curtis, 146–74 (Tokyo: Japan Center for International Exchange, 1998); Schoppa, *Bargaining with Japan;* Saori Katada, *Banking on Stability: Japan and the Cross-Pacific Dynamics of International Crisis Management* (Ann Arbor: University of Michigan Press, 2001); Henning, "Japan's Resistance to Macroeconomic Gaiatsu," on which this section draws.

32. This factor is emphasized by Peter J. Katzenstein, Kozo Kato, Ming Yue, and Natasha Hamilton-Hart, *Asian Regionalism* (Ithaca: Cornell University Press, 2000).

economic advancement of members of the region, East Asia as a whole and China in particular have largely replaced Japan as the focus of U.S. policy makers seeking to reduce U.S. external deficits.

U.S. officials began to scrutinize the exchange-rate policies of other East Asian countries in the 1980s. Taiwan, South Korea, and China became the focus of attention of the second Reagan administration when their central banks did not allow their currencies to float upward with the Japanese yen after the Plaza accord. These three countries were cited in the late 1980s by the Treasury Department, in semiannual reports mandated by the Omnibus Trade and Competitiveness Act of 1988, for manipulating their currencies to achieve unfair competitive advantage.[33] Their currency policies were publicly reviewed in hearings before the banking committees of the U.S. Congress. The Treasury Department pressed bilaterally and successfully for these governments to allow appreciation of their currencies.

Meanwhile, the dramatic rise of China in international trade and investment over the course of the 1990s intensified scrutiny of Beijing's exchange-rate policies. After receiving widespread acclaim for holding its currency steady against the U.S. dollar during the Asian financial crisis of 1997–98,[34] by 2003 Chinese authorities became the focus of U.S. as well as European pressure for revaluation or appreciation to facilitate adjustment.

In fact, the 1997–98 crisis (and profound resentment with the multilateral response) provided strong incentives for East Asian governments to cooperate on a regional basis.[35] A regional network of currency-swap agreements, known as the Chiang Mai Initiative, emerged as a direct consequence. Governments of China, Japan, Korea, and Southeast Asia (the ASEAN+3) concluded a framework agreement and sixteen bilateral swap agreements to help shield themselves against future crises.[36] Although their size appears to be modest, these swaps are large compared

33. See, for example, U.S. Department of the Treasury, *Report to Congress on International Economic and Exchange Rate Policy* (Washington, D.C.: U.S. Department of the Treasury, October 1988).

34. Hongying Wang, "China's Exchange Rate Policy in the Aftermath of the Asian Financial Crisis," in *Monetary Orders: Ambiguous Economics, Ubiquitous Politics*, ed. Jonathan Kirshner, 153–71 (Ithaca: Cornell University Press, 2003).

35. See Jennifer Amyx, "Japan and the Evolution of Regional Financial Arrangements in East Asia," in *Beyond Bilateralism: US-Japan Relations in the New Asia-Pacific*, ed. Ellis S. Krauss and T. J. Pempel, 198–220 (Stanford: Stanford University Press, 2004); Saori N. Katada, "Japan's Counterweight Strategy: US-Japan Cooperation and Competition in International Finance," in *Beyond Bilateralism*, 176–197; C. Randall Henning, "Systemic Contextualism and Financial Regionalism: The Case of East Asia," *American University and Institute for International Economics* (photocopy, August 2005); Jonathan Kirshner (chap. 7 in this volume).

36. East Asian financial cooperation is analyzed in Edwin M. Truman, "Remarks of the Assistant Secretary for International Affairs," presented to the 33rd annual meeting of the Asian Development Bank, U.S. Department of Treasury, press release, Washington, D.C., May 7, 2000; Barry Eichengreen, "What to Do with the Chiang Mai Initiative," *Asian Economic Papers* 2, no. 1 (winter 2003): 1–49; Gordon de Brouwer, "Financial Markets, Institutions, and Integration in East Asia," *Asian Economic Papers* 2, no. 1 (2003): 53–80; Yung Chul Park and Yunjong Wang, 2004. "Chiang Mai and Beyond," http://soback.kornet.net/~ycpark/pub/Chiang%20Mai%20and%20Beyond_Fondad_%200206% (accessed March 15, 2004); C. Fred Bergsten and Yung Chul Park, "Toward Creating a Regional Monetary Arrangement in East Asia," ADBI Research Paper no. 50, Asian Development Bank Institute, Tokyo, 2002, 112; Haruhiko Kuroda and Masahiro Kawai, "Strengthening Regional Financial Cooperation in

to Southeast Asian countries' quotas in the International Monetary Fund (IMF). Given the prodigious foreign-exchange reserves held by Japan, China, and Korea, the creditors under the Chiang Mai Initiative, the amounts of the swaps could easily be raised at short notice. Notwithstanding the formal agreement to link most disbursements to adjustment programs negotiated with the IMF, these arrangements lay the basis for members of the region to reduce their reliance on the United States and the IMF for balance-of-payments financing in the future.

Despite this progress toward regional financial cooperation and despite periodic advocacy on the part of some Asian leaders for an Asian Monetary Fund and even an Asian currency, some perspective is in order. The governments and central banks of East Asia have made little progress toward genuine exchange-rate or monetary cooperation. China does not appear to be attracted to Japanese proposals for the joint pegging of currencies within the region to a common basket. Mutual surveillance of economic and exchange-rate policy in the region is at a preliminary stage of development. The obstacles to regional monetary cooperation remain high, higher than within Western Europe during the 1960s, when the intra-European market was similarly integrated.

Nonetheless, any future U.S. pressure on East Asian states for adjustment would give the governments in the region a strong incentive to suspend (although not dismiss) their considerable differences and to reach a modus vivendi on financial questions of common interest. Irrespective of the economic merits of Asian currency appreciation, advocating those exchange-rate changes generates resentment on the part of target states and key private constituents. Regional cooperation and dialog, particularly within the ASEAN+3 group, potentially opens new options for East Asian states. The dramatic increase in foreign-exchange holdings by East Asian central banks, another unilateral aspect of the response to the 1997–98 crisis, moreover, gives material backing to additional financial agreements that governments of the region might eventually develop.

East Asia," paper presented to the European Central Bank seminar Regional Economic, Financial and Monetary Cooperation: The European and Asian Experiences, Frankfurt am Main, April 15–16, 2002; Masaru Yoshitomi and Sayuri Shirai, "Technical Background Paper for Policy Recommendations for Preventing Another Capital Account Crisis," Asian Development Bank Institute, Tokyo: July, 2000; Graham Bird and Ramkishen S. Rajan, *The Evolving Asian Financial Architecture,* Princeton Essays in International Economics no. 226 (Princeton, N.J.: Princeton University, 2002); C. Randall Henning, *East Asian Financial Cooperation,* Policy Analyses in International Economics no. 68 (Washington, D.C.: Institute for International Economics, 2002); C. Randall Henning, "The Complex Political Economy of Cooperation and Integration," in *Financial Governance in East Asia: Policy Dialogue, Surveillance and Cooperation,* ed. Gordon de Brouwer and Yunjon Wang, 83–101 (London: Routledge Curzon, 2004); C. Randall Henning, "East Asian Financial Cooperation and Global Adjustment: Building on the Chiang Mai Initiative," paper presented to the conference of the Institute for International Economics and Japan Economic Foundation, Economic Relations between the United States, Japan, and East Asia, Washington, D.C., 2004; Yunjong Wang, "Financial Cooperation in East Asia," paper presented to the Institute for International Economics, Korea Institute for International Economic Policy, and Korea Economic Institute workshop on The State of East Asian Financial Regionalism, Washington, D.C., February 2004.

United States

Important changes in the relative sensitivity and vulnerability of the world's major monetary actors are not limited to the leading partners of the United States; they have taken place within the United States as well. To begin with, consider the country's macroeconomic profile. Analysts are generally accustomed to thinking of the United States as a "large, relatively closed economy." But, although it is large, it is also considerably more open than it was four decades ago. The ratio of merchandise imports and exports to GDP has increased threefold, from 6.6 percent in 1960 to 20.3 percent in 2000. Including service imports and exports increases the ratio to 25.6 percent.[37] On this measure, the openness of the United States slightly exceeds that of Japan while remaining somewhat more closed than euro area.[38]

Greater openness alters the costs and benefits of using the exchange rate as an instrument of adjustment and coercion. Openness increases the impact of changes in the exchange rate on domestic output, employment, and prices and consequently increases the feedback effects of pushing the currency down (or up) to coerce others to pursue more expansionary (or restrictive) macroeconomic policies. For example, as a consequence of the larger share of imports in U.S. total expenditure, greater openness causes not only greater output and employment gains when the currency depreciates but also larger increases in the domestic price level.

U.S. financial markets have also become increasingly internationalized. As of March 2004, foreign ownership of U.S. Treasury securities has risen to about 50 percent of the total federal debt held by the public. Foreign official holdings, including the dollar reserves of central banks in East Asia, accounted for about 34 percent and foreign private holdings 16 percent of this total. Foreign official and private holdings of U.S. securities and corporate bonds together represent about 18 percent of U.S. bond market valuation. Foreign portfolio investment in corporate stocks amounts to about 11 percent of stock market valuation. Foreign-owned assets in the United States totaled $10.5 trillion at the end of 2003, roughly equal to U.S. GDP. The foreign assets–to–GDP ratio for the United States was thus roughly the same as for the euro area and considerably larger than for Japan.[39] The U.S. net international investment position at the end of 2004 was negative roughly $3 trillion, about 25 percent of U.S. GDP.[40] The greater the ratio of foreign-owned assets to total assets, the greater the possible increase in domestic interest rates in response to a depreciation of the dollar. These figures thus indicate that the po-

37. Calculated from U.S. Council of Economic Advisors, *Economic Report of the President* (Washington, D.C.: White House, February 2004), tables B-1, B-103, B-106.

38. The figure for the euro area during 2000–2 was about 38 percent. Robert Anderton, Filippo di Mauro, and Fabio Moneta, "Understanding the Impact of the External Dimension of the Euro Area," ECB Occasional Paper no. 12, European Central Bank, Frankfurt, April 2004, chart 1.

39. Anderton, di Mauro, and Moneta, "Understanding the Impact," 29, chart C.

40. Calculated or reported from U.S. Treasury Financial Management Service, table OFS-2 "Estimated Ownership of U.S. Treasury Securities," http://www.fms.treas.gov/bulletin/b25ofs.doc (accessed April 2004); U.S. Department of Commerce, Bureau of Economic Analysis, *US Net International Investment Position at Yearend 2003* (Washington, D.C.: U.S. Department of Commerce, 2004).

tential costs to the United States of deploying the exchange-rate weapon are increasing.

Adjustment Conflict in the Early Twenty-First Century

With the preceding analysis as background, let us consider the conflict over adjustment since 2003, the fifth major episode of macroeconomic conflict since the breakdown of the Bretton Woods regime. In several respects, this case displays the classic characteristics of conflict over U.S. current account deficits. Although China, with its pegged exchange-rate regime, is a new actor in the story, the central dynamic is familiar: the conflict between the deficit and surplus countries over measures to secure adjustment and the depreciation of the dollar.

A number of elements of the mid-2000s conflict, however, differ substantially from previous cycles. Unilateral countermeasures (such as reserve accumulation and Japanese direct investment), regionalism, and greater internationalization of the U.S. economy have combined to reduce the asymmetry in exchange-rate vulnerability among the United States, Europe, and East Asia. Put differently, the structure of international monetary relations has shifted substantially.

What are the consequences of these changes? We would expect structural shift to erode the effectiveness of the dollar weapon and, hence, the influence of the United States over adjustment outcomes. To be sure, we would not expect the dollar weapon to be completely impotent; it will continue to be at least partially effective vis-à-vis, especially, smaller and more vulnerable targets. But the scope of its effectiveness is likely to be significantly circumscribed.

Moreover, whereas the United States could make macroeconomic policy errors (overexpansionary monetary policy during the 1970s and overexpansionary fiscal policy in the 1980s) with near impunity in the past, similar macroeconomic policy errors could be more costly in international monetary terms in the future. Owing to the formation of Europe's monetary union, partial insulation of Japan, reserve accumulation in East Asia, and nascent financial cooperation in that region, the United States might well be confronted with greater penalties for policy errors in the future, including the erosion of the international value of the dollar or of the dollar's international role.

The year 1987 offers a potentially revealing comparison. Owing partly to the depreciation of the dollar since the Plaza accord of September 1985, private capital flows into the United States largely dried up in that year. The large current account deficit at that time was instead financed through foreign-exchange intervention by European central banks and the Bank of Japan. These central banks were willing to purchase dollars because they wanted to stem the appreciation of their own currencies and the reduction in their trade surpluses. By these actions, they hoped to maintain overall growth and employment in their domestic economies.[41]

Private capital markets have already balked at financing the U.S. current account

41. Henning, *Currencies and Politics*, 151–58, 205–8, 285–86.

deficit during particular moments over 2003 and 2004. East Asian central banks, of Japan and China in particular, filled much of the breach with unprecedented amounts of foreign-exchange intervention. If Asian central banks were to reduce their dollar purchases, the question of whether to finance the imbalance or adjust to it would be thrust on to U.S. and European officials. This time, however, the United States would face a consolidated monetary union rather than individual European monetary authorities. The euro area would be less vulnerable to exchange-rate fluctuations than the separate European countries were prior to the euro's creation. Europe might request joint intervention with the United States to support the dollar nonetheless, especially if European growth were anemic. But if the United States instead were to be the *demandeur*, European authorities would be in a stronger position than in any previous adjustment cycle to insist on U.S. policy adjustments as a quid pro quo. Any such insistence by euro-area officials would signal a new era in international monetary relations.

As of this writing,[42] China has maintained the renminbi peg to the dollar and Japan has succeeded in limiting the appreciation of the yen. With a potentially overheating economy, prodigious and growing foreign-exchange reserves, and a significant trade surplus, however, the economic case for the revaluation of the renminbi is strong.[43] The case strengthens as the dollar depreciates further against other currencies, principally the euro, taking the renminbi along with it. Because Japan, Korea, and Southeast Asian countries are reluctant to appreciate against their most feared competitor, the stakes are greater than simply China's role in the adjustment process. The revaluation or floatation of the renminbi is the key to wider participation in the adjustment process of East Asia as a whole.

The contrast between heavy Asian intervention and the absence of European intervention to date suggests that East Asia is more vulnerable to dollar depreciation than Europe. The heavier reliance of East Asian production networks on the U.S. market, the lingering threat of deflation in Japan, and the less advanced state of regionalism perpetuate a greater degree of vulnerability in East Asia than in Europe. Because the United States has an interest in adjustment, we might yet see the exchange-rate weapon deployed in East Asia before the present conflict is resolved. The weapon could, however, be counterproductive in deflation-prone countries or those with fragile banking systems, thus giving further impetus to forms of regionalism that could be antagonistic to U.S. interests. U.S. policy makers would therefore be wise to exercise caution in the deployment of exchange-rate coercion in this region.

Europe countenanced a substantial appreciation of the euro vis-à-vis the dollar during 2001–4. This movement strengthened pressures on European governments to pursue structural reform and on the European Central Bank to keep monetary

---

42. The final draft of this chapter was written in May 2004.

43. John Williamson, "The Renminbi Exchange Rate and the Global Monetary System," outline of a lecture given at Central University of Finance and Economics, Beijing, October 29, 2003; Morris Goldstein and Nicholas Lardy, "Two-State Currency Reform for China" (commentary), *The Wall Street Journal Online* (accessed September 12, 2003); Morris Goldstein, "Adjusting China's Exchange Rate Policies," Working Paper Series no. 04-1, Institute for International Economics, Washington, D.C., June 2004.

policy relaxed. Because EMU is still evolving, the full extent of the eventual change in the relative position of Europe and the United States remains unclear at this point, with Europe's position dependent in part on its ability to stimulate growth and streamline external monetary policy making. The outcome of the present conflict over global current account adjustment will reveal just how much the relative bargaining positions of the United States and Europe have changed.

Conclusion

The essential arguments of this chapter can be summarized in four points. First, during several conflicts over adjustment during the last forty years, the United States has used the exchange rate as an instrument to coerce partners to alter macroeconomic policy. This exchange-rate weapon is thus an important element of the dynamics of adjustment conflict and helps to explain the outcomes of such episodes. Exchange-rate coercion is specifically useful in explaining patterns of policy coordination and the distribution of the costs of adjustment.

Second, the deployment of the exchange-rate weapon creates strong incentives for targets to develop countermeasures. Such countermeasures include regional arrangements that reduce vulnerability to external exchange-rate shifts, such as EMU, and unilateral measures, such as reserve accumulation and production relocation through direct investment. Regional monetary integration is, of course, motivated by more than simply a desire to deflect exchange-rate coercion; but a desire to reduce exchange-rate vulnerability powerfully reinforces other motives to build regional cooperation. Countermeasures can take decades to develop, typically after multiple rather than single instances of exchange-rate coercion; but they can be developed nonetheless.

Third, these countermeasures—the monetary union in the case of Europe and a mix of unilateral action and regional cooperation in the case of East Asia—have collectively shifted the structure of the international monetary system so as to reduce the likely effectiveness of exchange-rate coercion by the United States on some of its major economic partners in the future. Structural shift has been accentuated by the progressive internationalization of the U.S. economy. Four decades of periodic exchange-rate coercion strongly suggest that, at least over the very long term, the exchange-rate weapon is a dissipating asset: if you use it repeatedly, you run the risk of eventually losing it.

Fourth, the exchange-rate weapon is nonetheless likely to have continuing relevance as an instrument of economic influence. The United States will continue to have residual power in this respect while Europe's monetary union, Japan, and China could conceivably begin to exercise a similar form of monetary statecraft in geographically contiguous areas (see Jonathan Kirshner, chap. 7 in this volume). The eventual resolution of the mid-2000s conflict over reduction of the U.S. current account deficit will provide useful insights into the future of the exchange-rate weapon.

CHAPTER SEVEN

Currency and Coercion in the Twenty-First Century

Jonathan Kirshner

$\mathbf{M}$ost scholarship on monetary power—and especially those studies that have focused on the manipulation of currency values and monetary arrangements to advance political goals, or what this volume terms monetary statecraft—have emphasized the experiences of the twentieth century, and in particular the years 1914–89, the period between World War I and the end of the Cold War.[1] In the early twenty-first century, however, two conditions, less salient during those seventy-five years, are of dramatically increased significance: globalization and unipolarity. How do these factors affect the prospects for and practice of monetary statecraft? In particular, has financial globalization—that is, the presence of very large, integrated and influential currency markets—radically circumscribed the capabilities of states to practice monetary diplomacy? This chapter argues that although the consequences of globalized finance are profound, they recast rather than reduce the significance of monetary diplomacy in contemporary international relations. True, the analysis must shift from an almost exclusive focus on state-to-state interactions to one that places much greater emphasis on the relationship between states and markets. But even in an era of globalization, international monetary relations remain an area of political competition. As long as there are states and money, states will attempt to manipulate monetary relations to advance their political objectives.

For helpful comments on earlier versions of this chapter I thank Rawi Abdelal, David Andrews, Scott Cooper, Eric Helleiner, Kathleen McNamara, Beth Simmons, and the participants in this project.

1. See for example Paul Einzig, *Behind the Scenes of International Finance* (London: Macmillan, 1931); Charles Kindleberger, "The International Monetary Politics of a Near-Great Power: Two French Episodes, 1926–1936 and 1960–70," *Economic Notes*, no. 1 (1972): 30–44; Jonathan Kirshner, *Currency and Coercion: The Political Economy of International Monetary Power* (Princeton: Princeton University Press, 1995). For a good critique of this literature, see Benjamin Cohen, "Money and Power in World Politics," in *Strange Power: Shaping the Parameters of International Relations and International Political Economy*, ed. Thomas C. Lawton, James N. Rosenau, and Amy C. Verdun, 91–113 (Aldershot, UK: Ashgate, 2000).

Two clarifying comments are in order. First, the catch word "globalization" captures a number of processes that occur across several dimensions, such as information flows, economic exchange, and marketization. But for the political analysis of monetary relations, one aspect of the intensification of economic exchange—financial globalization—is of paramount concern. To be clear, the analysis that follows does *not* presume that globalization is novel, irreversible, or irresistible. Rather, the point of departure is that it is here now and that it matters.[2] Second, contemporary globalization takes place in a specific political context, that of U.S. preponderance or unipolarity. Space constraints do not permit a lengthy elaboration of its consequences, but it is crucial to recognize that unipolarity powerfully shapes the possibility, politics, and nature of globalization and shapes the political practice of contemporary monetary power.[3]

This chapter proceeds in three parts, with sections that consider how globalization (and also unipolarity) recast the practice of currency manipulation, monetary dependence, and systemic disruption—the three principal instances of money statecraft that I consider in *Currency and Coercion.*[4] For each of these, I use a number of cases from the period since the end of the Cold War to demonstrate that although financial globalization is important in transforming the nature of monetary diplomacy, it does not reduce the significance of monetary power as a feature of world politics. The goals of this chapter are therefore to illustrate the continued role of monetary power and to assess the transformation of monetary statecraft that results from these changes in the global political and financial environment.

Currency Manipulation

Of the three aspects of monetary power mentioned above, the practice of currency manipulation would at first glance appear to be the one most inhibited in an era of globalization. This is a logical deductive inference. Given a floating exchange rate and the enormous size of financial markets, in most cases it will certainly be much more challenging for even the most powerful states in the system to successfully engage in the archetypical act of predatory currency manipulation—selling a target's currency on the open market to force depreciation as an act of coercion. The ratio

---

2. As David M. Andrews has argued, financial globalization (or more specifically, the level of capital mobility) "systematically alters state calculation and behavior." "Capital Mobility and State Autonomy: Towards a Structural Theory of International Monetary Relations," *International Studies Quarterly* 38, no. 2 (1994): 193–218, quotation on 202.

3. On globalization generally, see David Held, Anthony G. McGrew, David Goldblatt, and Jonathan Perraton, *Global Transformations: Politics, Economics and Culture* (Stanford: Stanford University Press, 1999). On globalization and the troika of information, exchange, and marketization, and for more on globalization and unipolarity, see Jonathan Kirshner, "Globalization and National Security," in *Globalization and National Security*, ed. Jonathan Kirshner (forthcoming).

4. I referred to these as types of monetary power in *Currency and Coercion.* Although I retain my original taxonomy, these concepts can be mapped onto the framework outlined by David Andrews (chap. 1 in this volume).

of government reserves to market transactions has diminished considerably (to the disadvantage of states), limiting the ability of governments, by dint of their own efforts, to significantly alter the value of a currency widely traded in free markets around the world.

However, there are a number of factors that caution against overstating the extent and novelty of the constraints placed on predatory currency manipulation under globalization. It was always understood that the opportunities for the practice of monetary power, in general, would be less common than other forms of economic coercion (such as trade sanctions) and that the market's response would influence the prospects for successful manipulation.[5] This remains the case, and obviously under globalization the market response will, in general, be of even greater importance. But when considered closely, this suggests not that predatory manipulation will necessarily be dramatically rarer but, rather, that it will be differently circumscribed.

Potential manipulators will find the ground relatively more fertile in settings where markets are thin, incomplete, and regulated, whereas efforts to nudge more robust currencies against the wind of market sentiment will be even less likely than ever to bear fruit. This observation, it should be noted, is consistent with the conclusions drawn by C. Randall Henning (chap. 6 in this volume). But the greater importance of market sentiment and market response, although reducing the vulnerability of some currencies, in fact cuts both ways. Given the proliferation of small states and new currency issues, markets are arguably more likely to exacerbate, rather than alleviate, the distress of many potential targets of currency manipulation.[6] In addition, there are techniques of predatory manipulation other than selling a freely floating currency. Given the disruptive nature of international financial markets, for example, many small states seek to employ devices to limit the fluctuations of their currencies. Realizing these objectives requires measures to sustain the arrangement chosen, efforts that are more, rather than less, vulnerable given challenges posed by the tides of enormous global financial flows. Once again, this suggests that globalization will recast rather than reduce the practice of currency manipulation. For example, these new vulnerabilities will almost certainly increase the demand for protective currency manipulation.

Thus, given the size and speed of contemporary exchange markets, whether floating or somehow pegged, the currencies of small states remain vulnerable. In addition, the proliferation of currencies and greater political contestation (especially in weak states) suggest that there will, in contemporary politics, typically be marginal currencies operating at the fringes of international markets. These settings will be conducive to the practice of currency manipulation, both protective and predatory. Indeed, despite the fact that predatory currency manipulation has been relatively rare in history, even this form of "good old-fashioned" currency manipulation has

5. Kirshner, *Currency and Coercion*, 31, 37–38.

6. The International Monetary Fund catalogs 146 separate currencies, with forty-one countries participating in "exchange agreements with no separate legal tender." International Monetary Fund, *Annual Report on Exchange Arrangements and Exchange Restrictions 2003* (Washington D.C.: IMF, 2003), 9–10.

been practiced in the era of globalization, as can be seen in the aftermath of the first Gulf War.

Plots against the Iraqi Dinar

After the first Gulf war, Iraq became a small hothouse of currency manipulation as several states, including Iraq, introduced various monetary schemes devised to advance their strategic goals. The first rounds in this conflict were aimed at Saddam Hussein's regime, as Iraq was especially vulnerable to currency manipulation due to an (unintended) consequence of UN sanctions. This, coupled with the vast array of hostile neighbors surrounding Iraq (with the sole exception of Jordan), not to mention the significant internal opposition to the regime, facilitated efforts to undermine the Iraqi dinar.

Reports of currency manipulation against Iraq surfaced in November 1991, when the governor of Iraq's central bank declared that "foreign quarters were behind the pumping of forged money for circulation in Iraq with the aim to sabotage the country's national economy."[7] Although the government declared victory over the would-be economic saboteurs, within months it was clear that the regime faced a serious counterfeiting problem. The Iraqi currency was relatively easy to copy because sanctions prevented the government from importing notes from Europe, as it had done in the past. (As is the practice of many states, Iraq had previously contracted out the production of its currency to foreign firms that specialized in the business.[8])

That the dinar was being counterfeited is beyond doubt; exactly who was behind the operation (or, perhaps, who was not) is less clear. The United States was most often considered to be the chief counterfeiter, under the auspices of the Central Intelligence Agency (CIA) scheme known as "Operation Meseraagh," (the Arabic word for laundry). This was certainly more than plausible; the United States was seeking to undermine Saddam Hussein's regime and had pulled this arrow from its quiver in the past, counterfeiting the North Vietnamese currency in the early 1970s.[9] But other reports claimed that separate operations were initiated by Saudi Arabia, Iran, and Israel, to name but a few.

Certainly there was a great deal of counterfeiting going on. Sixty miles south of the Arctic circle in the sleepy Swedish town of Pitea, for example, a counterfeiting ring produced about $28 million worth of fake dinars. In Bialystok, Poland, 30,000 fake banknotes were made at a printing plant on behalf of a mysterious figure who claimed the effort was designed to advance the Kurdish cause. But he soon ran afoul of the Polish authorities, which suspected that the man—known only as "Ibrahim S."—was simply in it for the money and planned to pass the notes in European exchange markets. No charges were brought against the representatives of the print-

7. "Iraq Combats Forgery of Its Currency," *Xinhua General News Service,* November 2, 1991.
8. The British firm De La Rue, for example, states that it is "involved in the production of over 150 national currencies."
9. Robert W. Chandler, *War of Ideas: The US Propaganda Campaign in Vietnam* (Boulder: Westview Press, 1981), 117, 123.

ing plant on the grounds that "the prosecution believes they were misled"—suggesting that, had the counterfeiting of the Iraqi dinar truly been in the service of the Kurdish cause, it would have been perfectly legal in Poland.[10]

Whatever the source, the notes were easily smuggled across the Jordanian, Saudi, Turkish, and Iranian borders and contributed to Iraq's monetary disorder, exacerbating an inflation already fueled by the government's excessive recourse to the monetary printing press. The forgeries were difficult to distinguish from the official notes issued by the government, and some accounts held that one out of every eight bills in the country was fake. The regime made numerous efforts to address the challenge, including the introduction of a new denomination, the 5-dinar note (which was also designed to deal with a shortage in small change). At the other end of the monetary spectrum, the commonly copied 100-dinar note was recalled and discontinued. The watermark on official currency was changed at least four times, and counterfeiting was made a capital crime (although this last measure was admittedly less extraordinary in context).[11]

Iraq found itself vulnerable to currency manipulation not only because its currency was so easily forged; there was also the problem of the so-called Swiss dinars—Iraqi currency that had been produced in Europe before the war and was still in circulation side by side with the government's new emissions. The "original" dinars (as the Swiss notes were often called) were easily distinguishable from the "dented" dinars printed in Iraq. In local currency markets, there was a high premium for original dinars, even though the regime made it a crime to distinguish between the two. Of great concern was that foreigners might try to foment monetary chaos in Iraq by playing the market to create instability in the rate of exchange between the two dinars. The government explicitly accused Saudi Arabia and Kuwait of accumulating billions of Swiss dinars, which Iraqi state-run radio described as "time bombs" that could be used to sabotage the economy.[12]

Parry and Thrust: The Iraqi Currency Exchange

Seizing the initiative, on May 3, 1993, Saddam Hussein's government announced a new currency maneuver. Effective immediately, all 25-dinar notes printed before

10. Youssef M. Ibrahim, "Fake-Money Flood Is Aimed at Crippling Iraq's Economy," *New York Times,* May 27, 1992, p. A1; Robert Aaron, "Is the CIA Flooding Iraq with Fake Dinar Bills?" *Toronto Star,* July 18, 1992, p. K4; "Fake Iraqi Cash Claim," *Herald Sun,* March 16, 1992; Kevin McKiernan, "Kurdistan's Season of Hope," *Los Angeles Times Magazine,* August 23, 1992 (which reported that "both the CIA and Iran [are] flooding Iraq with phony bills"); Ireneusz Dudziec, "Iraqi Dinars Forged in Poland," *Polish News Bulletin,* October 5, 1992; Associated Press, "Police: Ring Printed Counterfeit Iraqi Dinars," November 3, 1992.

11. Wilkinson, "First: Smart Bombs. Now: Funny Money," *Newsweek,* June 8, 1992, 37; "Iraq Issues New Currency Note to Fight Forgery," *Moneyclips,* March 9, 1992; Ibrahim, "Fake Money Flood"; Aaron, "Is the CIA Flooding Iraq?"

12. "The Money War on Iraq," *Mideast Mirror,* January 21, 1993; Agence France Presse, "Iraq Dinar Kurds," May 11, 1993; Agence France Presse, "Iraq Claims Triumph over 'Time Bomb' Dinars Stashed in Gulf States," May 11, 1993.

the war would no longer be legal tender in Iraq. The country's borders were to be sealed for one week, during which Iraqis would have the opportunity to exchange their Swiss dinars at face value for local dinars. The border closure was so abrupt that hundreds of travelers were stranded on both sides of the Iraqi–Jordanian border, Iraq's only open international frontier and its sole access to international markets (normally traversed by 1,000–2,000 Iraqis each day).[13]

The emergency measure was initially interpreted as last-gasp defensive maneuver, a "sign of desperation" and "evidence that the economy was crumbling under sanctions."[14] But it very quickly became clear that Hussein's parry was at the same time a powerful thrust, one that stuck terrible blows at two targets, Jordan and the Iraqi Kurds dwelling in de facto autonomy in Iraq's northern region.

The currency switch caused both panic and anger in Jordan. As Gresham's law (bad money drives out good) would have anticipated, many Jordanians had accumulated large stocks of Swiss dinars. These good notes—in fixed supply and difficult to counterfeit—were hoarded and held as a store of value (or traded in exchange markets for hard currencies, where they fetched more than three times what the new issues did), while the dented dinars were used as a medium of exchange. Thus, at the time the border was sealed, tens of thousands of ordinary Jordanians were in possession of vast stocks of cash whose value evaporated with the wave of a hand. Crowds overwhelmed local exchange houses, only to be turned away by currency dealers. Scenes from monetary disasters in history were briefly replayed on the streets of Amman, as some expressed their anger by lighting cigarettes with worthless notes bearing the image of Saddam Hussein. A few less fortunate, their life savings wiped out, succumbed to heart attacks.[15]

The Jordanian government appealed to Iraq to allow Jordanians to exchange their canceled notes, or at least to provide some compensation to those who collectively had lost an estimated $250 million. But Baghdad's central bank governor Tareq al-Tukmaji announced that no exceptions would be made for those holding Swiss dinars abroad; he suggested that any foreigners who held the notes did so illegally and with the intention of harming the Iraqi economy. This was a patently false claim; indeed, if anything, the reverse was true. The use of Iraqi currency in Jordan had been approved by the Baghdad government, and representatives of official Iraqi agencies routinely engaged in such transactions themselves, using the currency to buy essential goods only available to sanctions-constricted Iraq on the Jordanian market. In fact, reports circulated that Baghdad had smuggled huge amounts of Swiss notes

13. David Hirst, "Iraq Closes Border to Rescue Currency: Hundreds of Travellers Stranded on Jordanian Frontier," *Guardian* (London), May 6, 1993.

14. James Whittington, "Sanctions Bite Hard on Hungry Iraqis: Border Closure Is an Attempt to Halt Economic Collapse," *Financial Times*, May 6, 1993; Christopher Walker, "Iraqis Shut Borders and Ban Banknotes to Halt Speculators," *Times* (London), May 6, 1993.

15. Chris Hedges, "Fortunes in Iraqi Bills Gone Overnight," *New York Times*, May 16, 1993; Ed Blanche, Associated Press, "Iraq Invalidates 25-Dinar Banknotes, Closes Borders," May 5, 1993; Reuters, "Jordanians Mock Worthless Iraqi Banknotes," May 6, 1993; Agence France Presse, "Two Die of Heart Attacks over Iraqi Dinar Crisis," May 11, 1993. Many in Jordan (and elsewhere in the region) also apparently hoarded the Swiss notes, speculating that their value might rise when sanctions against Iraq were lifted.

into Jordan and exchanged them for dollars just days before they were declared invalid.[16]

Not surprisingly, the move led to considerable bitterness in Jordan, which had, almost alone, supported Iraq in the Gulf War (providing intelligence and spare parts) and after the war was widely considered to be lax at best in its enforcement of UN sanctions. However, rather than being an oversight, Baghdad's currency maneuver appears to have been purposely directed, at least in part, against Jordan's King Hussein, whose support of Iraq was wavering. For six months, the king had been backing away from his support for Iraqi regime—cautiously, given Saddam's broad popularity in Jordan. In numerous statements and interviews that were widely interpreted as suggesting that perhaps it was time for Saddam to go, the king had been calling for pluralism, democracy, and respect for human rights in Iraq. Baghdad's monetary stab in the back was designed either to serve as a warning to King Hussein or, having assessed that the relationship could not be salvaged, as part of an effort to bring down his regime. (This would also explain why Iraq took the additional measure of halting oil shipments to Jordan during the week the border was closed.[17]) Whatever its motivation, the move brought about a rupture in Jordanian-Iraqi relations as the king, capitalizing on the blow to Saddam's popularity in Jordan as a consequence of the currency exchange, publicly broke with Iraq, sought rapprochement with Saudi Arabia, and attempted to mend fences with the West.[18]

Saddam's Currency Manipulation against the Kurds

Jordan would have been the most vulnerable party in the repudiation of the Swiss dinar but for the imagination of the Iraqi regime. For Iraq not only sealed its external borders, preventing foreigners from participating in the currency exchange (and thus repudiating the claim those notes once held on Iraqi goods and services), it also sealed one of its internal borders. In northern Iraq, the Kurds, under the protection of the U.S. Air Force, enjoyed virtual autonomy from the central government in Baghdad. During the exchange week, those in the north were prevented from crossing into central Iraq and hence prohibited from participating in the currency exchange. Because the region, as part of Iraq, had no local currency of its own, the repudiation of the Swiss dinar wiped out the Kurds' international purchasing power.[19]

---

16. "Jordanian Columnist: Ban the Dinar," *Mideast Mirror,* May 7, 1993; United Press International, "Iraq Shuts Border to Canceled Currency," May 10, 1993; "Amman Stops Iraqi Dinar Dealings, with Jordan Times Questioning the Wisdom of Relying on Iraqi Oil," *Mideast Mirror,* May 10, 1993.

17. "King Hussein Urges End to Saddam's Rule," *Toronto Star,* November 8, 1992, p. B8; Hedges, "Fortunes in Iraqi Bills Gone Overnight"; "Amman Stops Iraqi Dinar Dealings"; United Press International, "Iraq Shuts Border to Canceled Currency."

18. Agence France Presse, "King Hussein Invited to White House in June," May 19, 1993; "King Hussein Says he Cannot Continue Supporting Baghdad," *Mideast Mirror,* May 24, 1993; "Jordan's King Urges Press to Jilt Saddam," *Guardian* (London) May 26, 1993, p. 10; Ruth Sinai (Associated Press), "Jordan's Hussein Calls for Democracy in Iraq," June 22, 1993.

19. This technique was used with great effectiveness by the central government in Nigeria during its civil war with Biafra in 1968. See Kirshner, *Currency and Coercion,* 102–6.

The Kurds had relied exclusively on the Swiss notes, disdaining the dented dinars produced in Baghdad as a symbolic gesture of their autonomy from Baghdad, and this only compounded the crisis. The blow "rocked the economy," creating a discombobulated present and an uncertain future. Petrol prices quickly tripled, and Kurdish officials told the UN that this "new economic war against Kurdistan" threatened the region with "economic devastation." By one estimate, one-third of the region's wealth "evaporated." Kurdish officials appealed for western help, asking the international community to force Iraq to allow for the exchange of notes held in Iraqi Kurdistan or to release frozen Iraqi assets to the Kurds as compensation. Neither measure was embraced.[20]

The Kurdish leadership faced multiple dilemmas. For an internal medium of exchange, they had little choice but to continue to rely on the Swiss notes; however, in communicating with the general public, explicitly promoting this course might encourage foreign merchants stuck with the worthless notes to dump them in the region. Nor could the Kurds simply introduce their own currency. As one Kurdish representative explained in calling for an international solution to the crisis: "we don't have the legal power to print our own money." Such a step would be seen as a major move toward independence, a white-hot political potato for most of the countries in the region. Indeed, Turkish officials saw the whole currency affair as an effort by Saddam Hussein to destabilize Turkey by forcing the Kurds' hand and "trying to confront Turkey with the prospect of an increasingly independent Iraqi Kurdistan, something Ankara has strongly opposed."[21]

One possibility that was considered was for the Iraqi Kurds to adopt the Turkish lira, creating a lira zone in northern Iraq. Fraught with its own complexities and political implications, this was nonetheless ultimately viewed as the least unattractive option by the Iraqi Kurds, and they formally requested that Turkey consider the option. The measure had some appeal for Turkey as it would presumably increase Turkish influence in the region and forestall any further momentum toward independence; for these reasons, the idea was endorsed by the *Turkish Daily News*. But the government was uncertain, divided, and inhibited by concerns for the lira itself; after all, inflation in Turkey was galloping along at 60 percent and the Turkish currency was no model of stability.[22]

Ultimately, inertia carried the day, and the Iraqi Kurds carried on with the Swiss

20. Agence France Presse, "Iraqi Kurds Seek Ways of Countering Baghdad's Monetary Moves," May 6, 1993; Hugh Pope, "Saddam's Dinar Ploy Bankrupts Kurds," *Independent* (London), May 15, 1993; Clare Pointon, "Banned Dinars Send Kurds Economy into a Tailspin: Leaders Need Western Backing to Continue to Use Currency," *Guardian* (London), May 10, 1993; Agence France Presse "Iraq Dinar Kurds."

21. Pointon, "Banned Dinars"; John Murray Brown, "Kurds Seek Access to Turkish Lira," *Financial Times*, May 28, 1993, p. 6; Agence France Presse, "Iraq Claims Triumph"; "Ankara Divided over Kurdish Request for Circulation of Turkish Lira in Northern Iraq," *Mideast Mirror*, May 18, 1993.

22. Andrew Finkel, "Saddam's Currency Tactic Steps up Pressure on Kurds," *Times* (London), May 17, 1993; "Demirel Urged to Push for Turkish Lira Zone in Northern Iraq," *Mideast Mirror*, May 21, 1993; Agence France Presse, "Iraqi Kurds Plead to Use Turkish Lira," May 15, 1993; "Ankara Divided over Kurdish Request."

dinar because the creation of a Kurdish currency remained too politically explosive while local currencies such as the Iranian riyal and the Turkish lira struggled with their own weaknesses and instability. The Swiss option was never satisfactory, however, especially because the notes diminished through wear and tear could not be replaced, creating a constant monetary shortage. In 2002, as an "emergency interim measure," the Kurdish authorities reintroduced stores of Swiss-printed 1-dinar notes that had long been retired; also U.S. dollars were used to buy up Swiss notes still in the hands of Turkish and Iranian merchants. Meanwhile, there remained the constant fear that Saddam Hussein (or, for that matter, the Iranians or the Syrians, as some rumors held) might dump the massive stores of Swiss notes he had held since the note exchange in an effort to cripple the Kurdish economy. The Iraqi government, on the other hand, periodically insisted that it was the victim of currency manipulation by Saudi Arabia and Kuwait. All of this was put to rest after the second Gulf War when the United States phased in, from October 15, 2003, through January 15, 2004, a "new Iraqi dinar" that replaced both the Swiss dinar still used in the north and the "old Iraqi dinar" circulating in the rest of the country.

Currency Manipulation under Globalization

As illustrated by these events, there is good reason to believe that currency manipulation will continue to be a feature of international relations under globalization, just as it was in the statist era. Globalization will, nonetheless, have two systematic effects on this aspect of monetary statecraft.

First, as suggested by the Gulf cases, it seems likely that predatory currency manipulation will be even less viable than it was previously against currencies that are widely traded and widely held but perhaps even more viable against less commonly held and traded currencies (of which there are now more than ever before)—especially where markets are thin and incomplete. According to the Bank for International Settlements, trade in five currencies accounts for 85 percent of all foreign-exchange transactions; adding the next five brings the total to 92.55 percent.[23] That leaves the vast majority of the world's currencies susceptible to predatory manipulation.

Second, more subtly and more important, globalization will recast the ways in which currency manipulation is most commonly practiced. After all, predatory manipulation is only one part of the currency manipulation story and, perhaps, the part of the story that is the least affected by the need to shift from a state-to-state to a state-system perspective. With this shift, as many surveys of international finance

23. The next fifteen currencies share about 4 percent of the market, which means that the top twenty-five currencies account for 96.6 percent of all currency trades. The rest of the world's currencies account for the remaining 3.4 percent, with the largest individual share in this group accounting for one-twentieth of 1 percent. Bank for International Settlements, *Triennial Central Bank Survey: Foreign Exchange and Derivatives Market Activity in 2001* (Basel: Bank for International Settlements, 2002), 9; Bank for International Settlements, "Central Bank Survey of Foreign Exchange and Derivatives Market Activity in April 2001: Preliminary Global Data," (press release) October 9, 2001, 6.

under globalization make clear, the system as a whole is more crisis prone and there is more, rather than less, politically consequential currency instability.[24] Under such conditions, the more salient change is that other forms of currency manipulation are likely to become both more common and more important—for those states in a position to practice them. In particular, what I have called "passive" and "protective" currency manipulation are each likely, under globalization, to attain increased political significance. Opportunities for passive manipulation (failing to provide help to a country in distress or extorting concessions in exchange for such help) as well as protective manipulation (the positive side of the same coin) proliferate in this context. The United States in particular is well placed to use its resources or to wield its enormous influence in international institutions, either to help out—or to fail to help out—those in distress. This will be a continuing, and likely even expanding, source of influence.

Monetary Dependence

The politics of international monetary arrangements centered around one currency are also transposed, not mitigated, by the consequences of unipolarity and globalization. Ironically, the relative increase in U.S. power generally since the end of the Cold War has made monetary conflict between competing currency areas more, rather than less, likely. Further, the pressures of and instabilities associated with globalization have made participation in such arrangements more, rather than less, attractive. And the traditional effort by leading states to cultivate monetary dependence in an effort to advance political goals continues uninterrupted into the twenty-first century.

The shift from bipolarity to unipolarity has increased the likelihood of economic conflict, including currency competition among the former participants in the anti-Soviet coalition: the United States, western Europe, and Japan.[25] The source of this emerging conflict is often misattributed; it is not that U.S. hegemony at the center of a stable Cold War alliance system allowed the United States, in particular, to disregard concerns for "relative gains." The pursuit of relative gains is not a function of anarchy—in fact, the pursuit of relative gains is virtually inherent in the process of negotiation between civil parties within states where there can be no plausible link back to fears for anarchy.[26] Rather, during the Cold War shared concerns for secu-

24. See, for example, Barry J. Eichengreen, *Financial Crises: And What to Do about Them* (Oxford: Oxford University Press, 2002); John Eatwell and Lance Taylor, *Global Finance at Risk: The Case for International Regulation* (New York: The New Press, 2000); Alexandre Lamfalussy, *Financial Crises in Emerging Markets: An Essay on Financial Globalisation and Fragility* (New Haven: Yale University Press, 2000).

25. Fred C. Bergsten, "America's Two Front Economic Conflict," *Foreign Affairs* 80, no. 2 (March–April 2001): 16–27.

26. The collective bargaining agreement of the National Basketball Association, for example, sets player's salaries at 48.04 percent of basketball-related income (BRI). But see, in contrast, Joanne S. Gowa, "Bipolarity, Multipolarity and Free Trade," *American Political Science Review* 83, no. 4 (December 1989):

rity provided an emergency brake on the economic conflict—all sides had strong incentives not to let such conflicts get out of hand lest they undermine crucial military alliances. Without this fear to rein in behavior, economic conflicts will become more uninhibited. Not only will this make conflicts over currency matters more likely, but the increasing recognition of the prospects for such conflicts will give an impetus to the coalescing of monetary areas.

Globalization will contribute further to this tendency by providing incentives for states to create, join, and support regional currency organizations. Again, this is more readily seen by shifting the focus from state-to-state relations to the state-system perspective. The awesome power of global financial markets creates often-unwelcome pressures for macroeconomic convergence; globalized markets are also remarkable conductors of financial instability. For these reasons among others, states will look to regional shelters from those monetary storms. For many states, ceding monetary authority to participate in a currency area will net more insulation and autonomy than going it alone.

The Search for Influence and Autonomy

One aspect of political behavior that has not changed as a function of either unipolarity or globalization is the efforts by states to extend their influence by situating themselves at the center of a regional monetary order. It remains difficult to quantify the benefits that states enjoy from such monetary leadership because the most important of these accrue from changes in perceived interests rather than from the exercise of overt coercion. This argument, which derives from Albert Hirschman's classic book *National Power and the Structure of Foreign Trade*,[27] is underappreciated in the literature on international relations. Hirschman was concerned with the political consequences of asymmetric economic relationships, and *National Power* illustrates this with a study of German trade strategy in the interwar period. Hirschman demonstrates, both theoretically and empirically, how asymmetric trade relationships can accrue political benefits to the larger state. For example, although trade between a large state and a small one can account for a very large percentage of the total commerce of the latter, it may represent only a fraction of the large partner's total trade. This asymmetry provides an imposing coercive lever because any interruption in the relationship will cause much greater distress in the small state than it will in the large one. Thus, threats to end or to interrupt the relationship, both explicit and implicit, provide power to the larger state.

This coercive potential is well recognized in the literature.[28] But there is much

---

1245–56; Joseph M. Grieco, "Understanding the Problem of International Cooperation: The Limits of Neoliberal Institutionalism and the Future of Realist Theory," in *Neorealism and Neoliberalism: The Contemporary Debate,* ed. David Baldwin, 301–38 (New York: Columbia University Press, 1993).

27. Albert Hirschman, *National Power and the Structure of Foreign Trade* (Berkeley: University of California Press, 1980).

28. See, for example, Stephen D. Krasner, "State Power and the Structure of International Trade," *World Politics* 28, no. 3 (1976): 317–43.

more to Hirschman's *National Power* than a story about coercion; there is also an important argument about influence.[29] Hirschman does develop the mechanics of the former more fully and systematically, but he also illustrates the crucial significance of the latter.[30] In practice, this less visible mechanism is the more common—and the more consequential—stuff of international relations.

As *National Power* shows, behind the headlines and with little fanfare, the pattern of international economic relations affects domestic politics, which in turn shapes national interests. This is always the case, but it is most significant in asymmetric relations, in which the effects on the smaller state can be quite considerable. A free trade agreement, for example, between a large state and a small state will, over time, shape the way in which the small state perceives its own interests; specifically, it will place greater value on the relationship with the larger state and see its interests as converging with those of its partner. Participation in the agreement will, by definition, strengthen those who benefit from it relative to those who do not, but these effects are likely to be magnified in the smaller state. Consequently, as the external relationship is sustained, the reshuffling of power, interests, and incentives among firms, sectors, and political coalitions in the small state will increasingly reflect these new realities. Private (and public) decisions based on the new incentives created by the agreement give firms and other actors a stake in their country's continued participation, and they will direct their political energies to that end. In Hirschman's words, "these regions or industries will exert a powerful influence in favor of a 'friendly' attitude toward the state to the imports of which they owe their existence."[31]

Although *National Power*, of course, focuses on trade relations, parallel arguments hold for currency arrangements as well.[32] It is this reason—chasing the prospects of political influence—that has led most great powers (and some not-so-great powers) throughout history to try and extend their monetary influence by positioning themselves at the center of an international currency nexus that will be attractive to at least some potential participants.[33] The significance of this sort of structural power is addressed by Eric Helleiner (chap. 4 in this volume) and discussed by David Andrews (chap. 1 in this volume) under the rubric of micro-level aspects of monetary power.

The larger point is that both globalization and unipolarity create additional incentives for states capable of considering some form of monetary leadership. Globalization presents risks of greater financial instability and reduced macroeconomic autonomy; the increased economic scale offered by regional monetary arrangements can provide some insulation from global shocks and, to an extent determined by the

29. Rawi Abdelal and Jonathan Kirshner, "Strategy, Economic Relations, and the Definition of National Interests," *Security Studies* 9, no. 1–2 (autumn 1999–winter 2000): 119–56.

30. Hirschman, *National Power*, 18, 28, 29, 34, 37.

31. Ibid., 29.

32. See Kirshner, *Currency and Coercion*, 115–69.

33. Note that the pursuit of this objective—political influence—can inhibit the practice of overt coercion. See Kirshner, *Currency and Coercion*, 168–69, 244; Scott Cooper (chap. 8 in this volume).

nature of the agreement, opportunities for coordination that can enhance the collective policy autonomy of the group as a whole. Unipolarity not only reflects the absence of a common threat (which would inhibit discord); it also leads to the inclination, however subtle, to lean against or at least mitigate U.S. influence—yielding two additional incentives for states to seek politically countervailing monetary arrangements. Thus, the stage is set for an increase in competition for monetary influence and for the coalescing of new monetary relationships. To be clear, this need not imply economic closure, draconian discrimination, or continuous economic warfare between competing centers of monetary influence. But it does suggest that there are now significant pressures toward a recasting of international monetary relations around regional arrangements, which will create new sources of political influence and new axes of economic conflict.

Competition for Monetary Influence in Asia

Japan's efforts (especially since the Asian financial crisis) to exert regional monetary influence, and the fierce opposition of both the United States and China to those efforts, reflect the high stakes involved in the struggle for monetary influence.[34] Since the late 1980s, Japan harbored aspirations to a greater leadership role in international monetary affairs to enhance its international influence and also to circumscribe U.S. monetary power.[35] These ambitions were put on the back burner with Japan's sustained economic malaise in the 1990s, but the Asian financial crisis created both an opportunity and an incentive to revisit the question of the internationalization of the yen and Japan's monetary leadership in Asia more broadly.

Global financial instability strengthened those voices in Japan that argued that an internationalized yen might insulate Japan from the increasingly crisis-prone system; moreover, there was broad dissatisfaction with the response of the International Monetary Fund (IMF) (and by implication, the United States) to the Asian financial crisis. Whereas officials in Washington attributed the crisis to fundamental flaws in the "East Asian model," in Tokyo the crisis was seen as reflecting problems inherent in a system of fully liberalized international capital. Government ministers in Japan repeatedly raised the issue that reform was required in the architecture of the international financial system and expressed displeasure at the invasiveness of IMF conditions.[36] Neither the U.S. government nor the IMF, however, would en-

---

34. C. Randall Henning (chap. 6 in this volume) also addresses this case, but focuses less on its geopolitical dimensions than does the analysis here.

35. On Japan's increasing assertiveness in the late 1980s, see Eric Helleiner, "Japan and the Changing Global Financial Order," *International Journal* 47, no. 2 (spring 1992): 434–37.

36. Kiichi Miyazawa (Japanese minister of finance), "Towards a New Financial Architecture," speech delivered at the Foreign Correspondents Club of Japan, December 15, 1998, http://www.mof.go.jp/english/if/e1e057.htm; Eisuke Sakakibara (Japanese vice minister of finance), "Reform of the International Financial Architecture," speech delivered at the Symposium on Building the Financial System of the Twenty-First Century, Kyoto, Japan, June 25, 1999, http://www.mof.go.jp/english/if/if004.htm; Haruhiko Kuroda (Japanese vice minister of finance), "Information Technology, Globalization, and International Financial Architecture," speech delivered at Foreign Correspondents Club of Japan, June 15,

tertain the notion that the crisis had an important international component or that perhaps some regulation of short-term capital flows was in order.[37]

The crisis thus reinvigorated dormant discussions in Japan about whether the time had come to promote the internationalization of the yen more aggressively. Although Japan was interested in claiming a greater leadership role in the region, viewing the behavior of the United States and the IMF as "a direct challenge to their country's economic and ideological interests,"[38] the debate was also, as William Grimes has pointed out, "fundamentally one about *insulation*" and the hope that an internationalized yen would "stabilize Japan's international environment."[39]

The most celebrated (and ill-fated) outcome of Japan's new assertiveness was Tokyo's proposal, floated in summer 1997, for an Asian Monetary Fund (AMF). The concept was never fully developed, but would have been bankrolled by $50 billion from Japan with an additional $50 billion in contributions from other Asian countries and, crucially, would have provided emergency loans to Asian states facing financial crisis without the types of conditions associated with IMF assistance.[40]

Leaders in both Tokyo and Washington understood that the stakes in the AMF were more geopolitical than economic—an effort to expand Japan's influence in the region at the expense of U.S. interests. Thus, the Ministry of Finance quietly coordinated its proposal exclusively with other Asian nations, leaving the United States to be "caught by surprise" by the plan, which only heightened tensions—as one account stated simply, "American officials were enraged."[41] In the end, the original AMF proposal never got very far, mostly due to "heated" and "vehement" U.S. opposition,[42] although other factors played a role as well—including the strong op-

---

2000, http://www.mof.go.jp/english/if/if018.htm. See also Michael Green, *Japan's Reluctant Realism: Foreign Policy Challenges in an Era of Uncertain Power* (New York: Palgrave, 2001), 259–60; Christopher Hughes, "Japanese Policy and the East Asian Crisis: Abject Defeat or Quiet Victory?" *Review of International Political Economy* 7, no. 2 (summer 2000): 241, 242.

37. Jonathan Kirshner, "Explaining Choices about Money: Disentangling Power, Ideas and Conflict," in *Monetary Orders: Ambiguous Economics, Ubiquitous Politics,* ed. Jonathan Kirshner, 270–79 (Ithaca: Cornell University Press, 2003).

38. Saori Katada, "Japan and Asian Monetary Regionalization: Cultivating a New Regional Leadership Role after the Asian Financial Crisis," *Geopolitics* 7, no. 1 (summer 2002): 86.

39. William Grimes, "Internationalization of the Yen and the New Politics of Monetary Insulation," in *Monetary Orders: Ambiguous Economics, Ubiquitous Politics,* ed. Jonathan Kirshner (Ithaca: Cornell University Press, 2003), 173, 181 (second quotation, emphasis in original), 185 (first quotation). See also Paul Bowles, "Asia's Post-Crisis Regionalism: Bringing the State Back In, Keeping the (United) States Out," *Review of International Political Economy* 9, no. 2 (summer 2002): 231, 248.

40. Eric Altbach, "The Asian Monetary Fund Proposal: A Case Study of Japanese Regional Leadership," Japan Economic Institute Report no. 47, December 19, 1997; Fred Bergsten, "Reviving the Asian Monetary Fund," *International Economics Policy Briefs* 98, no. 8 (1998).

41. Green, *Japan's Reluctant Realism,* 230–31, 245 (first quotation), 248; Paul Blustein, *The Chastening: Inside the Crisis that Rocked the Global Financial System and Humbled the IMF* (New York: Public Affairs, 2001), 165–66 (second quotation).

42. Altbach, "Asian Monetary Fund Proposal," 2, 10. See also Eric Helleiner, "Still an Extraordinary Power, but for How Much Longer? The United States in World Finance," in *Strange Power: Shaping the Parameters of International Relations and International Political Economy,* ed. Thomas C. Lawton, James N. Rosenau, and Amy C. Verdun, 229–48 (Aldershot: Ashgate, 2000), quotation on 236; Philip Lipscy,

position of China. Like Washington, Beijing interpreted the AMF proposal in geopolitical terms. Pursuing its own strategy of expanding political influence through the cultivation of economic ties, China saw the AMF as an effort by Japan to assert regional leadership at the expense of its chief Asian rival.[43]

The collapse of the AMF left Japan's monetary ambitions down but not out. In October 1998, Tokyo proposed the New Miyazawa Plan, at the center of which was the establishment of a fund of up to $30 billion to provide short- and medium-term loans to Asian nations. This was followed by other efforts, such as the Chiang Mai initiative to coordinate currency swaps. Compared to the AMF, these arrangements were modest and bowed to political realities; they were coordinated with both the United States and the IMF. But they reflected the underlying motivations that contributed to the original AMF proposal: a push for a greater international role for the yen in the wake of the instabilities reflected by the Asian financial crisis and, at the same time, an attempt to counter the influence of the United States and the IMF in Asia. In other words, they reflected Japan's reactions to globalization and unipolarity.[44]

The continuing divergence between Japan and the United States on questions of monetary order was reflected in their dramatically different responses to Malaysia's September 1998 decision to impose capital controls in response to the Asian financial crisis.[45] While officials from the United States and the IMF heaped scathing criticism on the Malaysian government, Japan fully supported the measure. In December, Japanese Finance Minister Kiichi Miyazawa stated publicly that in some cases it was appropriate to reintroduce or "maintain market friendly controls," and

"Japan's Asian Monetary Fund Proposal," *Stanford Journal of East Asian Affairs* 3, no. 1 (spring 2003): 93; Christopher Johnstone, "Paradigms Lost: Japan's Asia Policy in a Time of Growing Chinese Power," *Contemporary Southeast Asia* 21, no. 3 (December 1999): 377.

43. Katada, "Japan and Asian Monetary Regionalization," 87, 104, 105; Grimes, "Internationalization of the Yen," 173; Johnstone, "Paradigms Lost," 381; Green, *Japan's Reluctant Realism*, 230. For an example of China's ambitions, see Jane Perlez, "With US Busy, China Is Romping with Neighbors," *New York Times*, December 3, 2003.

44. Saori N. Katada, "Determining Factors in Japan's Cooperation and Non-Cooperation with the United States: The Case of Asian Financial Crisis Management, 1997–1999," in *Japanese Foreign Policy in Asia and the Pacific: Domestic Interests, American Pressure, and Regional Integration*, ed. Akitoshi Miyashita and Yoichiro Sato (New York: Palgrave, 2001), 155–74. Katada argues that domestic financial concerns that surfaced in Japan in 1997 also contributed to the demise of the AMF, suggesting that Japan would reassert its international ambitions as domestic economic pressures eased (161, 162, 169). See also Hughes, "Japanese Policy," 245–47; Bowles, "Asia's Post-Crisis Regionalism," 239, 240; Lipscy, "Japan's Asian Monetary Fund Proposal"; Council on Foreign Exchange and Other Transactions, "Internationalization of the Yen for the 21st Century," April 20, 1999, http://www.mof.go.jp/english/if/e1b064a.htm. On the Chiang Mai initiative, see C. Randall Henning, "East Asian Financial Cooperation," Policy Analyses in International Economics no. 68, Institute for International Economics, Washington, D.C., 2002; Hennings (chap. 6 in this volume).

45. On this episode, see Rawi Abdelal and Laura Alfaro, "Malaysia: Capital and Control," case no. N9-702-040, Harvard Business School, March 14, 2002; Prema-chandra Athukoralge, *Crisis and Recovery in Malaysia: The Role of Capital Controls* (Cheltenham, UK: Edward Elgar, 2001); Mark Beeson, "Mahathir and the Markets: Globalization and the Pursuit of Economic Autonomy in Malaysia," *Pacific Affairs* 73, no. 3 (2000): 335–51.

Malaysia became the first country to receive assistance under the New Miyazawa Initiative. After the country had sustained (with reasonable economic success) its controls for a full year, Malaysia "received cheers" from the Japanese government as well as from other parts of Asia.[46] Those cheers were not for Malaysia's economic endurance; rather, they were echoes from the arena of competition for global monetary influence.

The Continuing Politics of Monetary Geography

The competition for monetary influence is certainly not limited to Asia; indeed, many observers anticipate a global jockeying for influence between the world's two most important currencies, neither of which is produced in Asia—the dollar and the euro. How serious a threat the euro poses to the global supremacy of the dollar remains an open question. Some prominent commentators, such as Fred Bergsten, argue that the euro will almost inevitably become a peer competitor to the dollar. Although the incumbency advantages enjoyed by the dollar will delay this development, it is solely a matter of time; and some developments suggest that the euro may be gaining firmer footing, such as reports that some Asian central banks may increase their euro-denominated holdings.[47]

Others, such as Benjamin Cohen, remain skeptical that the euro will rival the dollar any time in the foreseeable future, suggesting that the lag time provided by incumbency advantages will be considerable. Further, the euro is hampered by a number of characteristics that make it ill suited to serve as the "world's currency"; for example, there is an anti-growth bias in management of the euro, rendering euro-denominated assets less attractive. Furthermore, as Kathleen McNamara and Sophie Meunier have noted, the formation of the euro left the currency without a clear political representation on the world stage—a "single voice" for the euro in the international arena. Cohen also points out that exchange-rate movements tell much less about the fate of key currencies than the extent to which they are used by private actors and held as reserves, two factors that continue to favor the dollar.[48]

The politics of monetary dependence will remain important regardless of how

46. Rudi Dornbusch, "Malaysia: Was It Different?" *NBER Working Paper* no. 8325 *National Bureau of Economic Research, Washington, D.C.*, June 2001, 1; Miyazawa, "New Financial Architecture," 3; Katada, "Japan and Asian Monetary Regionalization," 87 (quotation), 97; Abdelal and Alfaro, "Malaysia," 12.

47. Fred Bergsten, "The Euro versus the Dollar: Will There Be a Struggle for Dominance?" paper presented at the meeting of the American Economic Association, January 4, 2002; Mingqi Xu, "The Impact of the Euro on the International Stability: A Chinese Perspective," in *The Euro as a Stabilizer in the International Economic System*, ed. Robert Mundell and Armand Clesse (Boston: Kluwer Academic Publishers, 2000), 266. The IMF has also revised upward its estimate of the share of euros in foreign-exchange reserves; see International Monetary Fund, *Revised IMF Annual Report Data on Official Foreign Exchange Reserves* (Washington, D.C.: IMF, 2002).

48. Benjamin J. Cohen, "Global Currency Rivalry: Can the Euro Ever Challenge the Dollar?" *Journal of Common Market Studies* 41, no. 4 (2003): 575–95; Kathleen McNamara and Sophie Meunier, "Between National Sovereignty and International Power: What External Voice for the Euro?" *International Affairs* 78, no. 4 (2002): 850.

this competition plays out; however, a perspective that privileges the role of power in explaining monetary relations yields different predictions than do standard analyses. Rather than an incremental process, as suggested by both the euro-optimists and euro-pessimists already mentioned,[49] a power perspective would anticipate the more rapid emergence of significant currency rivalry as the joint effects of globalization and unipolarity produce a sudden violent shift away from the dollar.

One consequence of the capital market deregulation associated with financial globalization is that the attractiveness of the dollar as an international asset—one of the pillars that supports the currency's dominance—may prove to be a double-edged sword. The United States has been empowered (relative to other states) by the process of financial globalization, yet at the same time it has become more vulnerable to financial crisis than at any time since World War II. In particular, the oceans of dollars held abroad—over $1 trillion—could serve as fuel to a fire started by a relatively moderate financial crisis involving the United States.

Moreover, the wheels have been greased. The U.S. federal budget deficit has soared, and its trade deficit is setting record after record. However imperfectly theory meets with practice, these deficits wave red flags at dollar holders about the future value of the greenback as they imply pressure on both inflation and the exchange rate. These flags will loom large if a moderate-size financial disturbance involving the United States takes place. At the same time, unipolarity has contributed to both U.S. unilateralism and to wariness of U.S. power in ways that create political space between the United States and many other parts of the world.[50] Should the dollar buckle, instead of a rush to preserve the status quo there might be a more subtle movement to recast the monetary order to the detriment of the United States.

Whether or not this dollar doomsday scenario occurs, what is of greater significance for present purposes is the explicit recognition by most participants in this debate that whatever monetary conflict exists is of fundamentally political origin and political consequence. Or, in the words of Hubert Zimmermann, the euro is "based on the assumption that monetary power matters."[51] States do and will continue to seek to extend the international use of their currency in order to increase their political influence. In the contemporary era, the pressures of financial globalization in conjunction with the politics of unipolarity create additional incentives for this behavior. As Martin Feldstein has argued, there is "no doubt" that the real rationale for Economic and Monetary Union (EMU) is "political, not economic," as the aggregation of European resources provides some insulation from global instability while potentially providing an essential element of any political counterweight to the United States. This may become increasingly important if the divergent foreign pol-

49. See, for example, Benjamin J. Cohen, *The Future of Money* (Princeton: Princeton University Press, 2004), especially chap. 3.

50. Robert Jervis, "Understanding the Bush Doctrine," *Political Science Quarterly* 118, no. 3 (fall 2003): 365–88.

51. Hubert Zimmermann, "Ever Challenging the Buck? The Euro and the Question of Power in International Monetary Governance" (unpublished manuscript), Cornell University, 2003.

icy visions of the European Union and the United States create increasingly greater political space between the two entities.[52]

European monetary politics are also illustrative of a more general point. Regardless of the level of globalization, the geography of money—which currency is used where—continues to be governed by political rather than economic factors. Only politics, for example, can account for the monetary choices made by the republics established in the wake of the collapse of the Soviet Union; the economic costs and benefits offer little guide. Similarly, choices about dollarization in Latin America will also be made primarily in response to political factors because the economic costs and benefits of dollarization remain modest, ambiguous, and contingent. The "supply side" of this equation—U.S. pressure for formal dollarization—will also follow this same pattern, a function of international politics and, hence, unlikely unless it becomes seen as necessary as a defensive move against an increasingly assertive euro or in the wake of a sudden realignment of the global monetary order.[53]

Financial globalization also creates incentives for smaller states to affiliate with regional monetary associations or to seek cover by closely associating, in one way or another, with a great monetary power. Not counting the formal participants in EMU, twenty-nine countries have abandoned their own legal tender in favor of foreign currencies; another forty-two have fixed-peg arrangements against a single currency. These relationships create vulnerabilities that could conceivably be exploited by the monetary leaders in exceptional circumstances. In 1988, for example, the United States capitalized on Panama's use of the U.S. dollar as its legal tender, turning the Panamanian reliance on the greenback into an important economic weapon during the confrontation between the United States with the Manuel Noriega regime.[54] As previously discussed, however, the principal effect of such arrangements will be first to shape and then to reinforce political preferences in the weaker partners of these asymmetric relationships.

Systemic Disruption

Systemic disruption—threats to destabilize the system, in almost all cases in order to extort political side payments—also remains an important feature of international

52. Martin Feldstein, "The EMU and International Conflict," *Foreign Affairs* 76, no. 6 (November–December 1997): 60–73, quotations on 60, 72, 73; see also McNamara and Meunier, "Between National Sovereignty and International Power," 849; Cohen, "Global Currency Rivalry." On the possibility of emerging rifts between the United States and Europe, see Charles Kupchan, *The End of the American Era: US Foreign Policy and the Geopolitics of the Twenty-first Century* (New York: Knopf, 2002).

53. Marco del Negro, Alejandro Hernandez-Delgado, Owen Humpage, and Elizabeth Huybens, "Introduction: Context, Issues and Contributions," *Journal of Money, Credit and Banking* 33, no. 2 (May 2001): 310–11; Jurgen Schuldt, "Latin American Official Dollarization: Political Economy Aspects," in *The Dollarization Debate*, ed. Dominick Salvatore, James Dean, and Thomas Willett 238–65 (Oxford: Oxford University Press, 2003); Cohen, *Global Currency Rivalry*, in which he argues that "political considerations will be decisive" (236). See also Rawi Abdelal, *National Purpose in the World Economy: Post-Soviet States in Comparative Perspective* (Ithaca: Cornell University Press, 2001).

54. International Monetary Fund, *Annual Report*, 9. On Panama, see Kirshner, *Currency and Coercion*, 159–64.

relations.[55] As with currency manipulation and monetary dependence, however, it is necessary to recast the analysis to account for unipolarity and (especially) globalization. This can also be illustrated by refining what is still the best metaphor for strategic disruption—boat rocking—and Thomas Schelling's analyses of the manipulation of risk.[56] The state-to-state version of this fable focuses on the occupants of the boat and the explicit negotiations among them—one state rocking the boat, the other protesting (or pretending not to care). In the state-system fable, by contrast, rather than overtly rocking, one state—the state with the power to set the boat's course—intentionally steers the craft toward stormy waters.

Still a story about the manipulation of risk and still risky business, this maneuver changes the underlying setting in a way that privileges the most powerful. Thus, strategic disruption under globalization is transformed from an instrument of economic coercion allowing second-tier powers to take on those at the top into an instrument of the powerful, whereby those mighty enough to alter the very the rules of the game do so in a way that the benefits the strong at the expense of the weak. In short, strategic disruption from below is replaced by strategic disruption from above.

Awareness of this type of structural power can help explain U.S. efforts to render illegitimate any forms of international capital control and, likewise, its efforts to promote complete and comprehensive domestic financial liberalization abroad in the absence of evidence to support the proposition that such deregulation is optimal from an economic perspective and in the wake of spectacular and unanticipated disruptions such as the east Asian financial crisis.[57] For while a world of completely unregulated capital is risky, it is perhaps the least risky for the United States, given the hegemonic position of the U.S. economy. Despite the vulnerabilities previously discussed, the United States is a relatively less likely candidate for financial crisis, even in a world where such crises are more common. Indeed, financial crises elsewhere might contribute to a "flight to quality," with capital seeking refuge on perceived islands of relative stability such as the United States. Further, as the home of powerful private financial actors and with rich and deeply institutionalized domestic financial markets, the United States is especially well situated to thrive competitively in a world of deregulated international markets. For these reasons, the United States can afford to adopt a position of benign neglect in many cases of financial crises around the globe. Most pointedly, when crises do occur, given its resources and influence in international institutions such as the IMF, the United States can set conditions for those who seek help.[58] The resulting influence is clearly seen in the case

55. States may also seek to destroy the system (or undermine the viability of a subsystem) as an end in itself; in practice, however, strategic disruption is much more likely.

56. Thomas Schelling, *The Strategy of Conflict* (Cambridge, Mass.: Harvard University Press, 1960); Thomas Schelling, *Arms and Influence* (New Haven: Yale University Press, 1966).

57. See Kirshner, "Explaining Choices about Money," especially 270–71.

58. On the international politics that sustain a system of economic instability, see Mark Blyth, "The Political Power of Financial Ideas: Transparency, Risk, and Distribution in Global Finance," in *Monetary Orders: Ambiguous Economics, Ubiquitous Politics*, ed. Jonathan Kirshner (Ithaca: Cornell University Press, 2003), especially 239, 256. Great power indifference is characterized as "benign neglect" in Graham Bird and Ramkishen S. Rajan, "The Evolving Asian Financial Architecture," Princeton Essays in International Economics no. 26, Princeton University, Princeton, N.J., 2002, 7.

of IMF policy toward South Korea in the wake of the east Asian financial crisis, as the next section describes.

International Instability and Korean Domestic Reforms

When the Asian financial crisis reached South Korea in the closing months of 1997, Seoul sought the assistance of the IMF and was successful in reaching an agreement that provided unprecedented financial support. In exchange for that support, however, Korea agreed to a comprehensive set of conditions.[59] These conditions fell into two categories. One group of reforms was obviously related to the financial crisis, with provisions concerning the restructuring, prudential regulation, and transparency of the banking and financial sector. But the IMF insisted on a second set of reforms—including the elimination of ceilings on foreign holdings of bonds and equities, abolition of restrictions on foreign ownership of land, the dismantling of trade barriers and acceleration of capital account liberalization, and reduced restrictions on corporate borrowing abroad—that were just as clearly unrelated to the risk of financial crisis.[60]

The economic merits of this second set of measures have since come under criticism from many sources, including some mainstream ones. These critics acknowledge that the conditions required by the IMF might improve the long-term efficiency of the Korean economy, but it is "hard to see how they would either help resolve the crisis or prevent a future one."[61] According to Martin Feldstein, for example, the Korean economy, "an economy to envy," was suffering from a crisis of "temporary illiquidity rather than fundamental insolvency." This being the case, all the IMF needed to do was provide a bridge loan and help coordinate action by creditor banks. Instead, the IMF's reaction—insisting that the Korean economy was in need of basic structural reform if it was to have any chance at recovery—actually exacerbated Korea's difficulties. Feldstein therefore argues that the "IMF should eschew the temptation to use currency crises as an opportunity to force fundamental and structural reforms on countries," as was done in this instance.[62]

59. Uk Heo, "South Korea: Democratization, Financial Crisis, and the Decline of the Developmental State," in *The Political Economy of International Financial Crises: Interest Groups, Ideologies, and Institutions,* ed. Shale Horowitz and Uk Heo, 151–64 (London: Rowman and Littlefield, 2001); Kiseok Hong and Jong-Wha Lee, "Korea: Returning to Sustainable Growth?" in *The Asian Financial Crisis: Lessons for a Resilient Asia,* ed. Wing Thye Woo, Jeffrey D. Sachs, and Klaus Schwab, 203–25 (Cambridge, Mass.: MIT Press, 2000).

60. Chol-Hwan Chon (governor, Bank of Korea) and Kyu-Sung Lee (minister of Finance and Economy), "Letter of Intent of the Government of Korea," May 2, 1998, http://www.imf.org.external/np/loi/050298.htm. See also Ajai Chopra, Kenneth Kang, Merai Karasulu, Hong Liang, Henry Ma, and Anthony Richards, "From Crisis to Recovery in Korea: Strategy, Achievements, and Lessons," International Monetary Fund Working Paper WP/01/154, IMF, Washington, D.C., 2001, 55–56.

61. W. Max Corden, "The World Financial Crisis: Are the IMF Prescriptions Right?" in *The Political Economy of International Financial Crises: Interest Groups, Ideologies, and Institutions,* ed. Shale Horowitz and Uk Heo (London: Rowman and Littlefield, 2001), 59. Although offering a thoughtful and balanced assessment of the IMF's performance during the crisis, Corden reports "surprise" and even "amaze[ment]" at many of the provisions required by the letter of intent.

62. Martin Feldstein, "Refocusing the IMF," *Foreign Affairs* 77, no. 2 (March–April 1998): 24, 27, 31, 32. See also Jeffrey Sachs, "Fixing the IMF Remedy," *The Banker* (February 1998), 16–18; Ha-Joon

Whatever the economic merits of the IMF's demands, however, their political attributes are unambiguous. The agreement required Korea to concede on a host of issues that had been the subject of long-standing bilateral negotiations with the United States. For example, South Korea had always restricted foreign direct investment (FDI) and had also protected its financial service sector from foreign competition; the United States had been pushing for some time on these matters without success. U.S. export interests had likewise been pressing for greater access to the Korean market, another requirement of the IMF agreement. In sum, the measures required by Korea's letter of intent, as Robert Gilpin concludes, "included specific items that the United States had long demanded of Asian governments, and that the latter had rejected." Joseph Stiglitz states it more bluntly: the U.S. imposition of requirements from its trade agenda had little to do with the crisis and "was simply part of a crude power play."[63]

There are few observers in Asia (or elsewhere, for that matter) who do not see the IMF as an agent of U.S. influence; they regard bowing down to U.S. demands that the Korean market be opened as a quid pro quo for IMF assistance. The required structural reforms, according to Feldstein, touched on areas that were "among the most politically sensitive" in Korea.[64] Notably, U.S. government officials have not offered much that would contradict this perspective. It is widely understood that it was the United States that encouraged the IMF to focus increasingly on microeconomic reform and trade liberalization. As a result, then U.S. Deputy Treasury Secretary Lawrence Summers could boast that "the IMF has done more to promote America's trade and investment agenda in East Asia than 30 years of bilateral trade negotiations," and U.S. Trade Representative Mickey Kantor hailed the IMF a "battering ram" that was used to open Asian markets to U.S. products.[65]

The Prospects for Disruption

Technology and market forces have been important factors in the advance of financial globalization, but the promotion of global capital mobility has also been encouraged by the United States and these efforts have been of profound importance.

Chang, Hong Jae Park, and Chul Gyue Yoo, "Interpreting the Korean Crisis: Financial Liberalization, Industrial Policy and Corporate Governance," *Cambridge Journal of Economics* 22, no. 6 (1998): 739.

63. Joseph Stiglitz, "Failure of the Fund: Rethinking the IMF Response," *Harvard International Review* 32, no. 2 (summer 2001): 18; Robert Gilpin, *The Challenge of Global Capitalism: The World Economy in the 21st Century* (Princeton: Princeton University Press, 2000), 157, 159.

64. Feldstein, "Refocusing the IMF," 25. See also Donald Kirk, *Korean Crisis: Unraveling of the Miracle in the IMF Era* (New York: Palgrave, 1999), 35 (where he refers to "egregious imperialistic meddling"), 36–38, 43, 46; John Mathews, "Fashioning a New Korean Model Out of the Crisis: The Rebuilding of Institutional Capabilities," *Cambridge Journal of Economics* 22, no. 6 (1998): 752. Stiglitz, "Failure of the Fund," reports that the IMF is perceived to be "dominated by the political interests of the U.S. Treasury," (17); see also Marcus Noland, "Japan and the International Institutions," paper presented at Macquarie University, Sydney, Australia, July 6–7, 2000, 8, 19.

65. David Hale, "Dodging the Bullet—This Time: The Asian Crisis and US Economic Growth during 1998," *Brookings Review* 16, no. 3 (summer 1998): 24, Summers's quotation on 26; *International Herald Tribune*, January 14, 1998 ("battering ram").

As U.S. Deputy Treasury Secretary Summers stated plainly, "financial liberalization, both domestically and internationally, is a critical part of the US agenda."[66] Encouraged by an ideological commitment to capital deregulation, the promotion of financial globalization is also a policy that serves U.S. geopolitical preferences. In the public assessment of Alan Greenspan, the Asian crisis offers evidence that "market capitalism, as practiced in the West, especially in the United States, is the superior model."[67] Although many in the United States have held this view for a long time, the end of the Cold War and U.S. preponderance have provided the opportunity to act on this belief. During the bipolar confrontation with the Soviet Union, the United States did not have the luxury of taking on different styles of national capitalism—it is quite reasonable to assume that if the Asian financial crisis had occurred during the Cold War, aid to Korea would have come with fewer strings.[68] Similarly, in the current era, the ability of the United States to practice strategic disruption from above is to a large extent a function of the prospects for currency rivalry and monetary dependence. If the dollar doomsday scenario occurs, then the coalescing of spheres of monetary influence will reshape U.S. incentives and the main theater of monetary statecraft will shift from disruption to dependence. In this scenario, the United States and other monetary leaders will make efforts to cultivate influence with followers and will pursue more subtle, economically generous strategies, á la Hirschman, of entrapment—and thus be more cautious with naked monetary coercion. Until that time, however, a monetary power perspective expects the United States to continue to promote global financial liberalization and to take political advantage of those financial crises that do occur, following a strategy, á la Schelling, of parlaying that riskier environment that enhances U.S. interests relative to those of other states.

Conclusion

As suggested here, the politics of U.S.–boat rocking is most transparent when it is understood that the economic merits of complete financial globalization are ambiguous. That is, although capital mobility is generally economically efficient, the balance of evidence suggests that the optimal level of controls on the international movement of capital is greater than zero. Thus, the vehement reaction of U.S. officials to the Malaysian controls, declaring that "it would be a catastrophe" if other countries followed suit, makes little sense if the analysis is limited to economic costs and benefits.[69] The political benefits of financial globalization, on the other hand,

66. Quoted in Devesh Kapur, "The IMF: A Cure or a Curse," *Foreign Policy* 111 (summer 1998): 114–29.

67. Alan Greenspan, "The Current Asian Crisis," testimony before the Subcommittee on Foreign Operations of the Committee on Appropriations, U.S. Senate, Washington, D.C., March 3, 1998.

68. Bruce Cumings, "The Asian Crisis, Democracy, and the End of 'Late' Development," in *The Politics of the Asian Economic Crisis*, ed. T. J. Pempel, 17–44 (Ithaca: Cornell University Press, 1999), quotations on 18, 41.

69. Lawrence Summers, quoted in Abdelal and Alfaro, "Malaysia," 11. Other leading figures had similarly disproportionate responses to the Malaysian experiment; Michel Camdessus called the controls

are more certain: the United States on balance has much to gain and bears a disproportionately small share of the resulting risks.

Power in international politics is always relative; a system characterized by greater risk of financial crisis does in some ways leave the United States more vulnerable, but compared to other states its power is enhanced. With relatively less vulnerability and the best prospects for practicing strategic disruption—manipulating the risks of crisis as well as the nature of agreements to contain them—the international political power of the United States is enhanced by a world of globalized finance.

In sum, the contemporary international system is characterized by globalization and unipolarity. Financial globalization, in particular, recasts the nature of monetary power and the practice of monetary diplomacy. But it does not provide an escape from politics; even under globalization, international relations will continue to feature currency manipulation, monetary dependence, and strategic disruption. As long as there are states and currencies, the monetary system will remain an arena of political conflict.

"dangerous and even harmful," as reported in Robert Wade, "The Asian Crisis and the Global Economy: Causes, Consequences, and Cure," *Current History* (November 1998): 368. Alan Greenspan, in pointed testimony, quickly (and erroneously, at least in the Malaysian case) equated capital controls with "borders closed to foreign investment" and explained that states that implement capital controls would be "mired at a sub-optimal standard of living and slow growth rate." Alan Greenspan, "International Economic and Financial Systems," testimony before the Committee on Banking and Financial Services, U.S. House of Representatives, Washington, D.C., September 16, 1998.

CHAPTER EIGHT

The Limits of Monetary Power:
Statecraft within Currency Areas

Scott Cooper

Despite the abundant literature on individual currency areas such as the franc zone and the sterling bloc, there has been a dearth of comparative political analysis of how these areas work. One important exception is Jonathan Kirshner's analysis of how monetary power is exploited by leading powers within currency areas. He explains the mechanisms of dependence and analyzes the various ways a currency area's leader is able to gain power at the expense of follower states. He also uses detailed empirical examples to show how leaders have exploited the monetary dependence of followers.[1]

Although Kirshner's analysis and evidence are generally persuasive, it is striking how often modern currency areas seem to magnify the leader's weaknesses rather than enhancing its strengths. For example, the sterling area may have been a source of British power in the 1930s and 1940s, but by the 1960s sterling was more of a

I thank David Andrews, Michael Artis, Jeff Chwieroth, Benjamin Cohen, Eric Helleiner, Randall Henning, Matthias Kaelberer, and Jonathan Kirshner for helpful comments; Brooke Richards for research assistance; and Brigham Young University and the European University Institute for research funding.

1. Jonathan Kirshner, *Currency and Coercion: The Political Economy of International Monetary Power* (Princeton: Princeton University Press, 1995). Benjamin J. Cohen's work in part reinforces Kirshner's by emphasizing the importance of a dominant state as a key factor in sustaining a currency area, but it also goes beyond Kirshner's in pointing out that a dense network of institutional ties may sustain a currency area in the absence of a leading state. In effect, Cohen reminds us that some currency areas have relatively symmetrical control mechanisms. See Benjamin J. Cohen, "Beyond EMU: The Problem of Sustainability," *Economics and Politics* 5, no. 2 (1993): 187–203; *The Geography of Money* (Ithaca: Cornell University Press, 1998), 68–91; *The Future of Money* (Princeton: Princeton University Press, 2004), 51–61, 123–78. Other important comparative work on currency areas includes Andrew Walter, *World Power and World Money: The Role of Hegemony and International Monetary Order* (New York: St. Martin's Press, 1991); Carsten Hefeker, "Interest Groups, Coalitions, and Monetary Integration in the XIXth Century," *Journal of European Economic History* 24, no. 3 (1995): 489–536; Walter Mattli, *The Logic of Regional Integration: Europe and Beyond* (Cambridge, UK: Cambridge University Press, 1999).

problem for the United Kingdom than it was a solution.[2] The U.S.-led Bretton Woods system went through a similar period of decline in the 1960s, with mounting costs for the center state.[3] The Communauté financière d'Afrique (CFA) franc zone has not declined in the same way, but, on the other hand, it has not brought any appreciable new resources to France other than the intangible prestige of its existence.[4] Maintaining the post-Soviet ruble zone was such a drain on Russia that the Russian government essentially abandoned the attempt within two years.[5] U.S. reluctance to endorse a formal dollar area in Latin America seems similarly to be based on fears that codification of existing practices would be more of a burden than a benefit.[6]

Certainly Kirshner fulfills his goal of demonstrating the existence of currency coercion within these zones of what he calls "monetary dependence." But a more complete picture of currency areas, which includes both regional currencies (e.g., the euro or the franc zone) and the use of a leading currency internationally (e.g., the dollar area), must flesh out exactly who is coercing whom and under what circumstances. The central theme of this chapter is that, at least under some conditions, great-power currency areas may constitute a greater liability than an asset to their leaders. In other words, monetary statecraft is a reciprocal process: the creation and maintenance of currency areas creates influence opportunities for both followers and leaders.

Why are currency areas potentially problematic? The basic economic idea behind the politics is clear enough—currency issue is an asset when others are buying but a liability when they start selling. Although the issuer gains real resources in return for its currency, it does so at the cost of increasing potential future claims against itself; getting others to accept your IOU is a benefit that can become a burden if too many IOUs come due at the same time. Depending on institutional arrangements and on market conditions, currency areas may therefore burden rather than benefit even the issuers of significant international currencies. No study of the opportunities for influence created by currency issue should forget the corresponding constraints. Benjamin Cohen makes this point in a discussion of monetary insulation:

> Latitude for the issuing government is apt to be greatest . . . in the earliest stages of cross-border use, when its money is most popular. . . . Over time, however, policy will

2. Classic studies are Benjamin J. Cohen, *The Future of Sterling as an International Currency* (London: Macmillan, 1971); Susan Strange, *Sterling and British Policy: A Political Study of an International Currency in Decline* (London: Oxford University Press, 1971).

3. For an account making good use of primary sources, see Francis J. Gavin, *Gold, Dollars, and Power: The Politics of International Monetary Relations, 1959–1971* (Chapel Hill: University of North Carolina Press, 2004).

4. Kirshner, *Currency and Coercion*, 156.

5. John Lloyd, "Currency Change Puts Pressure on Republics," *Financial Times*, July 28, 1993, Lexis-Nexis, accessed October 30, 2002; Rawi Abdelal, *National Purpose in the World Economy: Post-Soviet States in Comparative Perspective* (Ithaca: Cornell University Press, 2001), 51–54.

6. Benjamin Cohen, "US Policy on Dollarization: A Political Analysis," *Geopolitics* 7, no. 1 (2002): 63–84. Postwar Germany and Japan were initially reluctant to allow the international use of their currencies for similar reasons; Cohen, *Future of Money*, 38.

be increasingly constrained by the need to discourage sudden or substantial conversions into other currencies. Ultimately, effective political power may on balance be decreased rather than increased—precisely the reverse of the conventional wisdom regarding the political value of hegemony.[7]

Building on the contributions of both Cohen and Kirshner, this chapter aims to elaborate the conditions under which leverage shifts from the currency issuer to currency users. Put differently, I examine the politics of monetary statecraft within currency areas.

There are two types of limits that a currency area can place on its leader: market limits and institutional limits. Most important, market forces deeply condition the most basic tool of monetary statecraft available to the leader of a currency area—its potential to recruit or expel participants from that arrangement. In particular, the political significance of the leader's threat to expel the follower—or, vice versa, of the follower's threat to exit—depends on the relative costs each actor thinks are likely to ensue. The leader must weigh not only the prospective loss of enforcement, extraction, and entrapment resources but also the possibility—to extend the metaphor of boat rocking introduced by Thomas Schelling—that the follower's departure will destabilize or even capsize the boat.[8] For their part, followers must weigh the loss of membership perks, both direct and indirect. For both, a crucial consideration is how the follower's economy would fare outside the currency area. Most analyses rely on the premise that the follower has the weaker position because it needs the area more than the area needs it. But there is no ex ante reason to believe that the follower will always be weaker—and there are plenty of examples to suggest the opposite, as this chapter demonstrates.

A second type of limit placed on a currency area's leader derives from the institutional arrangements of the currency area because these rules provide the basic parameters for bargaining. Formalized symmetric rules tend to guarantee a greater share of the benefits for followers and thus to place limits on the leader's potential for extraction. Rules that delegate some functions to third-party monetary institutions also reduce the leader's power. Less formalized systems, or systems that incorporate asymmetric rules, tend to give the leader greater scope for throwing its weight around. Of course, symmetric rules are a weak barrier to a leader determined to extract resources. But both theory and history suggest that the formal rules of currency areas may prove at least a temporary constraint on the actions of the leading state.

As a result, even currency areas with asymmetric rules that are led by great powers create not so much monetary dependence as monetary *inter*dependence. Both leaders and followers are to some extent dependent on the currency area for insulation from the larger monetary world (i.e., the power to delay adjustment), and that

---

7. Cohen, *Geography of Money*, 129; see also Cohen, *Future of Sterling*, 38–41.

8. On enforcement, extraction, and entrapment, see Kirshner, *Currency and Coercion*, 116–18. On boat rocking, see Thomas Schelling, *Arms and Influence* (New Haven: Yale University Press, 1966), 99, and Kirshner's application of this concept in *Currency and Coercion*, 172.

interdependence creates leverage on both sides. Recognizing this fact allows us to explore the conditions under which followers may have more bargaining power than leaders, at least with respect to particular issues. As a more general matter, careful consideration of the limits of monetary power is necessary to fully appreciate the dynamics of monetary statecraft.

This chapter is divided into four parts. The first section defines basic concepts while reviewing Kirshner's theory of the exploitation of monetary dependence, including his discussion of the limits of that exploitation. The second and third sections examine how currency areas condition the power of leaders relative to followers, focusing on market limits (generated by the relative costs of the follower's exit or expulsion from the area) and institutional limits (generated by the currency area's rules). The fourth section concludes.

Monetary Dependence and Its Limits

To begin with, some definitions are in order. Cohen differentiates between currency areas, which are products of formal, state-to-state action linking currencies or exchange rates, and currency regions, which exist whenever a country's currency is widely used beyond the boundaries of the country.[9] Kirshner's study of monetary dependence includes both currency areas (e.g., the sterling area and the franc zone) and currency regions (e.g., Latin American dollarization). In this study, I follow Kirshner by including both types of arrangements, referring to the entire set of cases by the more common term, currency areas. One contribution of the present study, however, is the explicit recognition that (formalized) currency areas and (informal) currency regions may create different configurations of power. Varying levels of rule formalization are an important part of the analysis that follows.

Currency areas also range on a continuum between symmetric and asymmetric ideal types with respect to their decision-making procedures. In this context, symmetry can be defined as the degree of shared control over seigniorage, interest rates, money supply, and so forth. I include attention to the entire continuum of control arrangements while noting that more symmetric rules give the leader less power by design. (Indeed, in a perfectly symmetrical currency region, there would no longer even be a leader, as the discussion here makes clear.) Attention to the entire range of decision-making arrangements is helpful because it facilitates comparisons among different types of currency areas. Because there is no natural cutoff point where a currency area's rules shift from symmetric to asymmetric, I treat the level of symmetry as a continuous variable.

For convenience and to be consistent with the rest of this volume, I use the terms *leader* and *followers* to refer to the members of the currency area. This use should not be taken to imply that the leader is always formally designated as such or that it

---

9. Benjamin Cohen, "The Political Economy of Currency Regions," in *The Political Economy of Regionalism*, ed. Helen Milner and Edward Mansfield, 50–76 (New York: Columbia University Press, 1997).

is necessarily the most powerful member in every specific circumstance. Instead, the leader is the state with the greatest control over decision making within the currency area, even though the central argument of this essay is that followers sometimes have greater influence over certain issues.

Kirshner's Model of Monetary Dependence

Kirshner provides the best elaborated model of monetary dependence in the literature. He defines the concept in terms of asymmetric economic vulnerability. The leader of the currency area has influence over smaller followers because they fear expulsion from the arrangement. Followers benefit from membership because it provides them with access to the accumulated credibility and prestige of the system, a degree of insulation from adverse trends in the international economy, and protection from currency manipulation by powerful states outside the area. Depending on the nature of the area, followers may also gain access to pooled reserves or balance-of-payments credit lines. Currency-area membership is also typically linked to other benefits for followers, such as economic aid, military safeguards, and preferential access to the home state's capital and goods markets. For all these reasons, followers may depend heavily on continued membership in the currency area.[10]

According to Kirshner, leaders exploit followers' dependence in four ways. First, they can enforce the rules of the system to sanction followers. For example, the leader might interrupt the flow of currency to a follower in order to convince it to change specific policies. Second, the leader can use the threat of expulsion to get a follower to change its behavior. Third, the leader may use its structural power within the area to extract concessions from followers.[11] Finally, the leader of the currency area also has indirect influence because followers' internal preferences are transformed by membership. For example, currency-area membership strengthens domestic interest groups in the follower that are closely tied to the leader. In a process Kirshner labels entrapment, followers' interests are changed over time from the inside.[12]

Kirshner also points out some of the limits of monetary power in a currency area. Leaders are loath to extract so many resources from followers that the latter opt out of the area. Leaders are similarly reluctant to threaten expulsion because the follower might in fact choose to leave the area and deny the leader future benefits. In fact, Kirshner argues that the structural benefits of extraction and entrapment are so valuable to the leader that it must carefully limit its own enforcement of the rules and threats of expulsion: "The practice of enforcement and expulsion risks tempting states to abandon the system. This would cause the core state to lose the power it derives from the very existence of the system."[13]

10. Kirshner, *Currency and Coercion*, 12–17.
11. For more on this subject, especially the notion that this constitutes an instance of structural power, see the discussion by Eric Helleiner (chap. 4 in this volume).
12. Kirshner, *Currency and Coercion*, 116–19.
13. Ibid., 117.

In addition, Kirshner argues that the level of monetary dependence varies according to global economic conditions and the nature of the bilateral relationship between the leader and the follower. During periods of general international prosperity, the follower's costs of exit from the currency area are lower. But when economic conditions outside the area are poor, "the greater the power of overt threats, and the more punishment will be tolerated without unilateral withdrawal from the system." Similarly, the economic and political relationships between the leader and follower condition the vulnerability of the follower. For example, militarily strong states may be able to bully weaker followers. Thus, Kirshner explicitly recognizes that monetary power has its limits (although he never systematically discusses those limits).[14]

Even so, Kirshner explicitly rejects the idea of interdependence in a currency area.[15] Drawing on the logic of Albert Hirschman, Kirshner notes that because the members of a currency area pool resources that all can draw on and because large states typically provide more resources than small states, the follower gains more from membership in the area than the leader.[16] Using pooled reserves as an example of the broader sharing of resources, Kirshner explains, "Given a two-state currency area, where country 1 provides $1 billion of reserves and imports $100 million a day; and country 2 provides $10 billion in reserves and imports $200 million worth per day, the magnitude of the asymmetry is actually twenty to one, not ten to one. If the area breaks up, country 1 loses a cushion of one hundred days, whereas country 2 loses a cushion of five days."[17] Thus, according to Kirshner, the key to the leader's leverage is that the follower state is far more dependent on the currency area than the leader.

It is no doubt true that small states do gain disproportionately from pooling resources with larger states. Thus, followers are more dependent on the pool, *ceteris paribus*—but all other things are *not* always equal. For example, if the leader is involved in a balance-of-payments crisis at a time when the follower enjoys healthy payments surpluses and strong foreign-exchange reserves, the leader may be unusually dependent on the follower state's reserves to delay adjustment by insulating the leader from global conditions. Under such circumstances, the costs to the follower of exiting the currency area would be low because it has the necessary resources to establish its currency outside the area. But for the leader, the follower's departure could be very harmful. Moreover, because currency markets are subject to herd behavior, the market reaction to the follower's departure could compound

14. Ibid., 119–21, 168, quotation on 120. Kirshner also points out that large followers may gain the ability to disrupt the currency area and that they could try to gain leverage from that ability. He acknowledges that systemic disruption is in some ways inversely related to the exploitation of monetary dependence, but argues that it is a weak tool for followers because it so difficult to implement successfully (275).

15. Ibid., 40.

16. Ibid., 13–15; Albert Hirschman, *National Power and the Structure of Foreign Trade* (Berkeley: University of California, 1945).

17. Kirshner, *Currency and Coercion*, 14–15. The "cushion" referred to is the number of import days covered by pooled reserves.

the problem far beyond the opportunity cost to the leader of lost access to the follower's currency reserves. Those problems could be further exacerbated if the follower decides to dispose of some of the leader's currency, held in the form of reserve assets. Thus, particular circumstances may nullify or even reverse the asymmetry between the leader and followers, even if asymmetrical interdependence clearly favors the larger state on average.

A simple historical example helps illustrate this principle. Although the sterling area provided important resources to Britain, effectively expanding Britain's power to delay adjustment, large sterling holders also had a degree of leverage over Britain. Thus at the time of Kuwait's independence in the early 1960s, Her Majesty's Treasury instructed British officials to encourage Kuwait to keep its existing sterling reserves but also not to increase them in the future. Kuwait's pro-Nasser foreign policy tendencies made it an uncertain prop under the British balance of payments, and British officials were opposed to Kuwait increasing its leverage by means of increased sterling holdings.[18] Kirshner provides a similar example in his discussion of Zambia's attempts to use its sterling balances to coerce Britain during the Rhodesian independence crisis. He classifies this as an example of systemic disruption, but both examples demonstrate clearly the reciprocal nature of monetary dependence: leaders as well as followers have much at stake in a currency area.[19]

The point is that, at least under certain conditions, leaders may find themselves ceding political leverage rather than obtaining it. The task is therefore to elucidate the conditions under which currency areas place limits on leaders and not just on followers. Put differently, what we need is not only a theory of monetary power (as offered by the chapters in part one of this volume) but a theory of monetary statecraft, and specifically of how currency areas reshape the relative influence of leaders and followers at particular times and with respect to particular issues. The best way to go about identifying limits placed on the leader is by looking at two primary factors: the relative costs of the follower's exit, or market limits; and the currency area's rules, or institutional limits.

Market Limits

The first key to understanding the relative power of the leader and follower is to look at the relative costs to the leader and follower if the follower exits the area. A twist on Kirshner's use of the lifeboat analogy is helpful here. In discussing the form of monetary power he labels "systemic disruption," Kirshner compares a monetary system to a lifeboat with one passenger rocking the boat in a way that risks capsizing it. The passenger's goal is not to capsize the boat but to manipulate the risk of

18. UK Public Records Office, Treasury 317/24, A. Mackay, 16 March 1961.
19. Kirshner, *Currency and Coercion*, 203–12. Notice that neither example suggests that followers are immune from monetary dependence. Any Kuwaiti threat to sell its sterling reserves would have been limited by the fact that the attempt to sell would have lowered the value of its own sterling as well as Britain's. The examples simply suggest that the relationship is reciprocal.

capsizing to increase his own relative influence. Systemic disruption, however, is but one of several techniques available to follower states in their efforts to extract policy concessions from the leader. Furthermore, as Kirshner points out, the utility of this technique is limited: if the leader is weak enough and the passenger (follower) strong enough that boat rocking gets the leader's attention, the likelihood of capsizing is very high, which defeats the boat rocker's intention of extracting concessions within the existing system.[20]

For a more complete understanding of monetary statecraft within currency areas, we should focus instead on the more significant threats of exit and expulsion. That is, who would lose more if the passenger jumped (or was pushed) overboard? The answer depends on the benefits accruing to the leader and the passenger while both are safely inside the boat. Is that boat a dinghy or a yacht? If the former, is the passenger good with the oars? How well can the passenger swim? How dangerous are the waters? On average, the follower's exit is probably more costly to that participant than it is to the leader. However, in some circumstances, the follower's exit threat may be more powerful than the leader's threat to expel. Three types of issues will shape this calculation: membership costs and benefits, the relative need for insulation, and domestic politics.[21]

Membership Costs and Benefits

The first such issue is the flow of costs and benefits within the currency area. As Kirshner emphasizes, even when power flows generally to the leader, economic benefits may be flowing in the opposite direction.[22] A clear example is the West African CFA franc zone, which entitles members to overdraft privileges at the French Treasury, preferential access to French markets for capital and goods, military protection against external and internal enemies, and various forms of aid and technical expertise.[23] Likewise, members of the ruble zone gained access to Russian markets for

20. Kirshner, *Currency and Coercion*, 170–215. As mentioned earlier, Kirshner's conception of boat rocking (see especially 172) explicitly builds on Schelling's discussion about "manipulating the *shared* risk." Schelling, *Arms and Influence*, 99.

21. A fourth consideration is the transitional cost to the follower of its own departure; see Benjamin J. Cohen (chap. 2 in this volume) for a discussion of the distinction between continuing and transitional costs. Depending on the nature of the arrangement, this may include such costs as issuing a new currency, backing that currency with reserves, creating a new central bank, and rewriting foreign-exchange regulations. Although these are essentially one-off costs, some very poor states may have trouble paying them and therefore be deterred from exiting a currency area. On the other hand, many small poor states have their own currencies, so transitional costs generally should not be seen as an insurmountable barrier. Moreover, again depending on the nature of the currency area, there might be corresponding benefits (such as new seigniorage revenues or a stronger national identity) that help balance these transitional costs.

22. The leader may actually be making economic sacrifices in order to gain leverage over the follower and insulation from the global economy; see Kirshner, *Currency and Coercion*, 13, 168. Cohen, in "Beyond EMU," also emphasizes the benefits provided by the leader as a key condition for the sustainability of most currency areas.

23. James Boughton, "The CFA Franc: Zone of Fragile Stability in Africa," *Finance & Development* 29, no. 4 (1992): 34–36; James Boughton, "The CFA Franc Zone: Currency Union and Monetary Stan-

their goods and to subsidized energy resources—by one estimate, ruble-zone members paid only 2 percent of the world market price for oil in early 1992 (and even then often defaulted on payments).[24] Some ruble-zone members also gained military support as a side benefit, as suggested by the 25,000 Russian troops stationed in Tajikistan in the wake of the Tajik civil war. Generous benefits to the follower make it less likely to leave the area, which is precisely why leaders offer such benefits. Leaders may, in effect, trade economic benefits for political leverage. The relative generosity or stinginess of those benefits should be a key consideration for followers.

The sterling area after the Basle reform of 1968 provides an extreme example of the lengths to which leaders sometimes go in order to keep members in the currency area. Sterling-area members pledged to keep an agreed percentage of their currency reserves in sterling in return for a British guarantee of the dollar value of those reserves. Britain had been repeatedly pressed by sterling-area members for such guarantees in the past, but had successfully resisted until the Basle negotiations. Beginning in 1968, however, Britain pledged to maintain the dollar value of 90 percent of each country's official sterling reserves. The formal quid pro quo demonstrated the extent to which Britain was dependent on the sterling area's nominal followers.[25]

Balancing these membership benefits are accompanying costs, including whatever resources the leader is able to extract from members and the diversion of resources that results from entrapment. For example, followers in the franc zone must submit to varying levels of French oversight on macroeconomic management, limits on trade outside the franc zone, potential interference in domestic politics by French troops, and so on. Sometimes, of course, the net benefits to the follower are negative rather than positive. For the Baltic states, cheap Russian oil and access to huge Russian markets in no way compensated for the ruinously inflationary ruble and— most important of all—the risk of being reintegrated into the Russian sphere of influence after a half century of involuntary association. From the perspective of the Baltic states, the ruble zone was a dinghy, not a yacht, and their decisions to leave the ruble zone as soon as possible—even before permanent currencies were printed in Latvia and Lithuania—was therefore hardly surprising.[26]

For the leader, the follower's exit or expulsion raises a similar calculation. In gen-

---

dard," *Greek Economic Review* 15, no. 1 (1993): 267–312; James Boughton, "The Economics of the CFA Franc Zone," in *Policy Issues in the Operation of Currency Unions*, ed. Paul R. Mason and Mark P. Taylor, 96–107 (Cambridge, UK: Cambridge University Press, 1993); Francis Terry McNamara, *France in Black Africa* (Washington, D.C.: National Defense University Press, 1989), 110–27; Strange, *Sterling and British Policy*, 23–28. Kirshner also discusses this case in some detail, although he pays far more attention to Mali, which tried to escape but failed, than to Guinea, which managed to jump out and stay out. See Kirshner, *Currency and Coercion*, 148–56.

24. Daniel Sneider, "Energy Price Hike Marks Further Russian Reforms," *Christian Science Monitor*, May 20, 1992, Lexis-Nexis, accessed October 7, 2005; Martin Wolf, "Russia Rolls the Dice of Reform," *Financial Times*, May 14, 1992, Lexis-Nexis, accessed October 29, 2002; Richard Pomfret, The Economies of Central Asia (Princeton: Princeton University Press, 1995), 140–51; Richard Pomfret, *Asian Economies in Transition: Reforming Centrally Planned Economies* (Cheltenham, UK: Edward Elgar, 1996), 118–28.

25. Cohen, *Future of Sterling*, 78–79; Strange, *Sterling and British Policy*, 74–75.

26. Grant Spencer and Adrienne Cheasty, "The Ruble Area: A Breaking of Old Ties," *Finance & Development* 30, no. 2 (1993): 2–5; Peter Garber and Michael Spencer, *The Dissolution of the Austro-Hun-*

eral, leaders prefer that followers remain inside the currency area because of the various benefits that accrue to the leader via extraction, enforcement, and entrapment. The magnitude of those benefits depends heavily on the rules of the system and also on the follower's size and economic development. For France, the departure of resource-rich Ivory Coast or Gabon from the franc zone would be much harder to swallow than the departure of Togo. However, even when the follower's membership in the currency area provides resources to the leader, those advantages must be weighed against whatever costs the leader incurs to provide currency-area members with incentives for membership.

In short, for the leader as well as for the follower, the key issue is net benefits. For the leader, does the follower pull its weight relative to the perks necessary to keep it in the area? For the follower, do the benefits of membership outweigh the costs? These calculations will vary over time and from one country to the next.

Relative Need for Insulation

In addition to evaluating the relative benefits of membership, both leaders and followers must weigh conditions outside the currency area. One purpose of a currency area is to provide insulation against the global economy, which helps explain why currency areas were relatively popular in the 1930s and why Asian states increased their discussion of a yen bloc after the east Asian financial crisis of the late 1990s.[27] In times of global prosperity, jumping out of the lifeboat is less risky for followers. Other relevant external conditions include the available supply of other leading currencies and whether those alternative leaders are more inclined to offer help to, or to take advantage of, a prospective new follower. Is the ocean smooth or stormy? Are there lifeboats nearby, or just circling sharks?

For example, a number of countries that were closely associated with sterling in the early post–World War II years joined the de facto dollar area in the 1960s and 1970s; these included the states of the East Caribbean and the Persian Gulf. Jumping out of the British lifeboat was facilitated by the proximity of the U.S. one. Likewise, when Estonia left the ruble zone it immediately pegged its new currency to the deutschmark, trading one leader for another.

Less obviously, leaders themselves must consider the degree of damage to the currency area that would be done by the follower's departure. As David Andrews (chap. 5 in this volume) suggests, leaders benefit from the insulation the currency area provides against global economic conditions even if they need such insulation less, on average, than do their followers.[28] But a currency-area leader facing a balance-of-

---

garian Empire: Lessons for Currency Reform, Princeton Essays in International Finance no. 191 (Princeton: Princeton University Press, 1994).

27. See the discussions by C. Randall Henning (chap. 6) and Jonathan Kirshner (chap. 7 in this volume).

28. As Andrews (chap. 5 in this volume) explains, this is not simply because leaders can borrow reserve assets from bloc members; rather, it is primarily because the existence of the currency area makes leaders at least marginally less sensitive to exchange-rate movements with other major currencies, allowing them to tolerate such movements more easily rather than changing domestic policy.

payments crisis, for example, may need the continued support of other members of the currency area far more than does a smaller follower with relatively healthy finances. Worse still, the exit or expulsion of the follower may undermine the stability of the entire area. Unlike Kirshner's notion of systemic disruption, in which the follower rocks the boat to gain leverage but prefers to stay in the lifeboat, some followers actually prefer to exit and may, intentionally or unintentionally, destabilize the boat as they jump out. For example, whereas Guinea's departure did not damage the franc zone appreciably, Ukraine's departure from the ruble zone sorely weakened that currency area and Australia's exit from the sterling area would have devastated the area in the 1960s. In short, relatively large followers may provide resources to the currency area that are crucial for its continued vitality and may damage the arrangement simply by the act of leaving.

It was Susan Strange who demonstrated the degree of Britain's dependence during the 1960s on six states with especially large sterling holdings: Australia, Malaysia, Kuwait, Libya, Hong Kong, and Ireland. A decision by any one of these states to convert its sterling balances to dollars would have substantially reduced Britain's ability to delay adjustment, thereby undermining the pound. Even worse, a sterling sell-off by one state would probably have touched off a market panic as other states and market actors rushed to unload their sterling first. Officials at the Treasury and the Bank of England constantly reminded political officers of the important support provided by newly independent colonies to the British balance of payments, and during the 1950s and 1960s British officials at all levels worked to keep former colonies solidly within the sterling area. Strange notes pointedly that the "major interest in avoiding a break-up [of the sterling area] during [the 1960s] was Britain's," not Britain's followers. She quotes Prime Minister Harold Wilson's November 1964 statement on the political importance Britain attached to the sterling area: "To turn our backs on the sterling area would mean a body-blow to the Commonwealth and all it stands for."[29]

In one particularly interesting case, the Wilson government tried in early 1966 to coerce Malaysia into negotiating a monetary union with Singapore. This coercive threat backfired when Malaysia responded with a threat to pull out of the sterling area. Malaysian finance minister Tan Siew Sin noted pointedly that his country was the largest net dollar earner in the Commonwealth and that it had kept its reserves in sterling "out of sheer loyalty . . . though at some risk to ourselves." The Malaysian government also stoked a harsh anti-British press campaign that hardened domestic public opinion and made it difficult for pro-British voices to be heard—an instance of a follower state successfully blocking efforts by the leader to rearticulate its domestic interests.[30] Because Malaysia's sterling reserves amounted to US$1 billion (or 14 percent of Britain's net liabilities to sterling-area countries), converting Malaysian sterling to dollars would have had disastrous consequences for Britain's

29. Strange, *Sterling and British Policy*, 74–128, quotations on 89.
30. For a discussion of the capacity of monetary relations to rearticulate actor interests and even to reconstruct actor identities, see David M. Andrews (chap. 1) and Eric Helleiner (chap. 4 in this volume). UK Public Records Office, Dominions Office 169/349/5, 27 Jun 66.

balance of payments, which was already under stress. As Tan Siew Sin explained shortly after the diplomatic crisis, "If we had effected such a move, it could well have tipped the scales against sterling in view of its admittedly precarious position." British decision makers quickly decided that their attempted coercion had been "counterproductive," dropped their previous demands, and retreated to a position of neutrality in the Malaysia-Singapore negotiations. They even began to publicly assert that they had never attempted to coerce Malaysia in the first place (despite a substantial paper trail to the contrary).[31]

In effect, Britain recognized that, at that moment of British weakness, Malaysia would survive better without the sterling area than the sterling area would survive without Malaysia.[32] More recently, Persian Gulf states have provided support to the U.S. dollar by holding the bulk of their reserves in dollars, holding financial assets abroad in dollar-denominated accounts, and pricing oil in dollars. Over the years, members have occasionally discussed punishing the United States for its foreign policy or for its depreciating currency by pricing oil in another currency. Such an action might not have catastrophic effects on the U.S. economy, but it would produce a sufficiently large effect to make the threat noticed in Washington.[33]

Calculations along these lines are complicated, however, because the exiting state might suffer collateral damage as a result of its own departure. Returning to the example of sterling in the 1960s, the six follower states had sterling holdings that were so large as to be partially self-deterring: any attempt to sell their sterling reserves suddenly and in bulk would have touched off a market panic drastically lowering the value of their own assets. Similarly, Persian Gulf states understood that weakening the dollar would also undermine the value of their own abundant dollar-denominated financial assets, and, even more important, weaken security ties to the United States.[34]

Even so, decision makers in London and Washington could not take such threats lightly. Thomas Schelling's analysis of threats and crisis bargaining explains why. For one thing, followers might in some circumstances be angry enough to take actions that would be economically irrational. As Schelling puts it, in order to make a threat credible "it does not always help to be, or to be believed to be, fully rational, cool-headed, and in control of oneself." Similarly, threats sometimes succeed precisely because the target is afraid the risks will get out of hand. "The fact of uncer-

31. UK Public Records Office, Dominions Office [DO] 169/431/462, 23 Apr 66; DO 169/431/476, 17 May 66; DO 169/431/487, 20 May 66; DO 169/431/489A, 23 May 66. For context, see Scott Cooper, "Third World Monetary Blocs: Small State Choice or Great Power Hegemony?" paper prepared for Annual Meetings of the International Studies Association, Montreal, March 17–20, 2004.

32. At the end of 1965, Britain's net sterling liabilities amounted to $7.3 billion with regard to sterling-area countries and $13.6 billion with regard to all countries and international organizations; Strange, *Sterling and British Policy,* 81.

33. "Call to Delink Gulf Currencies from Dollar," *Moneyclips,* March 11, 1995, Lexis-Nexis, accessed October 7, 2005; Xinhua News Agency, "Gulf States Consider to End Dollar Link," February 26, 1998, Lexis-Nexis, accessed October 7, 2005.

34. Scott Cooper, "State-centric Balance-of-Threat Theory: Explaining the Misunderstood Gulf Cooperation Council," *Security Studies* 13, no. 2 (2003–2004): 306–49.

tainty—the sheer unpredictability of dangerous events—not only blurs things, it changes their character."[35] In the case of Malaysia, regardless of whether the finance minister's threat made good economic sense, it was powerful because of the danger that the Malaysian government might, intentionally or accidentally, capsize the boat protecting sterling from global markets. The British were highly concerned about either possibility and chose to deescalate the situation rather than risk a mutually disastrous outcome.

Finally, as Kirshner (chap. 7 in this volume) argues, the globalization of financial markets only increases the appeal of regional blocs as providers of insulation. Accelerating capital mobility affects both leaders and followers, although smaller followers are at greater risk in the rougher waters of a globalized world. But there are risks for large states as well, perhaps best evidenced by the European exchange-rate crisis of 1992. As a result, the assessment of leaders' and followers' changing demand for insulation is likely to be of increasing importance in the political analysis of currency areas.[36]

Domestic Politics

A final element of the bargaining calculus concerns the domestic political consequences of exit and expulsion. In fact, all the considerations discussed so far must be filtered through some domestic political process as leaders and followers weigh costs and benefits; these calculations matter to the extent that they influence key domestic interests and constituencies.[37] For example, membership benefits may flow to groups with privileged access to government leaders, and insulation may be a high priority for finance officials within the government. Here I treat domestic politics as a separate category simply to emphasize that these issues cannot be handled as an exercise in cost-benefit accounting between abstract unitary actors; issues such as who benefits and who pays matter at the domestic level just as they do internationally.

Domestic political considerations are especially important for followers because currency areas are designed to entrap them, reorienting domestic interests toward the leader's economy. Over time, some important local financial and commercial interests are likely to have developed such attachments and will presumably resist any effort to jump ship—an example of rearticulation (see Andrews, chap. 1 in this volume). At the same time, we should not overstate this factor because, in some circumstances, domestic political interests might equally well push the follower away

35. Schelling, *Arms and Influence*, 37, 94.

36. On the causes and consequences of increased capital mobility, see John Goodman and Louis Pauly, "The Obsolescence of Capital Controls?" *World Politics* 46, no. 1 (1993): 50–82; David Andrews, "Capital Mobility and State Autonomy: Toward a Structural Theory of International Monetary Relations," *International Studies Quarterly* 38, no. 2 (1994): 193–218; Eric Helleiner, *States and the Re-emergence of Global Finance: From Bretton Woods to the 1990s* (Ithaca: Cornell, 1994); Susan Strange, *Mad Money: When Markets Outgrow Governments* (Ann Arbor: University of Michigan Press, 1998).

37. Andrew Walter (chap. 3), Henning (chap. 6), and Louis W. Pauly (chap. 9 in this volume) pay particularly close attention to how policy is filtered through domestic institutions.

from the currency area. Many a government has scored political points by targeting powerfully entrenched domestic financial and commercial interests, especially when controlled by unpopular minorities or expatriate communities (consider the experience of ethnic Chinese in Southeast Asia or of Jews in many places). The crucial issue is not how large the leader-oriented domestic sector in the follower is but how important it is to the government's political fortunes.

In addition, the domestic actor forced to sacrifice the most in a currency-area institution is typically the follower government itself, which loses a significant tool for domestic economic adjustment. Control of domestic monetary policy allows governments to respond to economic disturbances in order to minimize political fallout (even if such attempts fail or backfire). In a currency zone, this tool is diminished, if not abandoned. A follower government also typically reduces its immediate control over foreign-exchange reserves, which limits its flexibility in a crisis. Finally, the government often loses a significant political symbol by subordinating its currency to the leader's. As a result of all these factors, we should expect followers to remain attached to the currency area only as long as the benefits to the government or its important political constituents outweigh these significant constraints on its autonomy.

Similarly, there may also be political interests within the leader that are reluctant to see the follower leave the currency area. Because the leader is usually much larger than the follower, these follower-oriented interest groups are likely to be less important than leader-oriented groups within the follower. But David Stasavage's analysis of the franc zone demonstrates the possible impact of such groups. He shows that French commitment to subsidizing franc-zone members over the past forty years has been crucially influenced by a small group of individuals within the French presidency and executive bureaucracy with a vested interest in maintaining the franc zone. Only as that group declined in importance in the early 1990s were the French willing to cut back on the expanding stream of subsidies to franc-zone followers.[38] Thus, leaders as well as followers may have domestic political incentives to resist exit or expulsion.

Given these varying domestic political circumstances, the politics of currency areas are likely to be complex, with rising attention to institutional rules (as discussed in the next section).

Institutional Limits

The second link between currency areas and the leader's power is the set of rules that governs the area. It may seem unusual to discuss rules as a limit on power—those rules are in part a function of underlying power relationships between leaders and followers, and we expect the leader to ensure that the rules of the area are writ-

38. David Stasavage, *The Political Economy of a Common Currency: The CFA Franc Zone since 1945* (Aldershot, UK: Ashgate, 2003).

ten and interpreted to meet its own particular needs. Nevertheless, rules may in practice have causal impact on power relationships for at least three reasons.

First, bloc rules tend to regulate the leader's power to deflect transitional adjustment costs onto followers, but even strong leaders may need to agree to rule-based limits on this power as a condition for followers to join the institution. The leader may agree ex ante to certain constraints on future behavior in exchange for followers' acceptance of more significant constraints. Conscious of the shadow of the future, the leader may even comply with currency-area rules that disadvantage it at a particular point in time, calculating that the long-term results will be more favorable.[39]

Second, because leaders are unlikely to anticipate all future contingencies that will affect their interests, it is possible that the same rules that the leader initially approved will at a future date prove unwelcome to the leader. Alternatively, changes in government may bring in new decision makers with different preferences. Even if we assume that the rules will be written to favor the currency leader, problems of uncertainty, turnover, and incomplete contracting make it likely that the rules will occasionally counter the leader's current interests.

Third, the relative power of leaders and followers changes over time both because of changes in costs of exit (as discussed in the previous section) and because of changes in underlying openness and adaptability (as discussed by Cohen, chap. 2 in this volume). As power relationships fluctuate, the leader may find at a particular moment that its ability to bend the rules to its favor is lower than expected. Or, in a moment of weakness, the leader may find itself complying with rules initially intended to limit followers.

For these reasons, the rules of the currency area can be a potential constraint on leaders as well as followers. Of course, the rules are unlikely to constrain leaders indefinitely. As the costs of compliance rise, we expect the leader to use its underlying power to reinterpret or renegotiate rules to fit its interests more closely. In the end, we expect the leader to abandon any rule-based system that proves overly constraining relative to its costs of exit. For these reasons, currency-area rules are likely to be only a temporary constraint on the leader's power. But they are nonetheless a constraint.

Because the nature of the rules varies dramatically across currency areas, we can differentiate among three characteristics that affect the level of constraint on currency-area leaders: the degree of formalization, the degree of symmetry in decision making, and the role of third-party agents.

Formalization

The first distinction is whether the rules are primarily formal or informal. Sometimes the rules are highly formalized by multilateral or bilateral international trea-

---

39. G. John Ikenberry, *After Victory: Institutions, Strategic Restraint, and the Rebuilding of Order after Major War* (Princeton: Princeton University Press, 2001).

ties, as in the Bretton Woods system or the franc zone, respectively. At other times, the rules are less formal and more heavily based on past practice rather than on specific agreements—for example, the dollar area today or the rand area before 1974. Even the most formalized rules, however, rarely codify all aspects of the currency-area relationship (such as the level of side payments) that matter to participants. For example, the former Soviet ruble zone gave the Central Bank of Russia a clearly defined monopoly on currency issue, but was ambiguous about the conditions for delivering currency notes to the other national central banks. This ambiguity gave Russia a significant lever for influence because it could—and did—link the delivery of currency notes to other economic and political objectives. In addition, one key benefit of ruble-zone membership was access to Russian energy at subsidized prices, but the exact nature and price of that access varied over time, at Russia's discretion.[40] Similarly, the postwar sterling area included precise rules about reserve pooling and especially exchange control, but the amount of development and military aid Britain would provide to members was determined on an ad hoc and continuously negotiated basis. Thus, even formalized currency areas are marked by significant ambiguity and therefore require interpretation and negotiation.

Because we expect the largest economy to benefit most from negotiation, less formalized rule systems generally place fewer limits on area leaders. However, it should be emphasized that rules are only one restraint on power in a currency area. We should not expect those rules to completely constrain powerful states that have an interest in violating them. Powerful states may fail to comply with the rules or may use their power to adopt new rules more to their liking. Even in these cases, however, formally specified rules raise the costs to powerful states of pursuing their narrow self-interest. As a result, formalized rules tilt the playing field more toward followers than would otherwise be the case.

An example arises in the context of the European Union's Economic and Monetary Union (EMU), specifically the recent debate about whether Germany and France should be held to the same formal rules (i.e., the Stability and Growth Pact) as were the smaller states of Ireland and Portugal. Although, in fact, the rules were unequally applied, the case suggests that rules can raise the costs of leaders' behavior even if the leader is only weakly constrained. The very fact that members of the euro area engaged in a public argument about whether Germany and France were pursuing allowable economic policies, but members of the dollar area have not debated U.S. behavior in any parallel fashion, is evidence of the constraining role of rules.

A stronger example is the leading role of the United States in the Bretton Woods monetary system from its creation in 1944 until its collapse in the early 1970s.

40. Good descriptions of the ruble zone and its collapse include Spencer and Cheasty, "The Ruble Area"; Garber and Spencer, *Dissolution of the Austro-Hungarian Empire;* International Monetary Fund, *World Economic Outlook* (Washington, DC: IMF, 1993), 65–68; Patrick Conway, *Currency Proliferation: The Monetary Legacy of the Soviet Union,* Princeton Essays in International Finance no. 197 (Princeton: Princeton University Press, 1995); Abdelal, *National Purpose in the World Economy,* 45–75.

Despite the fact that the United States was, along with Britain, a key architect of the system, the dollar-exchange standard became increasingly uncomfortable for the United States as confidence in the dollar declined in the 1960s. Because the United States was unwilling to tighten its belt domestically and because it could not devalue its currency within the system without the acquiescence of its partners—acquiescence that was not forthcoming—the fixed exchange-rate system left the dollar overvalued and placed a high burden on U.S. exports. On the one hand, the fact that the United States tolerated these burdens for so long—throughout much of the 1960s up until August 1971—is evidence that formalized rules can reshape the behavior of even powerful states. Rather than ignoring the rules, the United States attempted to interpret the rules to its own advantage and to attain support for modifying the rules. On the other hand, that the United States in the end solved its dilemma unilaterally by breaking out of the system is evidence that formalized rules are an imperfect barrier to a determined leader.[41] Although formalization places more effective limits on leaders than do informal rules, it does not make those limits perfectly effective.

Decision-Making Symmetry

Second, currency-area rules can be differentiated according to how symmetrically they distribute decision-making control over questions concerning money supply, the distribution of seigniorage, external exchange rates, capital controls, and so on. As discussed previously, we can think of a continuum between perfectly asymmetrical and symmetrical end points and use this framework to compare arrangements within a region over time. For example, the South African rand zone was almost perfectly asymmetrical before 1974 because South Africa completely controlled the issue of currency in all four members (South Africa, Botswana, Lesotho, and Swaziland). But as the zone was formalized starting in 1974, it also became less asymmetrical. South Africa ceded greater control to the other members by allowing them the option of circulating their own parallel currencies and agreed to share seigniorage revenues with the smaller currency-area members according to their share of currency circulation. It did not, however, grant followers direct influence over the rand itself, which was issued solely by the South African Central Bank.[42] Among contemporary currency areas, the East Caribbean dollar (issued by the East

41. Even Gilpin, a well-known proponent of power-centered explanations, acknowledges Bretton Woods as a temporary constraint on the United States; Robert Gilpin, *The Political Economy of International Relations* (Princeton: Princeton University Press, 1987), 131–42.

42. On the several variants of the rand area, see John Stuart, *The Economics of the Common Monetary Area in Southern Africa* (Durban, South Africa: Economic Research Unit, University of Natal, 1992), 60–81; Mats Lundahl and Lennart Petersson, *The Dependent Economy: Lesotho and the Southern African Customs Union* (Boulder: Westview Press, 1991), 271–317; Colin McCarthy, "SACU and the Rand Zone," in *Regionalisation in Africa: Integration and Disintegration*, ed. Daniel C. Bach, 159–68 (Oxford: James Currey, 1999). Note that sharing seigniorage does not require symmetrical control. South Africa could have given its followers a share of the currency profits without also giving them some control over their domestic money supply.

Caribbean Central Bank) and Europe's EMU are the most symmetrical; unlike the rand zone, both involve shared control of the currency-issuing central bank.[43] Other highly symmetrical currency areas have involved separate central banks issuing interchangeable currencies, as in the East African monetary union of the late 1960s and the Scandinavian Monetary Union of the late nineteenth century.[44]

Recall that *symmetry* is defined here in terms of decision-making control, not economic or political outcomes. As Kirshner emphasizes, even in an asymmetrically governed system, economic resources may actually be flowing from the leader to the follower. Nor does formal control over decision making within the currency area necessarily give the leader practical power in all circumstances.[45] At the same time, there is a straightforward causal link between the degree of decision-making symmetry and actual power. The leader is often able to decide the issues over which it has the predominant voice—for example, money supply, interest rate policy, and exchange-rate policy—in a way that deflects the transitional burdens of adjustment away from itself and on to its followers. How this is accomplished varies according to the nature of the currency system, but examples are plentiful.

For instance, during World War II the British used their control over the sterling bloc's pooled reserves to slow the transfer of reserves outside the currency area until more than a decade after the war. The power to freeze sterling balances was not part of its ex ante portfolio of decision-making prerogatives but was instead a mechanism Britain seized on as a result of its established control over pooled reserves. Britain's blocking of balances had the effect of limiting followers' trade outside the sterling area, thereby tying followers more closely to the leader than they were before.[46] France in the 1980s and early 1990s used its decision-making control over the reserves of the West African franc zone in a somewhat different manner. Despite the

---

43. On the East Caribbean, see Cohen, "Beyond EMU"; E. Eustace Liburd, "Aspects of Multinational Central Banking in the OECS," in *The Experience of Central Banking with Special Reference to the Caribbean,* ed. Ramesh F. Ramsaran, 47–57 (Mona, Jamaica: Regional Programme of Monetary Studies, University of the West Indies, 1995); Novelette Davis-Panton, "Issues Relating to the Central Bank's Autonomy in Jamaica," in *The Experience of Central Banking with Special Reference to the Caribbean,* ed. Ramesh F. Ramsaran, 58–86 (Mona, Jamaica: Regional Programme of Monetary Studies, University of the West Indies, 1995). The many good descriptions of EMU include Horst Ungerer, *A Concise History of European Monetary Integration: From EPU to EMU* (Westport: Quorum Books, 1997), 199–255, 273–92; Emmanuel Apel, *European Monetary Integration: 1958–2002* (London: Routledge, 1998), 94–156; Kenneth Dyson, *Elusive Union: The Process of Economic and Monetary Union in Europe* (London: Longman, 1994), 112–73.

44. On East Africa, see Scott Cooper and Clark Asay, "Regional Currencies in Africa: The Domestic Politics of Institutional Survival or Dissolution," *Perspectives on Global Development and Technology* 2, no. 15 (2003): 131–60. On the Scandinavian Monetary Union, see Michael Bergman, Stefan Gerlach, and Lars Jonung, "The Rise and Fall of the Scandinavian Currency Union 1873–1920," *European Economic Review* 37 (1993): 507–17; Lars Jonung, "Swedish Experience under the Classical Gold Standard," in *A Retrospective on the Classical Gold Standard, 1821–1931, ed.* Michael Bordo and Anna Schwartz, 361–404 (Chicago: University of Chicago, 1984); Cohen, "Beyond EMU."

45. In other words, I treat symmetry as an independent variable and political power as the dependent variable.

46. Kirshner, *Currency and Coercion,* 143–46. It also had the effect of driving some followers, such as Egypt, completely out of the area.

franc zone's formal limits on lending to member states, France chose to funnel extra funds to client states in West Africa that were suffering serious balance-of-payments problems. Because the French Treasury managed franc-zone accounts, France was able to unilaterally bypass franc-zone rules (albeit with the hearty approval of impoverished African governments) to infuse liquidity into the system. However, when France unilaterally decided to reverse course in 1994, franc-zone governments were forced to accept a substantial currency devaluation.[47] In both cases, asymmetric control over currency-area decision making translated into broad power over monetary and political outcomes.

By way of contrast, currency areas with more symmetrical rules have reduced the leader's power over parallel outcomes, at least temporarily. For example, the initial design of the ruble zone—although far from the symmetrical ideal—nevertheless distributed decisions about credit creation fairly symmetrically across the fifteen national central banks. The various central banks quite predictably engaged in massive credit creation that undermined Russia's control of its ruble money supply. As a result, Russia eventually used its other powers to rewrite the currency area's rules unilaterally, demanding greater control over credit creation from followers that wanted to stay inside the ruble zone.[48] Similarly, the Scandinavian Monetary Union was highly symmetrical in allowing each of the national central banks of Sweden, Norway, and Denmark authority to issue gold coins and gold-backed currency notes. As the union was breaking down during World War I, the symmetry of the union worked to the disadvantage of Sweden, which continued to honor its previous agreements by exchanging devalued Danish and Norwegian notes and gold coins at parity. Despite its status as "first among equals," Sweden's lack of asymmetrical control over currency issue within the union effectively limited its control over its domestic money supply. Not surprisingly, however, Sweden's patience with such conditions was short-lived, and Stockholm eventually forced the disintegration of the union.[49]

In sum, symmetrical decision-making control, although hardly a perfect constraint, does reduce the leader's ability to derive benefits from the currency area and may even cause the leader to shoulder unexpected costs. The Russian and Swedish examples also reemphasize the limits of formally symmetric rules as a constraint on leading states: in the end, both leaders chose to force the disintegration of the union, much as the United States dismantled the dollar-exchange standard. Nevertheless, decision-making symmetry provided a temporary constraint on even relatively strong leaders.

Third-Party Agents

Third, the rules of some currency areas delegate functions to institutions that may be difficult for the leader to control. Some currency areas include a third-party

---

47. Stasavage, *Political Economy of a Common Currency,* 39–44.

48. Garber and Spencer, *Dissolution of the Austro-Hungarian Empire;* Spencer and Cheasty, "Ruble Area"; Abdelal, *National Purpose in the World Economy,* 45–59, 68–70.

49. Bergman, Gerlach, and Jonung, "Rise and Fall," 513–16; Cohen, "Beyond EMU," 199.

monetary institution such as a supranational central bank or currency board that is not wholly under any state's control. Ceteris paribus, we would expect such institutions to respond more to the currency leader than to followers, but there are good reasons to doubt that even the leader will retain effective control over the institution's behavior. Michael Barnett and Martha Finnemore, drawing from sociological theory, stress the organizational interests of the institution in furthering its own purposes and strengthening its own autonomy.[50] Alternately, rational choice theory stresses that delegation to an agent invariably involves some slippage between the principal's goals and the agent's actions. Daniel Nielson and Michael Tierney point out that agent slippage is made even more likely by the collective nature of the principal behind many international organizations; when the leader shares control over the agent with several other actors, the ability of this principal to monitor and sanction negligent agents decreases significantly.[51]

For both sets of reasons, currency areas that empower a third-party monetary institution place limits on the ability of the leader to control outcomes. Recent criticism by European governments of the European Central Bank, their chosen agent, for overly tight monetary policies exemplifies this possibility.[52] Another example is the East African Currency Board (EACB), formed after the independence of Kenya, Uganda, and Tanzania in the early 1960s. Because the leadership of the EACB had been recruited and trained by the region's former colonial power, Britain, the institution was only partially under the control of its nominal masters in East Africa. In an extreme case, one of the key EACB decision makers, J. B. Loynes, had been seconded from the Bank of England and seems to have routinely provided confidential information to British officials in the region, undercutting the EACB's negotiations with Britain.[53]

Additional examples can be found if we relax our state-centric focus. Both the sterling area and the ruble zone empowered partially autonomous monetary institutions *within* the leading state, the Bank of England and the Central Bank of Russia, respectively. In each case, political leaders lacked some degree of control over monetary decision makers within the state, complicating the efforts of these governments to gain desired benefits from the currency area. For instance, in July 1993 the Central Bank of Russia hastened the collapse of the ruble zone by largely breaking the link between the old rubles in circulation outside Russia and the new rubles in circulation within Russia itself. To minimize interference by the government, Russian monetary authorities timed their announcement to coincide with President Boris Yeltsin's vacation away from Moscow. The explicitly stated goal of Viktor Gerashchenko, central bank governor—"to determine who will stay in the rouble zone and who must leave"—clearly demonstrates the ability of implementing insti-

50. Michael Barnett and Martha Finnemore, "The Politics, Power, and Pathologies of International Organizations," *International Organization* 53, no. 4 (1999): 699–732.

51. Daniel Nielson and Michael Tierney, "Delegation to International Organizations," *International Organization* 57, no. 2 (2003): 241–76.

52. For example, Paul De Grauwe, "Challenges for Monetary Policy in Euroland," *Journal of Common Market Studies* 40, no. 4 (2002): 693–718.

53. UK Public Records Office, Treasury, 317/579 and 317/757.

tutions to usurp elements of decision making away from political leaders. The bank's *fait accompli* had substantial consequences for Russia's foreign policy in its "near abroad," but Yeltsin, after hurriedly returning to Moscow, eventually acquiesced to the action.[54] In short, third-party monetary institutions—whether national or supranational—can use their autonomy to undermine the ability of political authorities within the leading state to bargain effectively with followers.

Taken together, the rules of the currency area help set the parameters of leader-follower bargaining. Relatively formalized rule systems with fairly symmetrical control institutions place limits on the leader's ability to use its size within the currency area to extract resources from followers. When those systems also contain a third-party implementing institution, the leader's discretion is further diminished. The leader may still gain many of the available resources, but the system's rules prevent it from taking as much as it might like in a particular circumstance—at least until those constraints become so substantial that the leader itself abandons the system. On the other hand, when rules are less formalized and are not implemented by a third-party institution, there is more scope for explicit bargaining and, hence, more opportunity for the leader to exploit its size and resource advantages. Similarly, in currency areas with highly asymmetric decision-making institutions, leaders are able to use their larger share of control to their own advantage. Ceteris paribus, leaders face the fewest constraints in highly informal currency areas where they are unconstrained either by joint decision-making procedures or third-party institutions.[55] On the other hand, as Cohen emphasizes, such arrangements still place some constraints on the leader, such as marginal difficulty in regulating its money supply and the risk of political backlash.[56]

Conclusion

Leaders of currency areas, despite their leading role, face significant limits on their ability to manipulate monetary relations with their followers to their own benefit. As a result, the relationship between leaders and followers can best be characterized as interdependence, not dependence. Monetary diplomacy within a currency area is of course influenced by factors beyond the currency area, but the nature of the currency area itself has an important independent impact. We can understand that impact best by looking at the rules of the currency area (or the institutional limits on

54. Anne McElvoy, "Rouble Reform Leaves Little Change in Consumers' Pockets," *Times* (London), July 27, 1993, Lexis-Nexis, accessed October 7, 2005; Anatol Lieven and Anne McElvoy, "Rouble Panic Is Storm before Calm," *Times* (London), July 28, 1993, Lexis-Nexis, accessed October 7, 2005.
55. For example, dollarized economies such as Ecuador and El Salvador share none of the dollar's seigniorage revenues and have no influence over the U.S. Federal Reserve Bank. In this instance, however, the influence of U.S. political officials over the dollar area is limited by virtue of the Fed's status as a highly independent third-party agent.
56. Cohen, *Future of Money*, 74–81.

the leader's power) and especially at the relative costs of the follower's exit from the area (or the market limits on the leader's power).

Although many of the examples in this chapter have been drawn from formalized currency areas, the same logic applies to informal currency areas such as the dollar area. As I have suggested, informal currency areas place relatively fewer constraints on currency leaders and allow them greater scope to use their bilateral bargaining advantage vis-à-vis followers, especially when compared to formal currency areas with symmetrical rules. Nevertheless, the same basic principles apply.

In addition, although the analysis in this chapter has emphasized the limits of leaders' power, this should not distract attention from the tremendous benefits that currency areas can and often do provide to powerful states. The highly problematic last decades of the sterling area, for example, should not be taken as representative of its entire history. Still, the difficulties that Britain encountered in managing the sterling area, as well as the other examples of bargaining between currency-area leaders and followers that I have provided, should give us pause in assessing the leader's prospects for successfully engaging in monetary statecraft with its followers.

Future research is necessary to determine whether the benefits of leadership typically outweigh the costs. Politicians in the states that lead currency areas have certainly stressed these benefits as reasons for the maintenance of a leadership role, but there does not appear to be any literature systematically comparing the costs and benefits. Typical analyses of the sterling area, franc zone, or ruble zone suggest that the leader subsidizes followers economically in return for the prestige of having them in its monetary area and the possibility of occasional tribute. To his credit, Kirshner carefully separates the economic and political costs and benefits for the leader and acknowledges that, in many cases, economic resources on balance flow away from the leader. But he also asserts that leaders "covet" monetary areas and that "virtually every" potential leader has expanded its monetary influence because the leader gains so much more from entrapment and extraction than it gives up in economic subsidies.[57] These propositions cry out for qualification; future research should examine the conditions under which they are valid.

57. Kirshner, *Currency and Coercion,* 168–69.

CHAPTER NINE

Monetary Statecraft
in Follower States

Louis W. Pauly

Common sense suggests that successful leaders need willing follow-ers. Coercion can sometimes be effective, but, as every new parent soon learns, out-comes achieved through self-interested acquiescence tend to be more satisfactory and more enduring than those achieved through the application of brute force. Po-litical theorists typically focus on the concept of legitimacy when they evoke the quality that transforms the raw power of a strong actor into something more ac-ceptable to a relatively weaker one. Only when it is operative, we might even say, is the term *leadership* really appropriate. The authority relationship thereby invoked ultimately entails a fundamental respect for the autonomy of the follower.[1]

Early versions of this chapter were presented at the annual meeting of the International Studies As-sociation, March 17–20, 2004, and at the European University Institute, May 16, 2004, and released as a working paper by the Institute on Globalization and the Human Condition of McMaster University (GHC 05/8, April 2005). For constructive comments and suggestions, I am grateful to Stephen Harris, Beth Simmons, Bob Hancké, William Coleman, fellow conferees, two anonymous referees, and especially to Dave Andrews. For generously sharing original empirical material on the two main cases, I am deeply indebted to Dave Andrews and to Eric Helleiner. Eduard Hochreiter opened many doors for David and me in Vienna. Georg Winckler and Aurel Schubert provided valuable assistance to me during several trips to Austria. It was a privilege to interview Louis Rasminsky in Ottawa during the final years of his long life. Financial assistance came from the Social Sciences and Humanities Research Council of Canada and from the Robert Schuman Centre for Advanced Studies.

1. Research on the meaning of power and authority in international relations is rapidly expanding. For an overview, see Edgar Grande and Louis W. Pauly, eds., *Complex Sovereignty: Reconstituting Political Authority in the Twenty-First Century* (Toronto: University of Toronto Press, 2005). On legitimacy and par-ticular monetary orders, see Benjamin J. Cohen, "Balance-of-Payments Financing: Evolution of a Re-gime," in *International Regimes*, ed. Stephen Krasner, 315–36 (Ithaca: Cornell University Press, 1983); Jonathan Kirshner, ed., *Monetary Orders: Ambiguous Economics, Ubiquitous Politics* (Ithaca: Cornell Uni-versity Press, 2003); David Andrews, C. Randall Henning, and Louis W. Pauly, eds., *Governing the World's Money* (Ithaca: Cornell University Press, 2002). On the concepts of leadership and followership in this arena, see Rawi Abdelal, "The Politics of Monetary Leadership and Followership: Stability in the Euro-pean Monetary System since the Currency Crisis of 1992," *Political Studies* 46, no. 2 (1998): 236–59.

In a world characterized by both intensifying economic interdependence and continuing political disunity, the quest to establish rules capable of governing monetary power is as difficult as it is persistent. Leading and following states in many different periods during the past century repeatedly attempted to negotiate such rules. That they needed to do so, for example in 1944 and again after 1971, suggests the enduring temptation of unbridled power on the part of leaders. That they wanted to do so suggests the capacity of followers somehow to limit the power of leaders. As I employ the term in this chapter, *followership* involves an observable capacity for strategic choice. In this policy context, that capacity defines the contours of monetary statecraft. This chapter explores leader-follower dynamics by applying conceptions of monetary power and statecraft developed by David Andrews (chap. 1 in this volume), as well as the discussion of monetary leadership by Andrew Walter (chap. 3 in this volume), to two important and illustrative empirical cases of monetary followership in Canada and Austria.

National Policies and International Monetary Order

What a follower state basically wants from a monetary leader, it might reasonably be assumed, is a reliable monetary anchor or, more precisely, in recent times an external bulwark against inflation. Despite the integrative effects of economic globalization, however, few follower states have in fact ever demonstrated a complete willingness simply to trust systemic or regional leaders to maintain macroeconomic policies consistent with their own preferences. Certainly since 1945, key follower states in the middle of the pyramid of international monetary power have always insisted on taking out insurance.[2] Because these follower states feared that the leading states might force them to bear more than their fair share of the burden of adjustment to expanded trade and investment flows, collaborative institutions such as the International Monetary Fund (IMF) or the Group of Seven promised them greater symmetry when payments imbalances needed to be equilibrated. But follower states insisted on hedging their bets even further by retaining national control over specific policy instruments, either because they believed that multilateral instruments would be too weak or because they actually hoped that asymmetries might work to their own benefit. Capital controls certainly fell into such a category, especially in the early postwar years. During the past few decades, as most follower states moved decisively to open their economies to freer capital movements, other measures were developed to compensate for the absence of effective controls. Some governments,

---

2. Benjamin J. Cohen hypothesizes, in *The Geography of Money* (Ithaca: Cornell University Press, 1998), 116–17, seven layers in the world's currency pyramid, extending from the "top currency" (the U.S. dollar) and "patrician currencies" (the Japanese yen and German mark, now the euro) at the apex to the "permeated," "quasi-," and "pseudo-currencies" at the base. Roughly speaking, the universe of follower states to which my analysis is addressed comes from the remaining two layers between this base and apex; they range from Switzerland and Canada to Australia, South Korea, Austria, Malaysia, and Chile. Also see Benjamin J. Cohen, *The Future of Money* (Princeton: Princeton University Press, 2004).

for example, opted to combine capital decontrol with exchange-rate floats. Others, particularly inside the European monetary union, chose a combination of regional exchange-rate fixity and new collaborative mechanisms for managing external monetary relationships.

Such decisions construct policy buffers between followers and leaders. The purposes of those buffers are to limit monetary power conceived in relational terms and to constrain the instrumental use of such power. Most clearly, to employ the conceptual terminology employed in earlier chapters, such buffers work mainly to counter the leader's Power to Deflect the transitional costs of balance-of-payments adjustment, including the costs of maintaining a system designed to facilitate such adjustment. A perennial struggle among interdependent but ultimately sovereign states involves the attempted shifting of such costs on to others. Blunting the power of states to do so is equivalent to carving out a zone of autonomy in an interdependent relationship. This makes willing and self-interested followership possible.

In the Canadian and Austrian case histories summarized in this chapter, we see the struggle to limit monetary power, to practice monetary statecraft, up close. We also see very different policy choices being made, arguably with similar degrees of success. Beyond helping us understand how those choices constrain monetary power, a comparison of the underlying reasons for the differences between them suggests the importance of relational context. It also suggests the key role that continues to be played by distinctive domestic political and social arrangements, even in a policy arena commonly depicted as ever more completely dominated by free-wheeling systemic forces. In the end, the empirical evidence presented here points to the importance of conjoining research on the varieties of contemporary capitalism with continuing research on international monetary power and authority. More specifically, it highlights the broader significance of idiosyncratic arrangements for wage bargaining and other measures to redistribute internally the net benefits and costs of ever-deepening national involvement in external markets.[3]

Without attention to those idiosyncrasies, the very different exchange-rate regime choices of Canada and Austria represent an evident puzzle. Both countries have similarly asymmetrical, dependent economic relationships with their larger neighbors and leading trading and investing partners. They also have similarly complicated and historically fraught political relationships with those large neighbors. Prominent international political economists predict that currency politics in small, open economies will incline in the direction of exchange-rate stability.[4] Despite a

3. See, for example, Fritz Scharpf, *Crisis and Choice in European Social Democracy* (Ithaca: Cornell University Press, 1991); Herbert Kitschelt, Peter Lange, Gary Marks, and John D. Stephens, *Continuity and Change in Contemporary Capitalism* (Cambridge, UK: Cambridge University Press, 1999); Peter Hall and David Soskice, eds., *Varieties of Capitalism: The Institutional Foundations of Comparative Advantage* (Oxford: Oxford University Press, 2001); Bob Hancké and David Soskice, "Wage-Setting, Fiscal Policy, and Political Exchange in EMU," in *Institutionen, Wirtschaftswachtum, und Beschaftigung in der EWU*, ed. Hans-Böckler Stiftung (Düsseldorf: Hans-Böckler Stiftung, 2003); Linda Weiss, *The Myth of the Powerless State* (Ithaca: Cornell University Press, 1998).
4. As noted by Eric Helleiner, "The Fixation with Floating: The Politics of Canada's Exchange Rate Regime," *Canadian Journal of Political Science* 38, no. 1 (2005): 1–22 (see especially 2); see also Jeffry A.

rapidly increasing degree of integration with the United States when it comes to trade and investment, however, Canada confounded such expectations by jealously guarding its national currency and maintaining a floating exchange rate for all but thirteen of the years since 1945. It continues, moreover, to reject the logic of monetary union. In contrast, facing high levels of economic reliance on the German market for its exports, and despite the elegant theoretical logic of floating exchange rates in the context of ever more open capital markets, Austria has long followed precisely the opposite path.

Given this curious and persistent difference, surprisingly few comparative studies of these two follower states exist.[5] While helping to fill this lacuna in the empirical literature, this chapter suggests more generally that the efforts of follower states to limit the power of leaders significantly define and structure the relationships between them. If we conceive of the monetary system as a whole essentially as a complex network of such relationships, then future research on international monetary power will require deeper attention to intranational variables and their continuing variety.

The Canadian Case

Figures 9.1 and 9.2 suggest a straightforward story. With the significant exception of the 1962–70 period, in modern times Canada has relied heavily on the policy tool of flexible exchange-rate adjustment to manage its deepening interaction with its main economic partner. At three moments in living memory, strategic moves occurred not only in the actual exchange rates but in the very nature of the Canadian exchange-rate regime. In 1950, it broke away from its Bretton Woods commitment by floating the Canadian dollar. In 1962, it repegged (fig. 9.1). And in 1970, it returned to floating once more (fig. 9.2), a policy that continues to this day. Throughout the past three decades, the Bank of Canada even began moving away from attempts to manage the currency's value directly. After 1991, it held to an ever-deeper commitment to targeting monetary policy mainly on inflation, in the belief

Frieden, "Invested Interests: The Politics of National Economic Policies in a World of Global Finance," *International Organization* 45, no. 4 (1991): 425–51; C. Randall Henning, *Currencies and Politics in the United States, Germany, and Japan* (Washington, D.C.: Institute for International Economics, 1994).

5. The trailblazer here is Harald von Riekhoff and Hanspeter Neuhold, eds., *Unequal Partners* (Boulder: Westview, 1993); the volume includes a few paragraphs on Austria's exchange-rate policy by the distinguished economist Georg Winckler, but it has practically nothing on Canada. On the underlying concepts of leadership and followership applied in a broad comparison involving Canada, see Andrew Cooper, Richard Higgott, and Kim Nossal, *Relocating Middle Powers: Australia and Canada in a Changing World* (Vancouver, Canada: University of British Columbia Press, 1993). Although he does not focus on Canada, Peter J. Katzenstein proposes a directly relevant notion concerning successful small states in a globalizing economy: that their economic policies are shaped by broadly shared perceptions of vulnerability, by social learning, and by attendant efforts to construct effective tools for defending their national interests. See Peter J. Katzenstein, *Corporatism and Change: Austria, Switzerland, and the Politics of Industry* (Ithaca: Cornell University Press, 1984); *Small States in World Markets* (Ithaca: Cornell University Press, 1985); "Small States and Small States Revisited," *New Political Economy* 8, no. 1 (2003): 9–30.

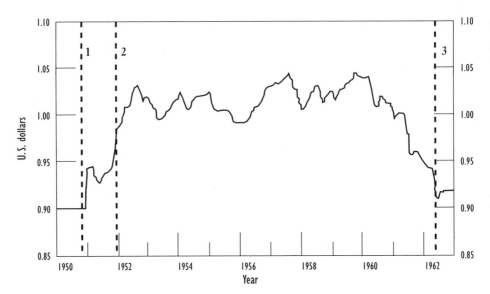

Figure 9.1 Exchange rate (monthly averages): Canadian dollar to U.S. dollar, 1950–1962. (*) 20 August 1957, modern-day Canadian dollar peak: CA$1.00 = US$1.0614.

1. September 1950, Canadian dollar floated
2. December 1951, exchange controls lifted
3. May 1962, Canadian dollar fixed

Source: Reproduced from James Powell, *A History of the Canadian Dollar* (Ottawa: Bank of Canada, 1999), 43.

that movements in the exchange rate would complement, or at least not entirely undercut, the macroeconomic consequences of movements in interest rates. There was no change in basic policy after 1998, even though the bilateral exchange rate soon bottomed out and returned to the $0.80 range by the middle of the next decade.

What lies behind the policy choices encapsulated in this brief summary? In the years just after World War II, Canadian ties with Britain attenuated, and the United States rapidly became the only partner crucial to its economic fortunes. Since 1971, an exceptionally deep economic partnership with the United States developed; this was finally acknowledged and even embraced in 1988 in the Canada-US Free Trade Agreement.[6] At present, nearly 90 percent of Canadian exports go to the United States, although in the wake of the integration of transport systems some of this huge proportion, as yet unmeasured by either Canadian or U.S. authorities, simply represents Canadian goods passing through U.S. ports. In terms of power conceived

6. See Louis W. Pauly, "Canada in a New North America," in *The Rebordering of North America: Integration and Exclusion in a New Security Context*, ed. Peter Andreas and Thomas Biersteker, 90–109 (New York: Routledge, 2003); Stephen Clarkson, *Uncle Sam and Us: Globalization, Neoconservatism, and the Canadian State* (Toronto: University of Toronto Press, 2002).

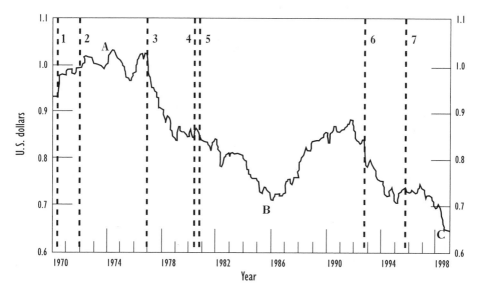

Figure 9.2 Exchange rate (monthly averages): Canadian dollar to U.S. dollar, 1970–1998. (A) 25 April 1974, Canadian dollar high: CA\$1.00 = US\$1.0443; (B) 4 February 1986, CA\$1.00 = US\$0.6913; (C) 27 August 1998, CA\$1.00 = US\$0.6311.

1. 31 May 1970, Canadian dollar floated
2. December 1971, Smithsonian agreement
3. 15 November 1976, election of Parti Québécois in Quebec
4. 20 May 1980, Quebec referendum
5. October 1980, National Energy Program introduced
6. 26 October 1992, defeat of Charlottetown accord
7. 30 October 1995, Quebec referendum

Source: Reproduced from James Powell, *A History of the Canadian Dollar* (Ottawa: Bank of Canada, 1999), 54.

in relational terms, this trade dependence obviously gives the United States enormous leverage.

But we need to back up a bit if we are to understand the monetary aspect of Canada's relationship with the United States. One method is to trace the rationales for the three principal changes in Canada's postwar international monetary policy regime.[7] A key source is the one person who was at, or very near, the center of policy decision from 1940 right through to 1973. Louis Rasminsky managed the Canadian Foreign Exchange Control Board during and immediately after World War II.

---

7. See A. F. W. Plumptre, *Three Decades of Decision: Canada and the World Monetary System, 1944–75* (Toronto: McClelland and Stewart, 1977); Paul Wonnacott, *The Canadian Dollar, 1948–62* (Toronto: University of Toronto Press, 1965); Douglas Fullerton, *Graham Towers and His Times* (Toronto: McClelland and Stewart, 1986); Eric Helleiner, *Towards North American Monetary Union? The History and Politics of Canada's Exchange Rate Regime* (Montreal: McGill-Queen's University Press, forthcoming).

He played an important role in the drafting of the Bretton Woods Agreement in 1944, served as the first Canadian director on the IMF Executive Board, and held the position of deputy governor and, from 1961, governor of the Bank of Canada until his retirement in 1973. Rasminsky lived a full life and was into his ninety-first year when it ended in 1998. He was physically frail but mentally extremely sharp when I had the opportunities to interview him in 1993 and once again a few months before his death. Those interviews, in conjunction with observations drawn from the secondary literature, provide the basis of the analysis of Canadian exchange-rate policy that follows.

The IMF Agreement and the Abandonment of Capital Controls

Rasminsky termed his presence at the 1942 London meeting where Keynes unveiled his draft plan for the postwar monetary system "the highlight of my international monetary career."[8] Like others at that meeting, he was convinced that deflation, recession, and competitive currency devaluation would be the chief dangers after the war ended. Keynes's ideas for "a clearing union and code of behavior based on non-discrimination and convertibility" made a deep impression on Rasminsky because they promised an elegant way to avoid recapitulating the dismal monetary experience of the 1930s. That the plan envisaged stable exchange rates was not the main attraction, however. Rather, it seemed to chart a politically feasible and economically sound path back to more freely flowing trade and international capital movements. "Non-discrimination and convertibility were so important to Canada because of the structure of our trade then: we had a surplus of imports from the United States, which we paid for through a surplus of exports to Britain and Europe, and some capital inflows from Britain but mainly from the United States."[9] Given these priorities, capital controls were never welcomed for their own sake, although they had proved essential during the war years. They came off again as soon as possible, a process completed in 1951.

Although Rasminsky personally favored the idea of exchange-rate stability embodied in the original Articles of Agreement of the IMF, he claimed always to have shared with other Canadian officials an overriding commitment to easing conditions for international capital flows. "We were always committed to freely flowing capital, both before [the IMF agreement] and ever after."[10] That commitment only deepened when the postwar economic reality turned out to be a boom and not a bust. With U.S. capital flows to Canada rising rapidly at both of the crucial turning points of 1950 and 1970, "we were always willing to sacrifice exchange-rate stability if need be." Canadian authorities did not relish breaching their Bretton Woods commit-

---

8. Louis Rasminsky, interview, Ottawa, August 11, 1993.
9. Ibid.
10. Ibid.

ments in either case, Rasminsky recalled, "But what could we do? When we floated, we floated up, so we could always deny competitive devaluation."[11]

Although some U.S. counterparts understood the Canadian position in both 1950 and 1970, rising tension existed at the official level, especially in 1970. For Rasminsky, this was nothing new. He had hopes even into 1944 that something like Keynes's politically neutral Clearing Union might succeed. In theory, such a mechanism could have reconciled the desires for both exchange-rate stability and capital mobility, and Canada could therefore have supported it. But Rasminsky soon concluded that the United States had no stomach for such a multilateral ideal, one which would give voice and, more important, automatic and certain financing to countries when they faced balance-of-payments adjustment problems. In the late 1940s, he complained about the niggardliness of IMF financing, and early on he worried that the IMF was condemned by the United States to be much less relevant than it could have been.

These concerns rested on his close observation of U.S. behavior in the crucial 1944–46 period. A remark he recorded during the 1946 inaugural meeting of governors of the IMF and World Bank in Savannah, Georgia, captured the lesson Rasminsky learned then and carried with him throughout his life: "We have all been treated to a spectacle of American domination and domineeringness through their financial power which has to be seen to be believed. . . . US foreign economic policy seems to be in the hands of the Treasury who are insensitive to other peoples' reactions and prepared to ram everything they want down everyone's throat."[12]

The 1950 Float

In 1950, when Canada found itself awash in U.S. dollar reserves, the necessary consequence of simultaneous export and investment booms, inflation was the rising threat. U.S. Treasury officials were not so much domineering as concerned. Even more worried were IMF staffers, who feared that a Canadian revaluation would set a precedent and undermine the central exchange-rate plank of the Articles of Agreement. Rasminsky saw the problem, but he also now saw serious design flaws in the structure of the IMF itself. His advice to the minister of finance, therefore, took the following line. Especially after the formal end of residual wartime exchange controls, Canada should embrace its full obligations to the IMF (entailed by Article VIII status). At the same time, however, the IMF should be asked to acknowledge the market conditions facing the country and quietly exempt it from any commitment to hold an explicit exchange-rate peg or even to any promise of reestablishing such a peg by a certain date.[13] This is exactly what happened. Fifty-three years later, Rasminsky was forthright in his rationale for the policy he advocated: "Our commit-

11. Ibid.

12. Bruce Muirhead, *Against the Odds: The Public Life and Times of Louis Rasminsky* (Toronto: University of Toronto Press, 1999), 111.

13. Ibid., 143.

ment to multilateralism mainly had to do with the desire to have a buffer between us and the United States. Negotiating head to head with them was never enjoyable. In a way, our position was like Switzerland's: an island of stability and a great haven for capital flows in a turbulent world. It was often best to keep our heads down."[14]

As Eric Helleiner points out, the decision to float in 1950 was certainly backed by the weight of opinion in the Canadian private sector.[15] It would be an exaggeration, however, to say that the actual decision to break IMF obligations and float the currency originated there. Nor was there much evidence of any particularly salient partisan influence or serious lobbying by provincial governments. Instead, the central governmental policy makers who actually made the final choice of assigning priority to monetary independence and capital mobility over exchange-rate stability enjoyed a significant amount of policy autonomy within the Canadian political system. We might argue that this choice made by the small group of Canadian policy makers was ideational or even ideological in origin.[16] It seems more accurate, however, simply to call it logical, both in light of market conditions and policy makers' understanding of the decentralized structure of the Canadian state and the regionally differentiated nature of the national economy. The only feasible alternative to floating the currency in 1950 would have been a combination of running a very loose monetary policy (risking accelerated inflation during an unexpected period of economic expansion) and reimposing capital controls. Price stability was even then seen to be in the national interest and so too was the development of manufacturing in Quebec and Ontario and of commodity-based businesses in the Maritimes and the West. Private U.S. capital inflows were the key to achieving these latter goals. If this meant that bankers in Montreal and Toronto had to continue living with some hot money, this seemed a small price to pay.[17] Was excessive currency speculation ever really a serious problem? Rasminsky was clear: "No. We didn't build very many long-term assets with short-term money."[18]

The 1962 Peg

In light of such reasoning, the decision to repeg in 1962 is anomalous. Unique circumstances explain it, but in retrospect the main conclusion Canadian policy makers subsequently drew was that it was a mistake.

Erratic domestic economic policy in 1961 set the stage. A trade deficit was exacerbated by an overly tight monetary policy that simultaneously depressed exports and attracted an avalanche of capital inflows. In the face of rising unemployment, a populist Conservative government tried to talk the Canadian dollar down, the United States and the IMF began complaining about competitive currency depre-

14. Rasminsky, interview, Ottawa, August 11, 1993.
15. Helleiner, "Fixation with Floating," 5.
16. Ibid.; Kathleen McNamara, *The Currency of Ideas: Monetary Politics in the European Union* (Ithaca: Cornell University Press, 1998).
17. I have seen no record of loud objections emanating from that quarter.
18. Rasminsky, interview, August 11, 1993.

ciation, and a politically tone-deaf central bank governor refused to loosen the monetary reins. That governor, James Coyne, resigned under pressure on July 14, 1961, and Rasminsky took his place ten days later.[19] His first order of business was to hammer out an historic understanding with the government concerning the future unique and depoliticized responsibilities of the Bank of Canada; his second task was to use the Bank's renewed mandate to help restore confidence in a Canadian economy beset by increasing unemployment.

For a brief period of time, it seemed that one prudent way to do so would be to accede to U.S. and IMF calls to repeg the exchange rate. There was also some pressure from the business community to take this route. Rasminsky emphasized the need "to eliminate uncertainty" when in May 1962 he announced the decision to fix the rate.[20] In later years, he insisted that the government, with advice from the Bank, would never have taken that decision if it had not believed that domestic circumstances themselves had warranted it. In the event, the new policy did not work. The rate immediately came under pressure as a deteriorating trade position convinced the markets that the Canadian dollar was overvalued. In order to defend the currency, the government found itself forced into the classic posture of imposing fiscal stringency, acquiescing as the Bank raised interest rates, and shoring up emergency reserves by borrowing from the IMF as well as the U.S. and UK central banks—all in the face of rising unemployment. Once committed, however, Rasminsky himself could see no other way out, except to urge the government to take even more direct measures to reduce the current account deficit. This necessarily implied reducing domestic production costs. He therefore urged that "cabinet should consult with business and labor."[21] But such consultations could not quickly reduce those costs, and the government relied instead on import surcharges. This antagonized the United States but also changed market psychology. The exchange crisis eventually subsided; later in the decade, the focus of policy attention shifted away from unemployment and back toward inflation.

The 1970 Float

By 1970, Canada faced again a situation very similar to the one in 1950. Confidence in the Canadian currency had long since returned, and capital rolling in from the United States made alternatives to refloating the Canadian dollar unpalatable. Defending the then-existing Canadian-U.S. exchange rate would have required massive official purchases of U.S. dollars and sales of Canadian dollars. This could easily have exacerbated inflationary pressures in Canada and set off a spiral of currency speculation.[22] In the event, Canadians were determined to float. Even under

19. James Powell, *A History of the Canadian Dollar* (Ottawa, Ontario: Bank of Canada, 1999), 44.
20. Plumptre, *Three Decades of Decision*, 168; Muirhead, *Against the Odds*, 196.
21. Muirhead, *Against the Odds*, 200.
22. Powell, *A History of the Canadian Dollar*, 49. As Powell further notes, "The authorities also considered asking the United States to reconsider Canada's exemption from the U.S. Interest Equalization Tax. Application of the tax to Canadian residents would have raised the cost of foreign borrowing and,

the most aggressive pressure from U.S. Treasury officials, especially from Secretary John Connally, Canada refused to support the U.S. attempt to shore up the Bretton Woods system in the negotiations following President Richard Nixon's decision to suspend the official convertibility of the U.S. dollar on August 15, 1971. Rasminsky recalled the key negotiating session vividly:

> Connally was very rude. We had to float, and I told him privately that we were not his problem. We were not draining US gold reserves, since we were holding much of our foreign reserve in the form of non-marketable T-bills. He began yelling about Canada always having its hand out for one thing or another but never being willing to help, and I raised my voice in anger. He stormed out of the room. In a public session later, Connally asked [IMF Managing Director Pierre-Paul] Schweitzer if Canada was contravening the Articles. He said yes. But we immediately intervened to ask Schweitzer if he thought that under the circumstances it would be possible for Canada to fix a durable par value. He said no. This probably helped put him in hot water with Connally.[23]

Continuity in Canadian Analysis and Policy

After the Smithsonian Agreement was announced in December 1971, Canadian unwillingness to participate in the repegging exercise was publicly and bluntly attacked by Paul Volcker of the U.S. Treasury and by Arthur Burns, then chairman of the Federal Reserve. Canada, according to Burns in 1972, "had not been prepared to be helpful to the USA in its time of need."[24] Underlying the adamant position of Canada, however, was the reawakening of a strong preference for monetary autonomy. The line of thinking was well articulated as early as 1932 by Clifford Clark, arguably the most important deputy minister of finance in Canadian history and the person who, along with central bank governor Graham Towers, originally recruited Rasminsky to government service:

> Under a policy of fixed exchanges, an upset in the country's balance of payments due to a crop shortage, or a change in foreign demand for one or more of the country's important products may have to be corrected by the painful process of restricting credit and reducing prices and personal incomes. This process appears the more ruthless when it is realized that many disequilibria in international balances of payments are temporary in nature. The question may be raised whether the policy of exchange stability in some cases does not involve the payment of too high a price for the advantage gained. . . . The arguments against a tie-up with New York and with London constitute the case for retaining our national autonomy in monetary affairs for the present at least. In particular, neither alternative offers any real assurance of price stability or the restoration of our prices to a level at which the burden of fixed debt upon the shoulders of industri-

---

hence, would have dampened capital inflows. This too was rejected, however, because of concerns that it would negatively affect borrowing in the United States by provincial governments."

23. Rasminsky, interview, Ottawa, August 11, 1993. See also Muirhead, *Against the Odds*, 293.

24. Muirhead, *Against the Odds*, 294.

alist and taxpayer will be appreciably mitigated. . . . If we retain our independence, we may choose our own objectives and plot our own course towards them.[25]

What we might call the Clark-Rasminsky shared narrative on Canadian external monetary and financial polices really extended from the 1930s straight through to the 1990s and beyond. In this narrative, there has been no basic change in the country's exchange-rate regime since 1971. If anything, the country made an even stronger commitment to floating in the aftermath of the negotiation in 1988 of a free trade agreement with the United States, when the Bank of Canada let it be known that it would not intervene in foreign-exchange markets to manage the rate. Such a commitment was harshly tested during the late 1990s when the exchange rate plummeted to historic lows against the dollar. To the surprise of many in the business community who continued to push the cause of fixed rates, even to the point of monetary union, that commitment held. The strong recovery in the exchange rate since then has tested it again from the opposite side. But the Clark-Rasminsky consensus survives.

In sum, policy autonomy remains the key Canadian priority. Sometimes, this means maintaining the ability to counter official insistence on obeisance to the changing policy preferences of the United States. More often, it means letting the exchange rate buffer the impact of monetary and fiscal policy changes in the United States. In the wake of the miserable experience of the 1930s and the shock to Canadian polity and economy posed by World War II and the rapid erosion of the British empire, there was a brief moment when the country's monetary policy makers were willing to consider new international arrangements that might have fundamentally compromised that autonomy. The need for national-level policy insulators might have been met by a radically new kind of international organization. But by 1946, it was crystal clear that no such organization could be created. Canadian policy makers were therefore left to confront the unmediated power of the United States. The historically tried and tested response has been to let the exchange rate be the main instrument for limiting that power, especially because there was no serious constituency for a permanent regime of capital controls.

In the meantime, Canada wanted to be as helpful as possible in the establishment of the Bretton Woods institutions and in their subsequent operation.[26] The government would take its day-to-day operations seriously, and it would send respected

25. W. C. Clark, "Monetary Reconstruction," 1932, National Archives of Canada, RG25 D1 v. 770 File 333, 145–46, 195; cited in Helleiner, "Fixation with Floating," 5.

26. Rasminsky had spent most of the 1930s working in the economic and financial department of the League of Nations. In the twilight of his life, he concluded that although Keynes's more ambitious plans for a currency union remained noteworthy, the creation of the IMF actually did represent something new and it was wrong to underestimate its role in postwar history. "What emerged was better than the League, and probably as much as the United States could ever stomach politically. The decisions made in Savannah in 1946 were bad ones, but Congress and the politicized environment in Washington likely made them unavoidable. In the end, the Fund can claim substantial credit for the prosperity of the golden age of 1945–1970." Interview, Ottawa, August 11, 1993.

senior officials to sit on their boards. Even when it failed to meet the spirit of its obligations to the IMF, it would go to great lengths (before the generalized shift to floating in March 1973) to ensure that the IMF formally acceded to its "temporary" derogations. But it would always defend its own way of dealing with the practical exigencies of U.S. monetary and financial power. Viewed from a less generous perspective, this sometimes meant defending Canada's own interest in bearing less of the load of system maintenance. Canadian senior monetary officials were, in short, pragmatic nationalists. Time and again, not wanting either to impede the capital inflows required to underwrite national prosperity or supinely to acquiesce in asymmetrical external constraints on their own monetary policy, they relied on the exchange rate as the principal buffer against U.S. monetary hegemony.

Ironically, the logic and consistent wisdom of this choice was starkly revealed when Canadian monetary policy makers made the unusual mistake of repegging in 1962. Fearing the consequences of quickly reversing course, they set out to uphold the peg—and immediately confronted the core political contradiction of the Canadian political economy. If external costs could not be adjusted rapidly as payments pressures mounted, internal production costs—and their major wage component—would have to adjust. But this simply could not easily be done in a liberal, continent-spanning economy marked by distinct regional differences and disaggregated unions fully capable of resisting downward wage pressures. The fact that the initial error was soon masked by the effects of an eventual inflationary boom in the United States in the 1960s should not confuse the basic issue. In 1970, Canadian policy makers once again squarely confronted their internal political constraints and reverted to their traditional external practices.

Canadian exchange-rate policy was therefore capable of being deployed unilaterally and swiftly in a deadly serious game always played on two dimensions. Internally, if business and labor could not be cajoled into negotiated concessions to keep national production competitive, then a change in the value of the currency could accomplish the same end less obtrusively, even if internal regional effects might be unbalanced. Externally, the same kind of change could shift some of the costs of adjustment on to others, or, more benignly, limit the shifting of such costs to Canada. Despite external political pressures, including most prominently those voiced in the early 1970s, Canadian policy makers steadfastly refused to rely on any other policy mechanism. Blaming financial markets for changes in living standards always proved a workable political strategy, and it certainly was more effective than relying on negotiating wage agreements in a complex and diffuse labor market. Call it the influence of a particular brand of liberal-market ideology, but this approach certainly did complement revealed policy preferences. It helped manage the irresolvable tension between equally enthusiastic demands from opposing domestic constituencies for continental economic integration, on the one hand, and for the retention of national political independence, on the other.

Despite tremendous changes in the real economy of Canada in recent decades, including those resulting from freer trade with the United States, the explicit adoption of inflation targeting in 1991, and dramatic fiscal restructuring in the mid-1990s, this

logic continues to hold.[27] External shocks continue to entail abrupt changes in foreign demand for Canadian goods and services, whose composition and production
vary markedly across the country's regions. In the face of such shocks, we could certainly imagine an alternative adjustment mechanism focused mainly on the continental movement of labor or on relative changes in sectoral wages. But even in a post–
North American Free Trade Agreement (NAFTA) era, the movement of labor and
other factors of production across the Canadian-U.S. border is still considerably more
difficult and less common than their movement within the country. It also remains
the case that relative wages across Canadian regions are sticky in nominal terms.[28]

The question of whether smoother and deeper continental adjustment will be
possible in the future is an open one, which overlaps with quiet expert debate on the
extent to which a separate currency now comes with mounting transaction and opportunity costs. Booming cross-border trade and investment during the past decade
suggest that such costs are low, but the jury is out until more empirical work is done.
In the meantime, the Clark-Rasminsky policy consensus continues to hold: as long
as Canadian monetary policy is disciplined, a flexible exchange rate facilitates macroeconomic stabilization with minimal political costs, both domestic and external. In
other words, it limits U.S. monetary power while carving out an acceptable degree
of political autonomy for the Canadian state and the decentralized national society
it still seeks to steer.[29]

The Austrian Case

Austrians understand what it means to confront power. When the democratic Republic of Austria was reconstituted on April 27, 1945, Germany had yet to surrender
and the country was occupied by the Soviet army. Allied troops were approaching
from the west, and their governments had yet to recognize the new state. Ironically,
although the country had been shattered by external forces even more thoroughly
than in 1918, the traumatic experience of the previous seven years effectively incu-
bated a new sense of national identity. In a hostile environment, a new nation and a
new state initiated a complicated process of mutual construction.

Especially after the State Treaty of 1955 finally ended the Allied occupation, monetary policy became an important instrument in that task. Whereas only 47 percent

27. Stephen Harris, once a senior official in the Bank of Canada, reinforces my point here by emphasizing that inflation targeting became especially attractive to Canada after the difficult era of rising
prices and high interest rates in the late 1980s. In its aftermath, dominant thinking in the Bank held that
if Canadian inflation performance could better that of the United States, interest rates could be made-
in-Canada. Hard experience in the 1990s and beyond undercut this reasoning. Personal correspondence,
March 31, 2004.

28. John Helliwell, *How Much Do National Borders Matter?* (Washington, D.C.: Brookings Institution Press, 1998).

29. For an exceptionally clear statement of this position and of the associated agenda for future research, see Lawrence Schembri, "Exchange Rate Policy in Canada: Lessons from the Past, Implications
for the Future," paper presented at the University of Victoria Conference, October 17–18, 2003.

of its people considered themselves to be members of an Austrian nation in the mid-1960s, within a quarter century some 80 percent embraced just such an identity.[30] The performance of the Austrian economy, and of the schilling, surely played no small part in this transformation. A small group of monetary policy experts understood from the beginning the deeply political nature of their own assignment. Like their Canadian counterparts, they may fairly be labeled pragmatic nationalists, but their pragmatism led them in distinctly different directions.

Reconstructing Monetary Autonomy

For those Austrian monetary policy makers who remember the postwar atmosphere (or who remember what their forebears told them about it), two vivid impressions stand out. The first is the pall cast over all discussions concerning money by the hyperinflation of the early 1920s and by the way it ended, with the state in receivership and the national financial accounts directly administered by a Dutch national assigned by the League of Nations.[31] The League commissioner left in 1926, but by then the new Austrian National Bank was firmly established. The law creating it on November 24, 1922, committed the Bank to one overriding objective: safeguarding the stability of the currency. Even though the subsequent fixed rate between the new schilling and gold had to be devalued by 28 percent at the start of the Great Depression, support for a hard currency survived until German troops arrived on March 12, 1938.

The fact that the Germans proceeded to loot the National Bank's reserves might have been forgotten if World War II had turned out differently. But the memory of that trauma proved useful to the builders of the Second Republic. During the predictable postwar inflation, the Austrian National Bank was resurrected, the schilling was reintroduced and devalued, and the Currency Protection Act of November 1947 was passed in rapid succession, initiating a process of monetary stabilization.[32] Underpinning the restoration of monetary sovereignty was the first of five wage-and-price agreements between organized Austrian industry and the national trade union association, the foundation of the modern "social partnership" and the core of a coordinated market economy.

Bitter memories of debilitating industrial and class conflict during the interwar years framed that progressive-sounding but distinctively illiberal idea.[33] Price infla-

30. Max Riedlsperger, "Austria: A Question of National Identity," *Journal of Politics and Society in Germany, Austria, and Switzerland* 4, no. 1 (1991): 48–71; Peter Katzenstein, "The Last Old Nation: Austrian National Consciousness since 1945," *Comparative Politics* 9, no. 2 (1977): 147–71.

31. Louis W. Pauly, *Who Elected the Bankers? Surveillance and Control in the World Economy* (Ithaca: Cornell University Press, 1997), 54–55.

32. See "Österreichische Geldgeschichte," Austrian National Bank website, http://www.oenb.at/, accessed June 27, 2004.

33. Katzenstein, *Corporatism and Change,* 28–29 traces its roots to nineteenth-century nationality conflicts in the multiethnic Austro-Hungarian empire and the syndicalism of Austro-Marxism. Add to that the social teachings of Christian democracy in the late nineteenth century and the establishment of a Labor Advisory Council within the Ministry of Commerce as early as 1898.

tion was also in the background, and not just in people's memories; it was not until 1952 that tightening monetary policies finally reined in prices. Exchange controls and a dual exchange rate remained until the next year, when a one-time devaluation of the schilling was matched with the declaration of a fixed link to the U.S. dollar. Although Austria joined the IMF on August 27, 1948, it took another ten years until it was able to end its dual exchange rate and accept the full obligations of IMF membership. In 1958, it moved with other European states to a regime of currency convertibility. By then, the social recommitment to the monetary orthodoxy of the late 1920s had been tested and found durable. Despite the rebirth of passionate debates over the famous Austrian black-red political divide, the base of support for price stability remained broad and deep. It found expression in a 1955 act affirming the continuity (since 1922) of the National Bank and recommitting it to currency stability. Among other things, the capacity of the Bank for independent action was widened through a grant of powers to regulate the minimum reserves held by banks and to conduct open market operations without prior approval from the government.

Interdependence and Austrian Social Partnership

If by the 1950s Austrians did not yet fully trust themselves to maintain a sense of national solidarity for internal reasons, external conditions—the familiar problems faced by small states in an increasingly open international economy—provided reinforcement. Social partnership came to mean that organized business groups, the national farmers association, and the trade union federation (Österreichischen Gewerkschaftsbundes, ÖGB) were authorized to make national bargains that were insulated from ideological competition. Domestic politics, in turn, was guided by principles of federalism, proportional representation, and the continual redivision of the spoils of power along red and black lines (the Proporzsystem).[34]

The fact that internal stabilizing measures had failed catastrophically before 1938 undoubtedly contributed to a continuing sense of national vulnerability. But so too did the long shadow of the Soviet Union. The postwar occupation of the country by the victorious allies lasted for ten years; ending it without the formal partition of the country depended on Austria pledging permanent neutrality on the model of Switzerland. This was not declared in the Austrian State Treaty of May 15, 1955, but it was directly noted one month earlier in a bilateral memorandum signed with Moscow. The subsequent constitutional law of October 26, 1955, stated that "for the purpose of the permanent maintenance of her external independence and for the purpose of the inviolability of her territory, Austria of her own free will declares herewith her permanent neutrality, which she is resolved to maintain and defend with all the means at her disposal."[35]

34. The rise of the Freedom Party and accession to the European Union later complicated these political understandings. See Albert Rothbacher, "EU Accession and Political Change in Austria," *Revue d'Integration Europeene* 19, no. 1 (1995): 71–90.

35. Marko Milivokevi, "Neighbours in Neutrality: Aspects of a Close but Delicate Relationship," *Journal of Politics and Society in Germany, Austria, and Switzerland* 3, no. 1 (1990): 69–83, quotation on

Although political neutrality was an existential necessity for postwar Austria, the practical priority was to recover and rebuild the economy as rapidly as possible. But how to do so? History and geography pointed only one way—to economic interdependence with Germany, together with the reconstruction of a robust and distinctly Austrian identity. Natural advantages and traditional networks reasserted themselves. Strong export-led growth was crucial, and for a land-locked country in the heart of central Europe, diversification options were limited. The path reopened after the war led within fifty years to an economy in which trade accounted for over 60 percent of GDP; nearly 40 percent of exports and imports were to and from Germany (with Italy a distant second at around 9 percent), and trade in goods resulted in a perennial deficit requiring balancing receipts from services (such as tourism) and investment.

Manufacturing, however, always played the central role in the strategy for recovery and prosperity. Prevented by its neutrality commitment from joining the European Community during the Cold War, few doubted the practical necessity of redeveloping bilateral linkages with Germany in such industries as machine tools, chemicals, metal goods, and steel. That basic idea certainly appealed to the labor unions in what had always been a highly organized workforce. At its root lay the logical necessity of keeping Austrian wages competitive with German wages. Logic is one thing, however, and natural human impulses another—how to manage the trick? Enter the exchange-rate regime.

Exchange-Rate Policy and the Austrian Model

The aim of Austrian authorities, like their counterparts in other small states, was to take the best from the external markets but to leave the rest. Peter Katzenstein traces the delicate processes through which Austrians went down precisely this road after 1955; but he spends surprisingly little time on the monetary dimension of their crafting of the institutional and then functional sinews of a secure nation.[36] In this regard, whereas the Canadians relied on a flexible exchange rate, the Austrians consistently made the opposite choice.

During the delicate years after neutrality was proclaimed, the independent design of the Austrian fixed exchange-rate regime was acceptable both to the Soviet Union and to the United States. Over time, however, such a regime proved stable because it tended to be underpinned by anti-inflationary monetary policies. Most important, the essential buffering mechanism—necessitated by domestic preferences for both economic openness and political autonomy—was internalized.[37] A hard-currency peg became part of the formula to stabilize postwar social arrange-

---

72; Audrey Cronin, *Great Power Politics and the Struggle over Austria, 1945–1955* (Ithaca: Cornell University Press, 1986).

36. Katzenstein, *Corporatism and Change.*

37. Beth Simmons demonstrates on various dimensions how the country proved incapable of just such internalization during the interwar years. See Beth A. Simmons, *Who Adjusts? Domestic Sources of Foreign Economic Policy during the Interwar Years* (Princeton: Princeton University Press, 1994).

ments for distributing the economic and political costs and benefits of gradually opening the country once again to the German economy.

It is true that there was no automatic consensus on the notion of fixing the bilateral Austrian-German rate at a level marginally favorable to the cause of Austrian competitiveness. Certainly no one could advocate the policy openly. For one thing, German workers would not like to hear it. For another, both before and after 1955 the Russians were highly attentive to such matters, and bilateral concertation tended to sound like a new *Anschluss* to them.[38] Austrian employer groups and industry leaders, moreover, were of two minds. They understood the logic of bilateralism, but they also hoped to create options for export diversification in the future. In this light, a flexible exchange rate, especially a downwardly flexible one, could in principle be of considerable assistance.[39] Along that second line, even labor unions focused on Germany could be tempted by the lure of devaluation.

During the 1960s, such matters were not so much the subject of academic disputation as of practical experimentation. In 1961 and again in 1969, broad revaluations of the deutschmark on world markets seemed to present opportunities. The schilling was then still formally pegged to the dollar and did not therefore automatically follow the deutschmark upward. The social partners—business, labor, and government—clearly hoped in each case that the resulting undervaluation of the schilling would open new markets for Austrian exports. What they wound up experiencing, in fact, was domestic inflation, with real and palpable wage losses. Pensioners and others on fixed incomes spoke darkly about the 1920s. For their part, central bank officials eventually used the experience of the 1960s to teach a lesson about real effective exchange rates to all who would listen. Whether or not social learning can really account for the depth of the subsequent political commitment to the peg, ever since 1969 only minor adjustments have occurred in the nominal bilateral exchange rate (see table 9.1). Since the early 1980s, indeed, the rate has been completely frozen.[40] The few nominal changes that preceded that period are nevertheless worth some attention because they marked the points at which buffering mechanisms were deemed most clearly to be needed between powerful economic forces and countervailing political exigencies.

After Bretton Woods

Central bank officials from the 1960s recall the governor and the finance minister spending considerable time with trade union officials, especially with the head of the ÖGB, explaining the wisdom of a productivity-based wage policy. Such a policy centered on the fixed link to the deutschmark and a follow-the-leader strategy on both interest rates and labor costs. The beauty of the Bretton Woods system, they

38. In interviews with senior monetary officials with memories of the 1950s and 1960s, Russian sensitivities come up again and again. It is clear that this weighed heavily on many minds for many years. Interviews by David M. Andrews, Vienna, March 2001.

39. Retired senior National Bank official, interview by Andrews, March 13, 2001.

40. See von Riekhoff and Neuhold, *Unequal Partners*, 164–65.

Table 9.1 Exchange rate: Austrian schilling to deutschmark, 1955–1995[a]

Year	Rate
1955	6.19
1960	6.19
1965	6.48
1970	7.09
1975	7.08
1980	7.12
1985	7.03
1990	7.03
1995	7.03

Source: Austrian National Bank data
[a]No change in later periods, and the same nominal rate was embedded in the final transition to the euro on December 31, 1998.

held, was that no one had to be explicit about such a strategy. The excessive inflation experienced after the deutschmark revaluations in 1961 and 1969 suggested that Austria should simply have realigned in lock-step, a lesson union leaders were eventually willing to acknowledge. But central bankers initially confronted resistance to this reasoning from business groups, from the chancellor, and from the IMF.

From the point of view of the IMF, the Austrian structural trade deficit suggested then, and well into the 1970s, the need for a devaluation of the schilling. The moment of truth came when the Bretton Woods arrangements finally began to break down. At one level, the 1971 devaluation of the dollar and the final decision to float in 1973 raised an obvious, awkward, and politically sensitive problem. Inside Austria, an understanding had emerged among the social partners concerning the basic industrial strategy decisively shaped by Austrian-German production networks. The straightforward monetary dimension of this reality before 1971 meant simply importing low inflation from Germany via a fixed link between the deutschmark and the dollar. To the extent this may sometimes have necessitated flexibility in wages and production costs inside Austria, the social partners finally stood ready to comply—and to the extent that they could better Germany's performance on inflation, to profit thereby.[41]

As the dollar ceased to be a reliable anchor for that core relationship, however, it was politically impossible to shift to an explicit schilling-deutschmark link. Two things were at work. First, the Russians were still interested and still watching; at the very least, Austrian policy makers were still absolutely convinced of their interest right through to the 1980s. Second, in its own deeply conflicted, historically conditioned way, Austrian nationalism was now a political fact. In the ironic phrase of one former governor, this meant (and still means) that Austrian policy had to be one

41. Note that the social partners were, and are, represented on the governing council of the National Bank.

of "autonomous solidarity" with Germany.[42] The solution that eventually developed, beginning in the early 1970s, was to explicitly tie the Austrian schilling to a basket of currencies while implicitly pegging it to the deutschmark. Inside the central bank, considerable analytical resources were devoted to calculating the basket rate on a daily basis and, whenever necessary to keep the implicit peg rigid, to rejigging the basket. For Bank traders engaged in actual open-market operations, however, the task was uncomplicated: the target was understood.[43] For those who set Austrian interest rates, somewhat more delicacy was required. Eventually, a standard practice emerged—the board would meet the same day the Bundesbank board met; and whenever the Bundesbank changed its base rate, the National Bank would within the hour "autonomously" decide to match it.

Only in 1975, in unusual political circumstances, was there a brief attempt to step away from this post–Bretton Woods consensus by allowing a slight depreciation of the schilling. Once again, certain business groups and trade union leaders were apparently tempted by a strengthening deutschmark. This seemed, at least to some, an opportunity to expand exports and to secure an extra wage increase, partly to compensate for price hikes occasioned by continuing actions by the Organization of Petroleum Exporting Countries (OPEC) in the world oil markets.[44] But when the National Bank chose not to follow the Bundesbank in a particular interest rate hike, a brief run on the schilling ensued, significant reserves were lost, and accelerating inflation again followed. The lesson of money illusion was relearned, and the fundamental consensus reasserted itself. One central bank official recalls that in the year following this incident, the chancellor for the first time explicitly defended the necessity of the fixed tie to the deutschmark in talks with senior trade union officials.[45]

One final political struggle occurred in 1978–79 when the chancellor and the finance minister took different sides on the question of how to restructure aging industries such as steel. The IMF and the Organization for Economic Cooperation and Development (OECD), in particular, were quite critical of the excessive rigidity introduced in this context by the deutschmark peg. As one National Bank official explained, "We knew that if we gave up the peg, it wouldn't have changed anything; we also noted the experience of Norway and Sweden, for they had abandoned external discipline but without positive results."[46] In the event, the Bank

42. Former National Bank governor, interview by Andrews, Vienna, March 12, 2001. As Andrews has pointed out to me, an additional dimension of this creative ambiguity developed in the late 1960s and early 1970s when a Socialist government in Austria opposed the formation of the European Economic Community and its underlying liberal-market principles and also criticized Germany for joining it; in such an environment, an explicit deutschmark link would have been especially problematic. The expanding literature on money and identity is relevant to this point. See, for example, Eric Helleiner, *The Making of National Money: Territorial Currencies in Historical Perspective* (Ithaca: Cornell University Press, 2003); Matthias Kaelberer, "The Euro and European Identity: Symbols, Power, and the Politics of European Monetary Union," *Review of International Studies* 30, no. 2 (2004): 161–78.

43. Retired policy makers and currency traders of the Austrian National Bank, interviews by Andrews, Vienna, March 2001.

44. Von Riekhoff and Neuhold, *Unequal Partners*, 165.

45. National Bank official, interview by Andrews, Vienna, March 14, 2001.

46. National Bank official, interview by Andrews, Vienna, March 15, 2001.

briefly delayed responding to a rise in German interest rates, a minor devaluation of the schilling ensued, and the skeptics were again proved right. Shortly thereafter, the devaluation was reversed and the exchange rate was rigidly (but unofficially) fixed at 7.03 schillings to the deutschmark. When a similar controversy with the IMF occurred in 1991, the government and the central bank rejected outright its advice to loosen the hard-currency policy, and they even demanded a rewriting of the IMF annual surveillance report on the country.[47]

Austria and the Euro

Throughout the 1990s and until today, the hard-currency consensus remains dominant, even though the success of the peg continues to be a subject of some debate both externally and internally.[48] It certainly has made issues of fiscal adjustment more difficult to avoid and contributed to recent political crises, especially those associated with the challenge of pension reform.[49] The rise of the Freedom Party and its frontal attack on the social partnership system brought underlying tensions to the fore in the mid-1990s. A few years later, however, we would have been hard-pressed to find compelling evidence of the dismantlement of that system.[50]

The end of the Cold War, the 1994 move to join the European Union, and the subsequent decision to become a founding member of Europe's Economic and Monetary Union (EMU) opened a new chapter in this continuing story. On one level, there is no puzzle surrounding the ease with which the schilling followed the deutschmark into EMU—the fixed link of both currencies to the euro simply replaced a bilateral connection. On another level, however, a subtle but important change was involved.

The full significance of Austria's efforts to move beyond the dogma of neutrality as the Cold War was ending, and to embrace European integration as it was deepening and broadening, goes beyond the scope of this chapter. For present purposes, it is necessary merely to note the clear-eyed perception of Austrian monetary policy makers as they oversaw the transition from the era of the hard schilling to the era of the euro.[51] At base, the move meant abandoning a reliable but relatively passive set

47. Interviews by Andrews, Vienna, March 15, 2001.

48. For an exhaustive look at the economic performance data over time, see Karl Pichelmann and Helmut Hofer, "Austria: Long-Term Success through Social Partnership," *International Labor Organization Employment and Training Papers* 51, Geneva, Switzerland: International Labour Organization, 1999. Note, in particular, the data on long-term interest rates, flexible real wage rates, and changes in productivity indicators, all of which closely track German equivalents.

49. For detailed comparative assessments of the common challenges and diverse responses of European welfare states, see Fritz Scharpf and Vivien Schmidt, *Welfare & Work in the Open Economy*, Vols. 1–2 (Oxford: Oxford University Press, 2001); Vivien Schmidt, *The Futures of European Capitalism* (Oxford: Oxford University Press, 2002).

50. Reinhard Heinisch, "Coping with Economic Integration: Corporatist Strategies in Germany and Austria in the 1990s," *West European Politics* 23, no. 3 (July 2000): 67–96.

51. For one thing, as Andrews concludes on the basis of his interviews, the National Bank made clear that it would not rely overtly on the European exchange-rate mechanism in the run-up to the start of EMU. Instead, autonomous solidarity with Germany remained the order of the day.

of policy practices. After all, once the euro was adopted, the notion of autonomous solidarity with Germany became a less ironic turn of phrase. By joining EMU, Austria gained a voice in the making of the monetary policy that it now explicitly shared with Germany and other European partners. To be sure, the volume of the Austrian voice would not match that of Germany in the arcane processes through which European monetary policy was set. But Austria had had no voice in the Bundesbank when it used to call the shots, and it now did indeed have a place at the table when the European Central Bank (ECB) made monetary policy decisions for all member states.[52]

Through EMU, Austria was able to maintain its hard-currency policy in relation to Germany. It therefore had two buffering mechanisms at its disposal as it confronted external markets and the raw economic and financial power of Germany: a cooperative multilateral institution, of which it was now an intimate part, and a continuing internal capacity to match changes in German production costs. But it had lost one as well: the implicit peg with the deutschmark had become explicit and was, thus, more easily subject to scrutiny and criticism by potential opponents of the social market consensus. How this aspect of the change in regime will affect the social partnership remains to be seen.

Conclusion

"Trust, but verify," Ronald Reagan is famous for advising U.S. policy makers when they sought new arms-control arrangements with the Soviet Union in the 1980s. If he had been a monetary policy maker in Canada or Austria at any time since 1945, he may similarly have opined, "Cooperate, but maintain room for maneuver."

As in other arenas of power, neither Canada nor Austria ever really wanted directly to challenge the international monetary priorities of the leading states on their borders. But they also were not supine dependencies with no choice but to accept the external effects of those priorities. Specific monetary decisions taken by those leaders affected them and could either be acquiesced in or countered. Canada and Austria wanted to get as much as they could for their societies from their most important economic relationships, but they also sought to build and maintain separate nations.[53] To accomplish their objectives, carving out as much practical autonomy as possible was the critical task. For these states, monetary statecraft meant crafting institutional and policy buffers. Those buffers specifically promised to limit the power of their lead partners to deflect on to them the transitional costs of bilateral adjustment and sometimes of system maintenance. They also worked to sustain distinctive national identities, although it remains difficult to assess their precise contribution to this effort.

52. Interview by Andrews, Vienna, March 16, 2001.
53. This theme deserves more extensive study. For background on the Austrian case, see John Breuilly, *Austria, Prussia and Germany 1806–1871* (London: Longman, 2002); on the Canadian case, see John Holmes, *Life with Uncle* (Toronto: University of Toronto Press, 1981).

In the face of such follower strategies, what was left for the leaders? Acquiescence to the buffers when the leaders were leading wisely and fruitless confrontation when they were not. As previously noted, the willing acquiescence of followers is commonly viewed as the key distinction between coercive power and authoritative leadership. In the two special relationships explored here, acquiescence by the leaders to the use of effective buffers by their followers was the best response. Coercive attempts to make the follower change strategic tracks, most overtly in the 1971 U.S.-Canadian dispute, failed. In other words, monetary power conceived in the relational sense confronted distinct limits.

In comparing the Canadian and Austrian cases, it is not the existence of buffers in the crucial bilateral currency relationships that varies but their character. This variance seems functionally related to the deeper historical trajectory of internal political economies. At particular times in both cases, windows opened on the possibility of serious participation in truly multilateral institutions that just might substitute for less subtle buffering mechanisms. Only very recently in the German-Austrian case did such a choice seem partially to meet the basic political requirements of the follower state. In terms of effectively responding to the Austrian insistence on having a real voice in making shared monetary policies, the ECB may satisfy Austria in a way not dissimilar from the way Louis Rasminsky once hoped a Keynesian currency union might satisfy Canada. Austria may, as a consequence, already wield more regional monetary influence than Canada does in its context. In the end, however, it remains doubtful that cooperative multilateral mechanisms have ever convinced many people in either country that they should be relied on as the ultimate political buffers. After all, Austria and Canada both retain their own central banks, and both continue, each in its own way, tenaciously to defend their room for maneuver in more deeply integrating regional economies.

In the Canadian case, the final buffer was always a flexible exchange rate; only once was another option briefly pursued. When Rasminsky advised the federal Cabinet to consult with business and labor groups on measures to support a repegged exchange rate, he meant coordinated measures to render domestic prices and wages downwardly flexible. This was a pipe dream because Canadian society has always lacked the sense of solidarity and social cohesion necessary either to design or to implement such measures; the Austrian ideology of social partnership has no counterpart in liberal Canada. But neither does the alternative ideology of neoliberalism resonate deeply in a dualistic nation built across a continent of diverse regions. A flexible exchange rate is the one instrument under national control that can limit the capacity of the United States to export the costs of bilateral adjustment and system maintenance. It is also the one instrument the state could reliably use to ameliorate the adjustment burdens generated within Canada and to distribute those burdens across a fractious society.

Austria could have pursued a similar course over the decades since World War II. Certainly many Canadian economists expected them to do so, as did the IMF. At times, even industrialists within Austria advocated exchange-rate flexibility. But actual experience reinforced the contrary view. Useful for those advocating a hard-currency policy were memories of the 1920s, but especially important was a remarkably enduring social consensus on the wisdom of keeping inflation low so as to ensure that Austrian production costs would always marginally undercut competing German costs. Even so, such a consensus would have meant little in the absence of workable political mechanisms for rendering real prices and wages within Austria seriously flexible when circumstances so required. The social partnership system born in the bloody class conflict of the interwar period proved robust enough to serve this purpose throughout the postwar era. Some skeptical observers now argue that the country's coordinated market economy is under serious threat because the necessity of pension reform and rising regional demands push it to the breaking point. Such a contention remains doubtful, at least with respect to monetary policy, and it downplays the historical success of negotiated flexibility within the Austrian economy.

It may be true that only certain follower states, mostly located in the advanced industrial core of the global system, can now craft, defend, and use such buffers at the interface of their societies and leading external markets; that is, it may be true that only a few states today can seriously contemplate monetary statecraft. There is, however, no reason to accept such an assertion without further empirical research. Certainly Scott Cooper (chap. 8 in this volume) suggests otherwise. Diverse monetary strategies certainly remain possible for some, and not only for the powerful. Moreover, the specific choices follower states can make, on the evidence of this chapter, appear to remain deeply conditioned by underlying institutional idiosyncrasies. Monetary power and its limits, the Canadian and Austrian cases also suggest, must be understood not only in straightforward relational terms but also in light of the various domestic political arrangements that continue to exist within modern capitalism. Future scholarship on the dynamics of monetary power, as well as on grand strategic projects to transform such power into meaningful authority, needs to take such domestic arrangements seriously.

INDEX

active mode of influence, 48–49

actor interests, 31, 44; power to rearticulate, *12,* 15–16, 72, 174; power to reconstruct, *12,* 15–16, 72

adaptability, 14, 47–49

adaptation, 92 n, 108

adjustment: autonomy and influence, 32–33; burden of, 12–14, 31–36, 79; continuing, 3, 11, 13, 36–38; domestic impacts of, 41, 122; macro-dimension of, 12–14, 31–36, 79; partisan mutual, 108–9; payments financing, 18–19, *19,* 23–24; process, 38–39; real, 23, 37, 92 n, 97; transitional, 3, 11, 13, 38–41. *See also* Balance of payments

After Hegemony (Keohane), 108–9

agent slippage, 181

Andrews, David M., 3–4, 17, 31–32, 34–35, 47 n, 49, 70, 72, 120, 150, 171; power, view of, 75–76

Article VIII status (IMF), 191

ASEAN + 3, 133–34

Asian financial crisis of 1997–98, 132, 134, 151, 153, 157, 171. *See also* East Asia

Asian Monetary Fund (AMF) proposal, 24, 134, 152

asset financing, 23

asymmetry, 103–6, 114, 122–23, 149–50; currency areas and, 164–66; limits of international monetary power and, 164–65

Australia, 172

Austria, 4, 20, 92, 186, 206; autonomy, 107, 113, 198–99; EMU and, 204–5; Germany and, 197–204; social partnership, 202, 206–7

Austrian National Bank, 198, 199

Austrian State Treaty of 1955, 197, 199

autonomy, 32–33; Austria, 107, 113, 198–99; Canada, 195–96; core importance of, 33–34; of follower states, 184, 195–96; globalization and, 149–51; modes of influence and, 34–35

balance of payments, 12–14, 99, 117; currency areas and, 171–72; current account as measure of, 36–37; disequilibrium, 10–11, 31, 47–49, 79, 97; openness and, 47–49. *See also* Adjustment; Exchange-rate weapon

Baldwin, David, 17

Baltic states, 170

Bank of Canada, 187, 190, 193

Bank of England, 56–58, 181

Bank of Japan, 136

Barings crisis of 1890, 56–57

Barnett, Michael, 181

benign neglect, 68, 92, 120, 157. *See also* Passive leadership

Bergsten, Fred, 153

bilateral exchange rate, 40

Blessing letter of March 1967, 56

boat rocking metaphor, 164

Bonn summit (1978), 9, 10, 14, 112, 125, 127

borrowing, 62–63, 65, 67

borrowing capacity, 42–45

Bretton Woods system, 20 n, 131; Austria and, 201–2; breakdown of, 125–27, 163; Canada and, 187, 190–91, 194–96; formalized rules and, 177–78; Germany and, 126–27; Japan and, 14, 126–27; monetary policy coordination and, 98–99, 105, 114. *See also* Bretton Woods system, United States and

Bretton Woods system, United States and, 25–27, 105, 114; breakdown of, 125–27, 163; Canada and, 190–91, 194–96; double standards and, 64–65; limits of monetary power and, 177–78. *See also* Bretton Woods system

Britain: currency leadership, 52, 55–57, 61–62, 67, 69, 100; gold standard and, 58–59; limited government, 57–58; monetary dependence and, 172–74; sterling and, 7–8, 67, 100; sterling area and, 67, 162–63, 177, 179, 181; Suez Canal incident and, 7–8

Bryant, Ralph C., 94–95, 100 n

Bundesbank, 65, 67–68, 128, 205; monetary policy coordination and, 98, 106–7, 113

Burns, Arthur, 25, 126, 194

Butler, Richard A., 7

Canada, 4, 186; 1950 float, 191–92; 1962 peg, 192–93, 196; 1970 float, 193–94, 196; Bretton Woods system and, 187, 190–91, 194–96; continuity in analysis and policy, 194–97; floating exchange rate, 20, 187, 191–94, 196; as follower state, 187–97, 205–6; inflation, 187–88

Canada-US Free Trade Agreement, 188

capital controls, 20, 59, 157, 185, 190–91

capital mobility, 21, 97, 119–21

Carter administration, 9, 127

Casino Capitalism (Strange), 78–79

Central Bank of Russia, 177, 181

central banks, 58; Austrian National Bank, 198, 199; Bank of Canada, 187, 190, 193; Bank of England, 56–58, 181; Central Bank of Russia, 177, 181; Europe and Japan, 136–37; Iraq, 144. *See also* Bundesbank; European Central Bank; Federal Reserve

Central Intelligence Agency (CIA), 142

Chiang Mai Initiative, 133–34, 153

China, 121, 133, 136–37, 151–54

Clark, Clifford, 194–95

Clark-Rasminsky consensus, 194–95

Clinton administration, 129

Cohen, Benjamin J., 3, 13–14, 57, 70, 103–4, 117, 121, 153; dollarization, view of, 85–86; on monetary insulation, 163–64; structural power, view of, 73, 76–78, 82

Cold War, 148–49, 160, 200, 204

Communauté financière d'Afrique (CFA), 163, 169

Connally, John, 25–27, 65, 194

continuing cost of adjustment, 3, 11, 13, 36–38, 169 n. *See also* Power to Delay payment

Cooper, Richard N., 13 n

Cooper, Scott, 4, 15, 22, 207

cooperation, 92–96, 108–10

coordination, 98–101. *See also* Monetary policy coordination

coordination failure, 111–12

counterfeit money, 142–43

credibility, 51, 53, 57–58, 61, 65–70

creditor governments, 43–44, 57

crisis periods, 56–57, 97, 100, 112. *See also* Asian financial crisis of 1997–98

Cuba, 88

currencies, international roles of, 121–22, 141, 163

Currency and Coercion (Kirshner), 9, 73, 77, 140

currency apartheid, 87

currency areas, 22, 73, 77–78; decision-making symmetry, 178–80; domestic politics and, 174–75; euro area, 129–31, 137; franc zone, 163, 175, 179–80; institutional limits on, 175–82; insulation, need for, 171–74; interdependence and, 164–65, 167–68; Kirshner's model of monetary dependence, 166–68; Kirshner's view of, 80–82, 174, 183; leadership and followership, 165–66; limits on, 163–64; membership costs and benefits, 169–71; membership in, 15, 80–82; monetary dependence and, 162–63, 165–68; optimum currency area theory, 3, 12 n, 16, 103; rand zone, 178; ruble zone, 163, 180–82; sterling area, 67, 162–63, 177, 179, 181; systemic disruption and, 168–69, 172; third-party agents, 180–82; weakness of leadership and, 162–63. *See also* Monetary statecraft

currency leadership, 54; Britain, 52, 55–57, 61–62, 67, 69, 100; as conservative, 59–60, 65–66, 69; credibility, 51, 53, 57–58, 61, 65–70; Europe, 67–68, 70–71; financial development and, 56–57, 70; as form of monopoly power, 52, 55, 66–68; institutional arrangements and, 51–52, 71; limitations on, 66–69; material incentives and, 55–61; normative convergence through socialization, 61–66; private-sector agents, 55, 63–65; United States, 14, 52, 55–56, 59–62, 67–69. *See also* Monetary leadership

currency manipulation, 4, 21 n, 77, 140–48; under globalization, 147–48; against Iraq, 142–47; against Kurds, 145–47. *See also* Monetary statecraft

Currency Protection Act of November 1947 (Austria), 198

currency pyramid, 14, 50, 69, 85, 185

currency regions, 165

currency relations, 18, *19,* 20–21; closing of gold window and, 25–27; economic geography and, 81, *84,* 87; influencing currency use, 22–23; symbolism and, 82–83, *84,* 86. *See also* Monetary statecraft

currency use, 18–19, *19*
currency values, 18, *19*
current account, 9, 36–37, 121

decision-making symmetry, 178–80
default, 57
deflation, 39–40
depreciation, 39–40, *84;* of dollar, 62–63, 69, 78, 136, 178; exchange-rate weapon and, 121–23
deutschmark, 9, 22, 60, 67, 70; exchange-rate weapon and, 127–28; monetary policy coordination and, 98, 100, 107, 114
dinar, 142–47
direct influence, 8–9
direct power, 76–77. *See also* Relational power
discord, 94, 104, 107, 112
dollar, 45–46, 56, 183; depreciation of, 62–63, 69, 78, 136, 178; international role, 78–79, 136; Persian Gulf states and, 173; preeminence of, 45, 66, 67, 85; recession of 1970s and, 9–10; structural power and, 78–79
dollar area, 163
dollarization, 23, 88–89; informal, 85, 183; social divisions and, 86–87; structural power and, 84–88
dollar standard, 56, 64
domain, 8
domestic institutions, 57, 61
domestic policy insulation, 20–21
domestic politics, 53, 196, 199, 206; currency areas and, 174–75; exchange-rate weapon and, 124; globalization and, 150; traded and non-traded sectors and, 122–23

East African Currency Board (EACB), 181
East African monetary union, 179
East Asia, 69; Asian financial crisis of 1997–98, 132, 134, 151, 153, 157, 171; competition for influence, 151–54; exchange-rate weapon and, 131–34, 136–37
East Caribbean dollar, 178–79
Economic and Monetary Union (EMU), 14, 67, 70–71, 129–31, 137–38, 155, 177, 179; Austria and, 204–5
economic geography, 81, *84,* 87
economic statecraft, 17
economic theory, 13, 36
economic variables, 13–14
Eden, Anthony, 7
effective exchange rate, 40
Egypt, Suez Canal incident, 7–8
Eisenhower administration, 60, 64
enforcement, 82, 86
English common law, 57, 71
entrapment, 15, 22, 80–81, 86, 166

Estonia, 171
euro, 45–46, 67–68, 70–71, 112, 153, 155; appreciation, 2001–2004, 137–38
euro area, 129–31, 137, 163
Europe, 14, 204; central banks, 136–37; currency leadership and, 67–68, 70–71; exchange-rate weapon and, 21, 130–31, 137–38; policy objectives, 63–64. *See also* Economic and Monetary Union (EMU)
European Central Bank (ECB), 22–23 n, 70, 137–38, 181, 205
European Commission, 130
European Community, 106
European Monetary System (EMS), 22, 65, 67, 130; monetary policy coordination and, 97–98, 100, 106, 114
exchange-rate manipulation, 20–21
exchange-rate mechanism (ERM), 100, 112
exchange rates, 9; Austria, 200–201, *202;* Canada, 20, 187, *188, 189,* 191–94, 196; closure of gold window, 25–27, 78, 97, 126, 194; fixed, 25–27, 39–40, 65; flexible, 121–22, 187; pegged, 39, 40, 47, 54 n, 100, 126, 192–93, 196, 200–201; political concerns, 39–41. *See also* Floating exchange rate
exchange-rate weapon, 4, *84,* 97; assumptions and preconditions, 122–24; concepts and mechanisms, 118–24; countermeasures, 118, 129–36, 138; depreciation and, 121–23; Europe and, 21, 130–31, 137–38; history of, 124–29, 136; Japan and East Asia, 21, 126–29, 131–34, 136–37; macroeconomic conflict and, 119, 123–24; policy adjustment and, 117, 120, 123; structural shift, 129–30, 138; twenty-first century, 136–38; two forms of, 117–18; United States and, 21, 135–36
expenditure-changing policies, 37, 39–40
expenditure-switching policies, 37, 40
extraction, 66, *84,* 87, 89, 166

Federal Reserve, 58–60, 63, 70, 88
Feldstein, Martin, 155, 158
financial development, 56–58, 70
financial markets, regulatory trends, 79–80, *84,* 88
financial relations, 18–19, *19,* 23–24
financial variables, 13, 42. *See also* International liquidity
Finnemore, Martha, 181
flight to quality, 157
floating exchange rate, 39–40, 65, 126, 140; Canada, 20, 187, 191–94, 196
follower states, 54, 57; Austria, 197–205, 206; autonomy of, 184, 195–96; Canada, 187–97, 205–6; incentives and, 55–61, 70; monetary

follower states (*continued*)
   policy coordination and, 99, 111; national politics and international monetary order, 185–87; threats to currency areas, 164, 167, 169–71, 172–74
foreign assets-to-GDP ratio, 135
foreign direct investment (FDI), 159
foreign-exchange markets, 21, 121–22
foreign reserves, 13
formalization of rules, 176–78
franc, 65, 107
France, 99, 107; decision-making power, 179–80; exchange-rate weapon and, 130; *grand gaffe*, 65, 98
franc zone, 163, 175, 179–80; West African, 170–71, 179–80

G-7, 68
G-10, 126
Gaulle, Charles de, 66–67
Geertz, Clifford, 101
geography: economic, 81, *84*, 87; monetary, 154–56
Gerashchenko, Viktor, 181–82
Germany, 22, 56, 62, 112; Austria and, 197–204; Bretton Woods regime and, 126–27; currency leadership, 65, 69, 70; exchange-rate weapon and, 126–28, 130; monetary policy coordination, 92, 100, 106, 107; recession of 1970s and, 9–10; reunification, 65, 129 n
Gilpin, Robert, 159
global capital markets, 42, 44
globalization, 4, 139–40; Asian competition for influence, 151–54; continuing politics of monetary geography, 154–56; currency areas and, 171; currency manipulation under, 140–48; exchange-rate weapon and, 136–38; as financial, 139; international instability and, 158–59; monetary dependence and, 148–56; political benefits of, 160–61; regional monetary policy coordination, 149–51, 156, 174; search for influence and autonomy, 149–51; structural power and, 74–75, 84, 89; systemic disruption, 156–60
gold standard, 55–56; 1960s debates, 63–64; Britain and, 58–59; United States and, 59–60, 63–64, 105
gold window, closing of, 25–27, 78, 97, 126, 194
government: criticism of, 39–40, 47–48; type of, currency leadership and, 57–58
Gowa, Joanne S., 25
grand gaffe, 65, 98
Great Society program, 64
Greenspan, Alan, 160
Gresham's law, 144
Grimes, William, 152

gross domestic product (GDP), 47, 135
Group of Five, 128
Guinea, 172
Gulf wars, 145, 147
Guzzini, Stefano, 74–76

harmony, 94, 98
hegemonic stability theory, 2 n.5, 52–53
hegemony, 34–35, 52–53, 68–69
Helleiner, Eric, 3, 15–17, 66, 129 n, 150, 192
Henning, C. Randall, 4, 14, 21, 24, 35, 67, 78–79, 97
herd behavior, 167–68
Hewitt, Virginia, 82, 83
hierarchy, 14, 91–93, 98, 101, 111–12, 114; benign neglect and, 92, 157; in monetary relations, 49–50. *See also* Monetary policy coordination
Hirschman, Albert, 15, 149–50, 160, 167
Hussein, King, 145
Hussein, Saddam, 142, 144, 145

identity, 3, 11, 13; rearticulation of, *12*, 15–16, 72, 174; reconstruction of, *12*, 15–16, 72; symbolism of currency and, 83, *84*
Ikenberry, John, 53, 61
imperialism, age of, 81–83, 90
import surcharge, 27
incentives, 55–61, 70, 150; security, 56–57
indirect institutional power, 75, 77
individual consciousness, 11
inflation, 39–40, *60, 63;* Canada, 187–88; monetary policy coordination and, 98–99; U.S. monetary policy and, 59–60, 79
influence, 16–17, 22–23, 32–33, *84;* Asian competition for, 151–54; direct and indirect, 8–9, 166; globalization and, 149–51; passive and active modes, 48–49
influence attempts, 34–35, 77
institutional limits, 164
institutions, 4; currency leadership and, 51–52, 71; domestic, 57, 61; formalization of rules, 176–78; indirect power, 75, 77; limits on currency areas, 175–82
insulation, 20–21, 82, 163–64; currency areas and, 171–74
interdependence, 46–47, 103, 198–200; currency areas and, 164–65, 167–68
interest groups, 47, 175
interest rates, 100
international liquidity, 13, 42, 49, 51, 82
International Monetary Fund (IMF), 7, 23–24, 43, 68, 97; Articles of Agreement, 190, 191; Austria and, 199; Canada and, 190–91, 195–96; East Asia and, 134, 151, 152; South Korea and, 158–59

international monetary order: national politics and, 185–87; reform negotiations, 1972–74, 64, 68

international monetary power, 1, 3; beneficiaries, 11, 15–16; core of, 33–34; definition, 8; forms of, 10–16; international monetary relations and, 8–10; monetary statecraft vs., 16–17; two hands of, 35–36. *See also* Currency leadership; Domestic institutions; Domestic politics; Hierarchy; Limits of international monetary power; Macro-dimension of international monetary power; Micro-dimension of international monetary power; Monetary leadership; Monetary policy coordination

international monetary relations, 1; competitive dimension of, 13, 139; cycles, 124–29; direct and indirect influence, 8–9, 166; hierarchy in, 49–50; monetary power and, 8–10; structural power and, 76–84

international relations theory, 1–2; monetary policy coordination and, 91–93, 108–10; structural power and, 73–76

intervention data, 120–21

Iraq, plots against dinar, 142–47

issue linkage, 8–9

James, Scott, 17 n, 34

Japan, 14, 69, 78, 112; Bretton Woods regime and, 126–27; closing of gold window and, 25–27, 97, 126; competition for monetary influence, 151–54; exchange-rate weapon and, 21, 126–29, 131–34, 136–37; international trade, 56; interventions, 2002–4, 121; recession of 1970s and, 9–10; symbolic use of currencies, 83

Johnson, Lyndon, 64

Kakuei Tanaka, 126

Kantor, Mickey, 159

Katzenstein, Peter, 200

Keohane, Robert O., 33, 46, 94–96, 103, 108–9

Keynes, John Maynard, 190

Keynesian economic ideas, 59

Kiichi Miyazawa, 153

Kindleberger, Charles, 52–54

Kirshner, Jonathan, 8, 15, 20–21, 24, 35, 162–63, 165; *Currency and Coercion* (Kirshner), 9, 73, 77, 140; currency areas, view of, 80–82, 174, 183; dollarization, view of, 86; lifeboat analogy, 168–69; monetary dependence, model of, 166–68; structural power, view of, 73, 77–78, 80

Krasner, Stephen, 108 n

Kupchan, Charles, 53, 61

Kurds, 145–47

Kuwait, 168

Lake, David A., 34, 50, 53, 91

Lasswell, Harold D., 17

Latin America, 86–87, 163

Latvia, 170

leadership: liquidity, 14, 54; passive, *12*, 14, 68, 92, 104, 107; as term, 184. *See also* Currency leadership; Monetary leadership

League of Nations, 198

legitimacy, 32 n, 53, 68, 184. *See also* Credibility

Lemon, Alaina, 87

lender-of-last resort lending, 80, *84*, 88

liability financing, 23

liberalization, financial, 68

liberal-market ideology, 196

lifeboat analogy, 168–69

limited constitutional government, 57–58

limits of international monetary power, 162–63; asymmetry and, 164–65; market limits, 168–75; monetary dependence and, 162–68. *See also* Currency areas

Lindblom, Charles, 94–96, 108–9

liquidity, international, 13, 42, 49, 51, 82

liquidity leadership, 14, 54

liquidity provision, 18–19, *19*, 23–24

lira, 146–47

Lithuania, 170

locomotive theory, 127

Louvre accord, 125, 128

Loynes, J. B., 181

Maastricht treaty, 130

Machlup, Fritz, 100

Macmillan, Harold, 7

macro-dimension of international monetary power, 3, 37; adjustment and, 12–14, 31–36, 79; core of monetary power, 33–34; exchange-rate weapon and, 119, 123–24; structural power and, 78–79, *84*

Malaysia, 20, 153–54, 160, 172–74

manipulated adjustment, 108

market limits, 164, 168–75

markets, 4, 85; foreign-exchange, 21, 121–22; global capital, 42, 44; as opinion polls, 44–45; regulatory trends, 79–80, *84*, 88; structural power and, 75–76

market sentiment, 141

McKinnon, Ronald, 64

McNamara, Kathleen, 154

Meunier, Sophie, 154

micro-dimension of international monetary power, 3, 11, 72–73, *84;* beneficiaries, 15–16; symbolism and, 82–83. *See also* Structural power

military statecraft, 17

Milner, Helen, 95 n, 96, 109

Mitterand, François, 65

monetary dependence, 15, 33; Britain, 172–74; currency areas and, 162–63, 165–68; fostering of, 77, 81, 86; globalization and, 148–56; Kirshner's model of, 166–68; limits on, 165–68

monetary followership. *See* Follower states

monetary leadership, 3, 13, 69–71, 107; as conservative, 51, 53, 57–60, 65–66, 69; definitions, 52–54; legitimacy and, 53, 68; limitations, 66–69; passive, 14, 68, 92, 104, 107. *See also* Currency leadership

monetary policy coordination, 3–4; abundance of coordination, 98–99; among multiple actors, 106–7; asymmetrical demand for, 103–6, 114; bargaining over, 101–7; constructing policy coordination, 110–13, *111;* cooperation, 108–10; crisis periods and, 97, 100, 112; discord, 94, 104, 107, 112; European Monetary System and, 97–98, 100, 106, 114; failures, 103–4, 111–12; harmony, 94, 98; international relations theory and, 91–93, 108–10; negotiating dynamics, 102–5; paucity of formal negotiations, 91, 96–98, 114; policy adaptation, 98, *105,* 105–7, *106;* procedural, 93–101, 108, 111. *See also* Hierarchy; Regional monetary policy coordination; Substantive coordination

monetary power. *See* International monetary power

monetary statecraft, 1, 3–4, 49, 117, 139, 162; defined, 16–17; domestic policy insulation, 20–21; elements of, 18–24, *19;* exchange-rate manipulation, 20–21; financial relations, 18–19, *19,* 23–24; influencing currency use, 22–23; liquidity provision, 18–19, *19,* 23–24; monetary power vs., 16–17; objectives, 18–19, *19;* payments financing, 18–19, *19,* 23–24; recession example, 9–10; as reciprocal process, 163; Suez Canal example, 7–8; tools of, 25. *See also* Currency areas; Currency manipulation; Exchange-rate weapon; Follower states; Globalization; Macro-dimension of international monetary power; Monetary dependence

money, as social convention, 15–16, 62, 83–84

monopoly power, currency leadership and, 52, 55, 66–68

mutual indifference, 112

Mwangi, Wambui, 83

Nasser, Gamal Abdel, 7

National Power and the Structure of Foreign Trade (Hirschman), 149–50

negotiating dynamics, 102–5; paucity of formal monetary negotiations, 91, 96–98, 114

New Deal era, 59

New Miyazawa Plan, 153–54

Nielson, Daniel, 181

Nixon, Richard, 27, 194

Nixon administration, 27, 64

Nixon shocks, 25, 68, 126

Nobuhiko Ushiba, 127

nonintentional power, 16–17, 75–80, *84,* 88. *See also* Passive leadership

nontraded goods sectors, 122–23

Noriega regime, 86, 156

normative convergence, 53, 61–66, 68

North, Douglas, 57

North American Free Trade Agreement (NAFTA), 197

Nye, Joseph, 33, 46, 103, 108 n

oil markets, 48, 121, 203

oil shocks, 112, 126, 127

Omnibus Trade and Competitiveness Act of 1988, 133

openness, 14, 47–49, 120, 122, 135

Operation Meseraagh, 142

opinion polls, markets as, 44–45

optimality, 43, 44

optimum currency area theory, 12 n, 16, 103

Organization for Economic Cooperation and Development (OECD), 65, 203

Organization of Petroleum Exporting Countries (OPEC), 203

Organizing the World's Money (Cohen), 73

original sin literature, 67

Österreichischen Gewerkschaftsbundes (ÖGB), 199, 200

overt power, 73, 77

owned reserves, 43

Panama, 86, 156

Paris Club, 43

partisan mutual adjustment, 108–9

passive currency manipulation, 147–48

passive leadership, *12,* 14, 68, 92, 104, 107. *See also* Nonintentional power

passive mode of influence, 48–49

pass-through, 37 n

path dependency, 123–24

Pauly, Louis, 4, 20–21, 98, 107

payments financing, 18–19, *19,* 23–24

Persian Gulf states, 173

Plaza accord, 125, 128, 133, 136

Poland, counterfeit money and, 142

policy adaptation, 98, *105,* 105–7, *106, 111*

policy convergence, coordination vs., 99–101

policy instruments, 17

policy subordination, 110

political economy theory, 3

politics: monetary geography and, 154–56; national, international monetary order and, 185–87; traded and nontraded sectors and, 122–23

power, 21, 92; direct, 76–77; domain of, 8, 32;

external and internal dimensions, 32–33; indirect institutional, 75, 77; limitations, monetary leadership and, 66–69; monopoly, 52, 55, 66–68; nonintentional, 75–80, *84*, 88; overt, 73, 77; process, 73, 76–77, 82; relational, 2, 17n, 73–74, 76; scope of, 8, 32. *See also* International monetary power; Power to Deflect payment; Power to Delay payment; Power to Rearticulate interests; Power to Reconstruct interests; Structural power

Power and Interdependence (Keohane and Nye), 33, 46, 103

Power to Deflect payment, *12,* 13–14, 31, 36, 51, 118, 186; asymmetrical demand and, 103–4; Canada and, 196; currency leadership and, 66–67; openness and adaptability, 47–49; passive and active modes of influence, 48–49; sensitivity and vulnerability, 46–47; structural power and, 79

Power to Delay payment, *12,* 13–14, 31, 36, 38, 41–42, 49, 51, 78, 118; asymmetrical demand and, 103–4; borrowing capacity, 42–45; international liquidity, 42; owned reserves and, 42; United States and, 45–46

Power to Rearticulate interests, *12,* 15–16, 72, 174

Power to Reconstruct interests, *12,* 15–16, 72

private-sector agents, 11, 15, 132, 192; currency leadership and, 55, 63–66; third-party, 180–82

procedural coordination, 93–101, 108, 111; increase in, 98–99

process power, 73, 76–77, 82

propaganda, 17, 82

protectionism, 124, 128

protective currency manipulation, 147–48

public goods theory, 55

public-sector creditors, 43–44

pulling power, 79, *84*

rand zone, 178

Rasminsky, Louis, 189–97, 206

rational choice theory, 181

Reagan, Ronald, 205

Reagan administration, 128

real adjustment, 23, 37, 92 n, 97

reciprocity, 92, 99, 101

regional currencies, 163

regional monetary policy coordination, 97–98, 130, 138, 174; East Asia, 132–34, 137; twenty-first century, 149–51, 156. *See also* European Monetary System

regulatory trends, 79–80, *84*, 88

relational power, 2, 17 n, 73–74, 76. *See also* Direct power

relative gains, 148

renminbi, 137

reserves, 43–44, 49

resources, 10–11, 37

Roman Empire, 87

Roosevelt administration, 59

Rose, Andrew, 81

ruble zone, 163, 169–70, 180–82

Ruggie, John, 53, 61–62, 64

Russell, Bertrand, 16–17 n

Russia, 87; Austria and, 200–201, 202; Central Bank of Russia, 177, 181; ruble zone, 163, 169–70, 180–82

sanctions, 27 n, 49, 86; currency areas and, 164, 166

Scandinavian Monetary Union, 179, 180

Schelling, Thomas, 157, 160, 164, 173–74

schilling, 107, 198–99, 201–3

Schmidt, Helmut, 127

scope, 8

security incentives, 56–57

seigniorage, 22, 82, *84,* 86

sensitivity, 46–47

side payments, 23, 156–57

Simon, Herbert, 17 n

Singapore, 172–73

Smithsonian Agreement, 25–27, 126, 194

social convention, money as, 15–16, 62, 83–84

social divisions, dollarization and, 86–87

socialization, normative convergence through, 61–66

social power theory, 2

South Africa, 178

South Korea, 24, 133, 158–59

Special Drawing Rights (SDRs), 23, 64

Stability and Growth Pact, 177

stabilization programs, 43–44

Stasavage, David, 175

state-to-state relations, 49, 77, 91, 97, 149

sterling, 7–8, 67, 100

sterling area, 67, 162–63, 177, 179, 181; Britain's monetary dependence, 172–74

Stiglitz, Joseph, 159

stimulus and response, 47

Strange, Susan, 1, 25, 35, 172; *Casino Capitalism,* 78–79; nonintentional power, view of, 75, 77–78, 88; regulatory trends, view of, 79–80; structural power, view of, 73–78, 84–85; U.S. as nonterritorial empire, 85–87

Strauss, Robert, 127

structural power, 88–90, 129 n; in age of imperialism, 81–83, 90; benefits, 81, 88–89; causal mechanisms, 74–75, 77; dollarization and, 84–88; entrapment and, 80–81, 86; global political economy and, 74–75, 84, 89; international relations theory and, 73–76; macro-dimension monetary applications, 78–79, *84;* micro-level applications, 79–84; regulatory trends and,

structural power (*continued*)
79–80, *84*, 88; study of international monetary relations and, 76–84; symbolism and, 82–83, 86; transaction costs and, 81, *84*, 87. *See also* International monetary power; Power
structural shift, 118, 129–131, 136, 138
structure, as term, 129n
structure power, 73
substantive coordination, 93–101; abundance of, 98–99; construction of, 110–13; policy convergence and, 99–101
substate actors, 11
Substitution Account, 62, 64
Suez Canal example, 7–8, 24
Summers, Lawrence, 159–60
Sweden, 180
Swiss dinar, 143–47
Swiss franc, 107
Switzerland, 61, 62
symbolism, 82–83, *84*, 86, 175
symmetry, defined, 179
systemic disruption, 77, 156–60; currency areas and, 168–69, 172

Taiwan, 133
Tajikistan, 170
Takeo Fukuda, 127
Tan Siew Sin, 172–73
tariffs, 27
Tierney, Michael, 181
time-inconsistency problem, 93
Tokyo round of trade negotiations, 9
Towers, Graham, 194
trade, 3–4, 56, 81; adjustments of volumes, 36–37; asymmetric relationships, 149–50; money vs., 91–92, 102–3; sectors, 122–23
transaction costs, 16, 81, *84*, 87
transitional cost of adjustment, 3, 11, 13, 38–41. *See also* Power to Deflect payment
Treasury bonds, 69
Treasury Department, 133, 191
treaties, 176–77
trust, 83, *84*
Tukmaji, Tareq al-, 144
Turkey, 146–47
twenty-first century. *See* Currency manipulation; Globalization

Ukraine, 172
unemployment example, 39
unipolarity, 139–40, 148, 157
United States: borrowing, 62–63, 65, 68–69; Bretton Woods system and, 25–27; credibility, 65–69; currency leadership, 14, 52, 55–56, 59–62, 67–69; current account, 127, 136–37; departure from fiscal conservatism, 67–69; domestic politics, 124; exchange-rate weapon and, 21, 135–36; financial crisis and, 80, 155, 161; financial development, 58; foreign assets-to-GDP ratio, 135; gold standard and, 59–60, 63–64, 105; gold window, closing of, 25–27, 78, 97, 126, 194; hegemonic coerciveness, 68–69; hierarchy of monetary relations and, 50; inflation and monetary policy, 59–60, 79; interest rate hike, 1970s, 79; limits to monetary leadership, 67–69; as nonterritorial empire, 85–87; Power to Delay, 45–46; recessions, 9–10, 128–29; regulatory trends and, 79–80; Suez Canal incident and, 7–8; unipolarity, 139–40, 148, 157. *See also* Bretton Woods system, United States and; Dollar; Exchange-rate weapon; Federal Reserve
U.S. Treasury–Federal Reserve Accord of March 1951, 59

Volcker, Paul, 25–27, 60–61, 63, 194
vulnerability, 46–47

Walter, Andrew, 3, 14, 23, 79
Waltz, Kenneth, 108n
Webb, Michael, 35
wedge effect, 131
Weingast, Barry, 57
West African franc zone, 169, 179–80
West Germany. *See* Germany
Wilson, Harold, 172
World Bank, 55, 68
World War I, 58
World War II, 197, 198

Yeltsin, Boris, 181–82
yen, 127, 128, 132

Zambia, 168
Zimmermann, Hubert, 155